Bill Wolfe

# LEGENDARY GEMS
## or
# Gems that Made History

# LEGENDARY GEMS
## or
## Gems that Made History

**ERIC BRUTON** • F.G.A.

CHILTON BOOK COMPANY • RADNOR, PENNSYLVANIA

Cover: The Great Globe of Nasir-ul-Din.
(Courtesy of the Royal Ontario Museum, Toronto, Canada;
photo by Varouj Yazejian, Photo Vahe, Tehran.)
Designed by William E. Lickfield
Manufactured in the United States of America

*Library of Congress Cataloging in Publication Data*
Bruton, Eric,
Legendary gems, or, Gems that made history.
Bibliography: p.228
Includes index.
1. Gems.  I. Title.  II. Title: Legendary gems.
III. Title: Gems that made history.
TS756.B78  1986  553.8  86-47612
ISBN 0-8019-7511-5

1 2 3 4 5 6 7 8 9 0    5 4 3 2 1 0 9 8 7 6

# Contents

# List of Illustrations

## Colorplates

## Figures

# Acknowledgments

In writing a book such as this, it is impossible to acknowledge all sources because, in most cases, the exciting finds were made and the dramas played out so long ago that records are few, incomplete, and often contradictory. About the only exceptions are more recent large diamond finds in Africa. Past and present owners of such portable–as well as desirable–items as gems with extremely high values are naturally secretive about their possessions unless the owners happen to be museums.

Editing *The Gemmologist* (now, alas, defunct) for many years brought into my hands much useful information. Although I was able to visit and see most of the places and processes concerned, as well as to handle many of the diamonds referred to in my book *Diamonds*, the opportunity of seeing a legendary gem not in a museum is very rare. I had, therefore, to rely largely on past authors, records, and friends with special knowledge when writing this book so that I am naturally very much in their debt. I am also grateful to Helen Robb for her untiring efforts in obtaining the elusive photographs of legendary gems that grace this book.

For anyone wishing to pursue a particular interest, these are the books I found of particular value. Lord Twining's massive volume, *A History of the Crown Jewels of Europe* (London, 1960), contains a wealth of detailed and thoroughly researched information; it is a true sourcebook. On specialized subjects, the following are of particular value although the subjects are approached by the authors in quite different ways: *The Crown Jewels of Iran* by V. B. Meen and A. D.Tushingham (Toronto, 1968) started as a cataloging and research project of a largely unknown collection but became a readable book with some exceptional pictures; *The Koh-i-Noor Diamond* by Stephen Howarth (London, 1980) has many interesting sidelights with an historical approach and provides a number of new sources of information; *Blue Mystery. The Story of the Hope Diamond* by Susanne Steinem Patch (Washington, D. C., 1976) has an amount of personal information not generally known, and *The English Regalia* by Martin Holmes and Maj. Gen. H.D.W. Sitwell (HMSO London, 1972) is both factual and fascinating.

The earliest and most rewarding sourcebook is the work of the 17th century French gem dealer and traveler, J.-B. Tavernier, which is referred to in some detail in the main text. The original text of *Travels in India* was in French, and the English version I found full of interest — not the least because of the numerous annotations — was the two-volume second edition edited by William Crooke and published by The Oxford University Press in 1925. It may take a while to trace a copy, but it is well worth the effort. That comment also applies to Edwin W. Streeter's *The Great Diamonds of the World*, the second edition of which was published in London in 1882. It is a rare book to find today. Streeter proudly announced on the title page, "The MS. of the 'Koh-i-Nur' graciously read & approved by Her Majesty the Queen. The accounts of the 'Pitt' and the "Eugenie' revised by Her Majesty the Empress Eugenie."

A useful book to have at hand for summarized and accurate general information is *An Illustrated Dictionary of Jewellery* by Harold Newman (London, 1981). For similar information on diamonds alone, there are the booklets *Famous Diamonds* by Iain Balfour (De Beers, London), as well as Balfour's more detailed articles on famous diamonds in "INDIAQUA," the industrial diamond quarterly, and *Notable Diamonds of the World* (N. W. Ayer, New York). There is also the more extensive book *Diamonds, Famous, Notable and Unique* first published in 1966 by the Gemological Institute of America.

Eric Bruton, F.G.A.

# LEGENDARY GEMS
## or
# Gems that Made History

Beauty, durability and rarity; such are the three cardinal virtues of a perfect gemstone.
Stones lacking any of them cannot aspire to a high place
in the ranks of previous stones. . .
*G. F. Herbert Smith (1872–1953)*

# *Introduction*

**A**N illogical aspect of human nature is that some bright or colorful pebbles found in an ancient riverbed or on a desolate desert floor have had a more lasting influence on human destiny than the words or actions of many rulers — military, ecclesiastical, or political. Some stones were powerful because of their supposed mystical properties; others acquired such value that they financed armies and changed the balance of power among nations. The love of precious stones created vendettas and bloody murder at least as vicious as those created by the love of man for woman.

The gemstone is inert, lifeless, immobile: it wields its influence only through the human mind. Men and women die, yet gemstones exist forever unless destroyed by a sharp blow or by fire, They exert their influence throughout many generations unless, perhaps, they eventually come to rest in a museum. The story of the museum that was ruined by the evil influence of a gemstone in its collection has still to be told; the Smithsonian Institution in Washington, D.C., has continued to thrive since it acquired the ill-omened Hope Diamond.

The power of a famous gemstone really lies in what those who know of it believe, but that, in many ways, adds to the fascination of the history of famous stones. It is true, too, that not all stories are of disaster, but happy connections are apt to be forgotten along with the mundane when a drama is unfolded.

Today is the time of mass production and the mass market, and the influence of the precious stone has changed in accordance with these circumstances. The wealth of a country depends on its effective resources —

people and assets. Diamonds are among nature's most valuable natural resources. The economic power of South Africa was based on diamonds while the U.S.S.R. spent many years of extensive and expensive field exploration in the wastes of Siberia seeking sources of diamonds, which they found in the 1950s. The Soviet Union is now one of the largest producers of gems as well as industrial diamonds, which provide the nation with a powerful economic lever and a valuable source of foreign exchange.

Botswana, dependent for so long on cattle bred on the fringes of the Kalahari desert that covers most of the land, found sudden wealth under the desert sands, where diamonds had been hiding for a hundred million years. In the Congo, Zaire, and Angola, civil war was inspired partly by diamond riches, and the rivalry of East and West in their support of these new regimes is concerned almost entirely with natural resources. Perhaps the only revolutionaries untouched by such wealth (or by economic sense) were the Kymer Rouge, who in sweeping through Cambodia to the borders of Thailand, dropped bombs on the small ruby and sapphire mines that had covered the ground like myriads of well holes. They even destroyed the Pailin mines, historically famous for fine sapphires, and set all the miners to work in the fields.

So gems still have a powerful influence on the modern world, enlightened, as it is said to be, largely because the sale of gems at high prices makes the major contribution to mining industrial stones, at least as far as diamonds are concerned.

In the past, it was not gems en masse but individual gems that influenced the lives of people. So what, one may ask, makes one gem more famous than another? For that matter, when does a mineral or some other substance become a gem? Those kinds of questions were never asked until the scientific age, and, in the case of precious stones, not until a discipline called "gemology," the science of gem identification, was born in the first years of this century.

A gem is defined as a substance, usually a mineral, that is natural and has beauty, rarity, and durability. That it has to have beauty is obvious today, but it was not always so. In the past, rarity had a greater value. To have something that no one else possessed was the desire of egocentric rulers in ancient days. Some coveted relics of battle, for example, were great treasures then but are gruesome objects today. Beauty is often relative to time and current belief; in other words, it can follow fashion, and that can lead to tragic decisions, as was the case with one of the world's most historic diamonds, the Koh-i-Noor, which was recut in Victorian days because it was not bright enough.

Rarity is a relative term. A gem miner might say that the mineral diamond is not rare compared with certain other gem minerals because about seven tons are mined every year, but it is rare to someone who does not have the money to buy one and would become rarer to someone who did have the cash if everyone suddenly demanded diamonds. The human desire for something rare has not changed, but in a consumer society where rarity can be manipulated, it is called "novelty" or "newness" or "fashion," which can be enjoyed in the same way, at least for a short time.

Gems were not, of course, the only objects in the past coveted by those with power. There were various artifacts of man, such as rich tapestries and, from the 16th century, extraordinary mechanical devices like the organ with an aviary of mechanical singing birds sent by Queen Elizabeth I of England to the Turkish Sultan, Murat III, in 1599. In India and Ceylon, a special prize was a Coco de Mer shell, an enormous double coconut shell that is just like a female torso. The giant trees from which the coconut shells came grow only in a certain valley in one of the islands in the Seychelles group, and the coconut shells are carried by currents across the Pacific. Even the now-common metal aluminum was once so rare that one of the French kings had jewelry made from it.

In gems, rarity has to be combined with what is commonly referred to as hardness, although "durability" is a better word because some gems are quite durable but certainly not hard (e.g., pearls and amber) and a few gems are hard but brittle (topaz and zircon) so that they can be splintered by a blow that will not even mark the surface. The hardest and most durable of all materials, natural or man-made, is diamond, without which modern industry would soon come to a halt.

When diamond was first discovered—no one knows how or when, but probably it was in India in or near the bed of a river—it must have been obvious that it was different from other pebbles. It would have been bright, transparent, and attractive, but most of all, it would have appeared quite unworn compared with other pebbles. It might well have been a double four-sided pyramid (an octahedron) with sharp edges. In the world of today's wonders, the layman is always amazed on seeing a well-formed rough diamond for the first time. Although it may have been jostled around rocks, pebbles, and sand for millions of years, it still looks new. Some have natural facets as bright as those put on a polished diamond. That is why a diamond is said to be "forever."

The next hardest material after diamond is what mineralogists and gemologists call "corundum" but jewelers call "ruby" or "sapphire." Corundums are red, blue, yellow, pink, green, purple, violet, and colorless.

The red ones are rubies and the rest sapphires. All have the same hardness, which is hard indeed since they will scratch the hardest steel. Even so, diamond is an astonishing one hundred times harder and can be scratched only by another diamond.

Men and women who lusted for power when it was gained by the sword admired gems because the immense value of a single stone, worth perhaps a kingdom, was concentrated in a small piece of stone or a pearl that could be carried or concealed quite easily when fleeing from danger.

The point was dramatically illustrated by the great traveler, Marco Polo (1254–1324), as related by Giambattista Ramusio, his biographer, in 1553, as translated by Ronald Latham in *The Travels of Marco Polo* (The Folio Society, London, 1968). When Polo returned with two kinsmen to Venice from his journey to China, "they repaired to their own house, which was a noble palace, and found several of their relations still living in it, who. . .(considered them) from their coarse and common attire, poor adventurers returned to be a charge upon their families." Marco Polo organized a grand banquet, and the three received their guests wearing rich oriental garments of crimson satin. When water had been served for hand washing before the meal, the Polos changed into richer robes of crimson damask, and the first dresses were cut up and distributed among the servants. After the first course, they changed again, this time into crimson velvet, and the damask dresses were cut and distributed. At the end of the feast, they changed into the Venetian clothes of the day, and again their previous apparel was cut up and distributed. As Ramusio recounted in Latham's translation:

> The guests were lost in astonishment, and could not comprehend the meaning of this masquerade. Having dismissed their attendants, Marco Polo brought forth the coarse Tartan dresses in which they had arrived. Slashing them in several places with a knife, and ripping open the seams and the linings, there tumbled forth rubies, sapphires, emeralds, diamonds, and other precious stones, until the whole table glittered with inestimable wealth acquired from the munificence of the Grand Khan, and conveyed in this portable form through the perils of their long journey.

The durability of diamond obviously gave rise to the belief in its invincibility, although it was known from Roman days that even the invincible diamond could be subdued by a blow, which would shatter it. A diamond has directions of grain, called "cleavage planes," along which it can be split as one would split a piece of wood. Only a blow at the right angle will make the diamond split or break. Squeeze it in a powerful engineering vise and it will become embedded in the hardened steel jaws.

We accept facts like this today; but a few centuries ago, there was no clear division between fact and fiction. That process did not begin until the 17th century and is still far from complete today. There was, for example, no clear distinction between the animate and the inanimate. Some inanimate objects with special interest or attraction, such as gems, were assumed to have human, even superhuman, attributes and powers that they transferred to the owner or wearer.

This discussion is partly guesswork because tantalizingly little is known about when certain minerals became precious stones and what significance this label had to their owners. At least it seems reasonably certain that the early historic stones with which this book is concerned were not at first prized as much for personal adornment as for their magical powers of being able to fend off evil, protect, and bring good luck.

They were also treasured for the medicinal properties they were believed to possess because of their resonance with the sun and planets, which related to people's horoscopes. Usually, the stone was crushed into powder and added to a drink, but later a beaker made of the gem material and filled with water or wine was given to a patient in the belief that the virtues of the beaker were transmitted to what it contained, a superstition from which the legend of the Holy Grail was perhaps derived.

Nostrodamus (1503–1566), the French physician and astrologer, quoted the alchemist Pierre de Boniface: "The Diamond renders a man invisible; the Agate of India or Crete, eloquent and prudent, amiable and agreeable; the Amethyst resists intoxication; the Carnelian appeases anger; the Hyacinth provokes sleep; and various properties are in a similar manner ascribed to other kinds."

It has been suggested that the collection of pretty stones by primitive tribes from all countries of the world was in the same nature as painting their bodies and dwellings with color, and all are associated with the seasons. Rites welcoming the coming of spring are known to have been significant, and the retention of bright and colored objects was supposed to be associated with spring flowers and coming fruit. It has been pointed out with some truth that adorning the body seemed to be almost as compulsive a need of the early human race as seeking food and shelter, so the argument whether or not stones were first worn as talismans or as adornment is still open. But at least it is now reasonably certain that men were the first wearers of gemstones and that women began to wear gems symbolically because they were monarchs, not because they were women.

Alexander the Great (356–323 B.C.) had his breastplate set with precious stones and his mantle embroidered with gold thread and gems. Caesar and Cleopatra are supposed to have met in a tortoise-shell-lined hall studded with emeralds. A century later, the mad Emperor Caligula adorned his horse with a pearl collar. In more recent times, the Russian czars had not only their own mantles but the saddle cloths of their horses embroidered with thousands of diamonds while the reins were set with large fine emeralds.

Nearly all the famous historical diamonds were found in India, which is probably why precious stones have played an important role in the traditions, mythologies, legends, and poems of the Hindus. The Vedas, the four sacred Hindu writings that date back some 3,500 years, refer to a place illuminated by rubies and diamonds giving out a light as radiant as that of the planets. The two great epics of Hindustan, the Ramayana and the Mahabharata, the world's longest poem of 100,000 verses when it was completed between 500 B.C. and 500 A.D., make frequent mention of people decorating themselves with stones and pearls.

Among ancient peoples, the Mogul conquerors of India and the Persians who destroyed the Mogul empire were especially fond of precious stones, which cannot be disentangled from their histories. The fabulously bejeweled Peacock Throne, the most precious and valuable seat of all time, was conceived and originated by the Emperor Jahangir and completed by his son, Shah Jahan, who will be remembered for building for his wife Mumtaz the most beautiful tomb — if not the most beautiful building of any kind in the world — the white marble Taj Mahal on the banks of the Jumna River at Agra, south of Delhi. Perhaps the Peacock Throne was as remarkable in its own way. The Persians took it when they conquered the Moguls, and it was later destroyed, although the thousands of gems that had been set in it had been removed. There are thrones of the same name, but none comes close to the original.

Historical stones are nearly all large, which is one factor making them unique. Some are pure; others have unusual colors. Some stones found in recent times have become famous simply because they are extra large. They may become historical, but still, they cannot compete in interest with the earlier gems that became entangled with raw history in the making.

Many treasures removed by the Nazis during the Second World War have been recovered, but the troops never found the great Regent Diamond, which had been hidden behind a stone panel during Hitler's invasion of France. The Soviets also took some famous stones, including the Dresden Green Diamond, from Germany, but these have now been returned. The

British, who collected a number of famous gemstones during the reign of Queen Victoria, took none in the last war so had nothing to return, but there have been calls for the return of the Koh-i-Noor Diamond. The argument about whether the United Kingdom has a right to it and whether it should be returned to India is not recent. It has been going on for more than a century, but one fact has not changed—the law forbids the U.K. government from sending the Crown Jewels out of the country.

That law was passed because, ever since rulers collected gems, they have used them to raise money or win friends when they were in trouble. A gem that has become famous is a very highly concentrated form of wealth. It is possible to hold quite easily in one hand something that is not large or heavy yet could be worth a million or more pounds in today's terms. No wonder monarchs who sat uneasily on their thrones grabbed some of the gems from the Crown Jewels when they had to flee. During the English Revolution, Queen Henrietta Maria, consort of Charles I, slipped away with two famous diamonds among other items to raise money for the Royalist army, but it did not save Charles from the scaffold. Ironically, he wrote a poem the night before his execution in 1649, which included the lines:

In the King's name the King's himself uncrowned
So doth the dust destroy the diamond.

He referred to the fact that only diamond dust will cut diamond. Diamonds had certainly failed to save him.

They failed also to save King Louis VI and Queen Marie Antoinette, who were caught by the revolutionaries fleeing with some of the French Crown Jewels and who suffered the same fate as Charles. Napoleon, however, was more practical. He pawned the Regent Diamond in order to finance his armies in the field and then paid off the loan with the spoils of conquest, so that he redeemed the diamond in order to have it set in his sword hilt for his coronation.

## The Birth of a Gem

When first used for adornment or as talismans, gems were retained as they were found. Most were picked up or mined nearby or in active rivers or in places where rivers had flowed perhaps millions of years ago and had later become desert. These areas are called "alluvial" sources. Precious stones were also found in areas where, during the earth's formation, rocks had formed by the cooling of magmas—molten rock material deep within the earth. In rare conditions, the magma cooled slowly and instead of a rock of many tiny crystals, one or more large crystals formed, often beautiful, symmetrical, and exquisitely colored, in a seam or pocket of coarse rocks called a "pegmatite." Rare gems like the emerald, aquamarine, and topaz are formed in this way and are exposed by nature's or man's mining.

Diamond, always the exception, was formed deep in the earth — 100 miles (160 kilometers) or so down — probably from carbon dioxide. Diamond crystals were created from exposure of the carbon to great pressures and temperatures for long periods then brought to the surface in a semimolten rock. This rock, solidified, is the primary source of diamonds and is what miners call "blue ground." Other gems of mineral origin came into existence through a combination of volcanic processes, torrential rains, and the shrinking of the earth when it cooled. Such forces broke down the early igneous rocks and caused the sedimentation of rock debris into the beds of the great seas along with the formation of new minerals as a result of the pressures and temperatures imposed on these sedimentary rocks during the upheavals that subsequently formed the lands and mountains as the earth's crust cooled still further.

Another group of gems, known as "organic gems," is animal or vegetable in origin. They are primarily found by or in the sea and include pearls, amber, coral, and jet. Even these can be ancient. Amber, which is picked up on the shores of the Baltic Sea, is a fossilized resin that oozed from conifer trees perhaps as long ago as 120 million years. Nearly all historic pearls came from the Persian Gulf, so perhaps that is why the Persians coveted gems so much. Oysters were food, and the first pearl to be found must have been a byproduct of eating.

One organic gem material that is still growing is animal ivory, mainly from elephants' tusks. In spite of the fact that it is very much part of the trappings of the great in India and China, ivory is not featured in this book. Although most Western countries today ban its import (and enlightened African countries ban its export), elephants are still being slaughtered in large numbers by ivory poachers since the Chinese continue to have substantial factories of ivory carvers. It is hoped that before long, all countries of the world will turn their attention to the preservation of the world's ecology.

Not to be forgotten is a treasure of the ancient world: the horn of the unicorn. The legendary unicorn, with the body and head of a horse, hind legs of a stag, tail of a lion, and long, cornet-shaped horn growing out of its forehead, was so important that it has for a long time been featured in the Royal coat of arms. It was no myth to those who bought genuine twisted ivory horns up to nine feet (nearly three meters) long. They were genuine horns of excellent ivory, but they came from the narwhal, a sea mammal found in northern seas that Greenlanders hunted for its blubber.

Uncut gems were set into precious metals perhaps as long ago as 3000 B.C. because the Phoenicians, those great sailors and traders in the Mediterranean, brought trinkets studded with amber to the Greeks. Certainly in Crete, the Minoans, the earliest of the Greek-speaking peoples, were cutting beads out of stone during those times. A number of famous gems, however, were left and still remain uncut, the Black Prince's Ruby being one of them. It has a partially drilled hole in it, the reason for which is unknown. As well as being set in mounts (bands of metal) in crowns and jewelry, gemstones were also suspended, which meant they had to be drilled. Drilling was obviously more difficult with the harder stones than the mainly organic softer ones. Ruby and sapphire are particularly hard to drill, but the Black Prince's Ruby was the softer red spinel.

It is possible that engraving on gems — achieved by a form of drilling — is as old as faceting them. The Egyptians may have been the first to polish a flat surface on a hard stone by rubbing it on the natural flat surface of another larger stone that was not as hard and had been covered with the paste of a powdered mineral from the Island of Naxos in the Greek Cyclades group. The powder was what is called "emery" today along with comprised particles of corundum and some other minerals. As corundum (ruby) is the hardest mineral apart from diamond, it will grind other minerals. Applied to the end of a tiny stick oscillated by a bow, it can be used to make hollow carvings in the flattened surface of the gem. The Israelites may have learned the art from the Egyptians, who then taught the Greeks and Romans, but whatever their history, engraved gems had great importance in the ancient world, mainly as seals.

An intaglio (hollowed out) symbol or picture on a gem (Figure I–1), of-

Fig. I–1 Egyptian Intaglio Carving. Used to make an impression on sealing wax or to authenticate a document. Engraved gems had great importance in the ancient world, many as seals, since they could not readily be forged. *(Courtesy of Otto Frello, Copenhagen, Denmark, from* Gems and Jewelry in Color.*)*

ten set in a ring, was used for making an impression on the wax sealing a letter or for authenticating a document, hence, the seal and the signet ring. It could not be forged except by a seal engraver of equal skill, of which there were very few. Garnet, beryl, and the quartz minerals — amethyst, rock crystal, chalcedony, cornelian, and jasper — were commonly carved. Emery was no match for diamond's hardness and would make little impression on ruby and sapphire. Meantime, in China, similar arts were being learned independently and on a larger scale by jade carvers. The harder stones of ruby and sapphire, and even diamond, were engraved with the names of their owners and with messages using a pen tipped with a fragment of diamond. Claims to several famous stones were established so.

## The Diamond Mystique

Diamond, which figures prominently in this book, was probably the last precious stone to be altered in shape by man. It is possible that Indian lapidaries first discovered that fragments of diamond could be powdered in a mortar using a pestle and that the powder, mixed with oil or just spittle, would grind flats on a rough diamond when the diamond was presented in certain ways and rubbed in certain directions. In other directions, the powder had no effect at all no matter how long or how hard the rubbing. Thus, the mystique of the diamond polisher began and was kept a close secret until relatively recent times.

The Indian lapidary was apparently concerned not so much with making the diamond symmetrical by facets or improving its brilliance as with removing superficial flaws. This attitude may be rooted in the warning by the writer of the 14th century Indian book on the art of the lapidary, *Agastimata*, who was the first to point out that diamond could be worked by other diamonds. He stated that a diamond polished on a wheel would lose its magical powers. The Indians may have introduced the grinding wheel or mill to replace laborious grinding by rubbing to and fro, but it is more likely that the Venetians made this vital contribution.

The first known references to diamond are in the Old Testament of the revised edition of the Bible, if one takes the translations as accurate. The Hebrew word used was *jahalom*, and earlier translators gave it the meaning of crysolite, now an archaic term applied to various kinds of yellowish and greenish-yellow stones. Certain contexts imply that the *jahalom* (translated as "adamant," which is diamond) is extremely hard. There are two references in Exodus 28:18 and 39:11, dated about 1200 B.C., to the twelve engraved precious stones in the breastplate of the High Priest (Figure I–2). The breastplate was actually a bag containing the sacred lots, the Urim and

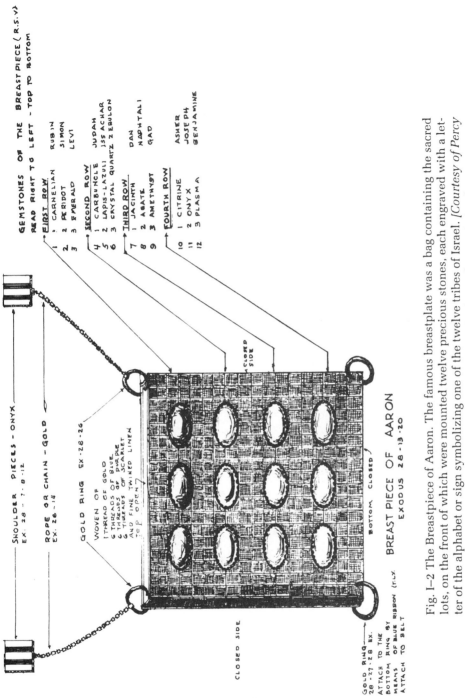

GEMSTONES OF THE BREAST PIECE (R.S.V.)
READ RIGHT TO LEFT - TOP TO BOTTOM

FIRST ROW
1 CARNELIAN     RUBIN
2 PERIDOT       SIMON
3 EMERALD       LEVI

SECOND ROW
4 CARBUNCLE          JUDAH
5 LAPIS-LAZULI       ISS ACHAR
6 CRYSTAL QUARTZ     ZEBULON

THIRD ROW
7 JACINTH       DAN
8 AGATE         NAPHTALI
9 AMETHYST      GAD

FOURTH ROW
10 CITRINE      ASHER
11 ONYX         JOSEPH
12 PLASMA       BENJAMINE

SHOULDER PIECES - ONYX
EX. 28 - 7. 8 - 12

ROPE OR CHAIN - GOLD
EX. 28 - 14

GOLD RING EX 28 - 26

WOVEN OF
1 THREAD OF GOLD
6 THREADS OF BLUE
6 THREADS OF PURPLE
6 THREADS OF SCARLET
AND FINE TWINED LINEN
TOP OPEN

CLOSED SIDE

CLOSED SIDE

BOTTOM CLOSED

GOLD RING
28 - 27 - 28 EX.
ATTACH TO THE
BOTTOM RING BY
MEANS OF BLUE RIBBON (T.L.)
ATTACH TO BELT

BREAST PIECE OF AARON
EXODUS 28 - 13 - 20

Fig. 1–2 The Breastpiece of Aaron. The famous breastplate was a bag containing the sacred lots, on the front of which were mounted twelve precious stones, each engraved with a letter of the alphabet or sign symbolizing one of the twelve tribes of Israel. *[Courtesy of Percy H. Perkins, Jr., in Gemstones of the Bible, 1981 (2nd ed.), with permission.]*

Thummim, on the front of which were mounted twelve precious stones, each engraved with a letter of the alphabet or sign indicating one of the twelve tribes of Israel. The revised version lists the stones as: sardius, topaz, carbuncle, emerald, sapphire, diamond, ligure, agate, amethyst, beryl, onyx, and jasper.

## *Of Religion and Gems . . .*

All the great religions use or have used the symbolism of the gem, even esoteric Hinduism and Bhuddism, which reject all attachment to sense-objects. The third eye is represented in idols by a precious stone in the forehead, and the famed Idol's Eye Diamond may have been such. Kissing the Pope's ring as an act of homage is a custom that has persisted until today. The Pope's lesser seal is a carved stone in a signet ring, known as the "Fisherman's Ring" because the engraving represents Saint Peter fishing from a boat.

Despite the close links of church and monarchy during the Christian era and symbolic links through jewels, particularly at coronations, monarchs were much more interested than high churchmen in acquiring valuable gems, at least outwardly, with the exception of the Roman Cardinals who followed the Roman Emperors. Another exception was the Italian-born French Cardinal Mazarin, who owned a unique private collection of diamonds, many bought from the French jeweler and traveler, Jean-Baptiste Tavernier, who also sold a collection to King Louis XIV. Mazarin left his collection to the King, and the French Crown Jewels at this time are said to have been the finest in Europe, if not the world.

From the middle of the 16th century, the Spaniards conquered Mexico, Peru, and Colombia and took back to Europe, not just Aztec, Inca, and Pre-Colombian gold but huge quantities of gems, especially fine emeralds. The most common Royal jewel was then the pearl, and paintings of the kings and queens of European countries show their costumes smothered with that particular gem.

An interesting portrait of Henry IV (painted about 1400) in the National Portrait Gallery, London, shows him with two large bluish stones mounted on his sleeves. The octahedral shapes are strongly suggestive of rough diamonds, and even allowing for artistic license, they must have been magnificent stones and particularly rare if they were, indeed, blue because the very rare blue diamonds are not normally octahedra.

In paintings of Henry VIII and his daughter Queen Elizabeth I, their costumes are smothered in pearls. The richness of jewels worn by a monarch at a coronation was so prestigious that some Crown Jewels were considered too meager; thus, the Royal Exchequer, in England, at least, had to stand rental on additional expensive personal ornaments. Indeed, so many jewels were rented at a cost of £1,000,000 in 1727 for Queen Caroline at the coronation of George II that a pulley system had to be rigged to pull up her petticoat like a curtain to allow her to kneel because it was so stiff with sewn on jewels. It was not until Louis XIV's day that the diamond superseded the pearl and was also used in large numbers.

Against the background of such a wealth of gems, famous stones had to be outstanding in and of themselves. But beyond their beauty, most are still marveled at today because of their imagined as well as their real history and the influence they had on the minds and actions of those who owned or coveted them in the past — in short, mainly on their influence as talismans.

Such jewels cannot be bought. Either they are won in battle,
or they are passed on as an honourable gift.
*Attributed to the 16th century Mogul Emperor, Humayun.*

---

## Chapter One

# Diamonds of Destiny

𝒯HE Koh-i-Noor Diamond probably has a history more entwined than any other stone with intrigue, battle, greed, and power. It and another large diamond of a similar name, the Darya-i-Noor, about which much less is known, were referred to as "the stones of destiny" by a French diplomat, whose name has been forgotten although his comment, like the diamonds, has endured. Today, the Koh-i-Noor is as safe as anything can be in the 20th century, locked up but on view to visitors along with the Crown Jewels of the United Kingdom.

The rough stone, about the size of a large walnut, was almost certainly found in the Kollur mines in India, where many other large and subsequently famous diamonds were discovered in alluvial mud and gravel, including the Great Mogul, the Regent, and the French Blue. The River Kristna (Figure 1–1) cuts a huge gorge in the land at Kollur, and as early as the 16th and 17th centuries, thousands of miners are known to have worked there. A share of the diamonds they recovered, or of their value, went to the local ruler. The better stones were taken to the village of Karwan, outside the fortified city of Golconda, for rough shaping with facets to remove exterior blemishes and were then sold within the city walls, where merchants met buyers. Golconda was in the old Kingdom of Golconda, northwest of the city of Hyderabad, and was destroyed in 1687 on the orders of one of the owners of the Koh-i-Noor, the Mogul emperor Jahan.

It is not known when the first Indian diamond, or the first from any country, was found, because in this age "found" means "identified." It used to be said cynically that discovery occurs when Western man, prefer-

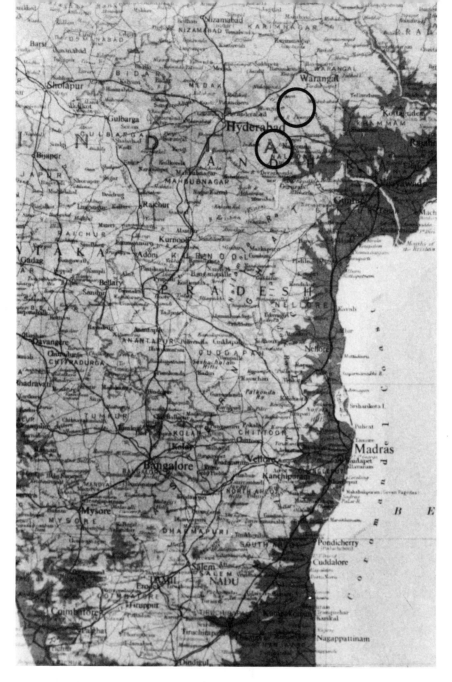

Fig. 1–1 Kollur Mine Area. The famous Koh-i-Noor Diamond was almost certainly found in the Kollur Mines in India. The River Kristna cuts a huge gorge in the land at Kollur; thousands of miners worked there in the 16th and 17th centuries.. *[With permission from INDIAQUA (Industrial Diamond Quarterly) and the Honorable Iain Balfour, author of the "Famous Diamond Series" in INDIAQUA.]*

ably white, first sets foot on someone else's land. Attitudes toward precious stones are the same. The first finder of a pretty stone now called "a diamond" could have been an Indian, a West African witch doctor, a Bushman in South Africa, a Wild Man from Borneo, or even a West Indian in Brazil. The fact that later we called it a diamond is really irrelevant to its actual discovery as being different from other stones.

India is known to have traded in diamonds as early as 800 B.C. and may have done so long before that. In the second century A.D., the Greeks invaded and ruled part of India. At that time the astronomer Ptolemy, a citizen of Alexandria, the port and center of learning, wrote the first important book on geography, in which he referred to a "river of diamonds" in India. Diamonds were exported overland from India and also by boat via Alexandria to Rome; some of the diamonds were reexported during the first five centuries of the Christian era to China for use in tools to shape jade, which was the beginning of the diamond industry.

So the Koh-i-Noor could have been found at any time during the course of many centuries. Its association with the great gems that are featured in ancient Sanscrit poems and writings sacred to the Hindus is not to be taken too seriously. The most likely possibility is that it was recovered from the Kollur mines at some time in the 17th century.

## *Barbur's Diamond*

India has been invaded many times and occupied for many centuries during its history. The first known mention of a big diamond that could possibly have been the Koh-i-Noor was after the Mongolians under Barbur swept south from Kabul in Afghanistan to face the armies of the Turkish Sultanate that had ruled from Delhi for more than three centuries. With two conquerors of India, Genghis Khan and Tamerlane, in his lineage, Barbur, at the age of fourteen, commanded the army that took Samarkand, but he lost it a year later. When he approached Delhi in 1519, he found his 12,000 men confronted by an army of 100,000 Indians supported by 100 elephants and commanded by Sultan Ibrahim Lodi. The mobility of his army and his generalship enabled Barbur, as he related in his memoirs, to crush and rout the Indians in no more than half a day.

His son, Humayun, swept south to Agra following a battle in which both the Sultan Ibrahim Lodi and the Rajah of Gwalior, ruler of Agra, were killed. The triumphant Mogul troops began pillaging and looting everything of value, and Humayun found the family of the slain Maharajah in hiding in an Agra fort. He put a stop to the rampage and placed the family under his own protection.

Because of this, the family presented him in 1526 with a large diamond. Humayun passed it on to his father, but apparently Barbur was unimpressed with material treasures as his passions were reserved for conquest and for the beautiful gardens he had created at Kabul. He wrote at the time that as a tribute, his son was presented with many precious stones, including a great diamond said to be worth "the value of one day's food for all the people of the world." He recorded that the diamond had once belonged to the Sultan Ala-ed-din, who had acquired it in 1304 from the Rajah of Malwa. Barbur's Diamond, as the stone was called although he only held it momentarily, is claimed by some researchers to have been the Koh-i-Noor, but this is very uncertain.

The spoils were so great from the plunder of Delhi's and Agra's treasuries that even after the generals, officers, soldiers, and even the camp followers had been amply rewarded, there were still huge quantities of precious metals, jewels, cloth, and slaves to be sent back to Kabul.

Barbur lived only four years as sultan before being succeeded by his son. Although Humayun was nominally the ruler from 1531 to 1556, his reign was punctuated by battles in which he lost and regained territory so often that he had to spend much of his life in exile. In 1544, he had to flee to Persia to seek refuge with the Shah. He was feted as the Emperor of India, although at the time deposed, and took with him to reward his host a number of jewels and gems he had inherited, including Barbur's Diamond.

On the journey to Persia, as Lord Twining wrote in his *A History of the Crown Jewels of Europe* (London, 1960), Humayun is said to have made the comment, "Such jewels cannot be bought. Either they are won in battle, or they are passed on as an honorable gift." He had repulsed several lesser Indian princes who had sought to buy the diamond, but a courtier (presumably representing one of the princes) posing as a diamond merchant to gain access was rebuked by those mild words from Humayun. Presumably, Humayun believed he had received the unique stone from the family of the man his army had killed as an "honorable gift" and gave it to the Persian Shah in the same spirit.

Humayun has been described in Lord Twining's book as a "scholarly, generous and merciful man, but at the same time tactless, irresolute and eminently unfitted to consolidate the conquest his father had bequeathed him." He regained his throne, but only two months later, he rushed out of his library, fell down the steps, and killed himself. He is commemorated by a great red sandstone and marble palacelike tomb southeast of Delhi.

The history of Barbur's Diamond comes to an end at this point because it has not been positively identified with any known diamond, although it could have been the Koh-i-Noor. There is no evidence but only the suggestive fact that the story of one diamond ends before the other begins and that each name refers to a large diamond known to have been in the possession of the Mogul emperors.

Persian documents in the British Museum studied by H. Beveridge in 1899 indicate that Humayun presented Barbur's Diamond to Shah Tahmasp of Persia as a token of appreciation for his help and that Tahmasp sent it to Burhan Nizam Shah of Ahmadnagar, who belonged to the Moslem Shi'ite sect, like himself. Unfortunately, it disappeared in 1547, and one supposition is that Tahmasp's envoy stole it.

## The Peacock Throne

As originally faceted, the Koh-i-Noor was dome-shaped with a pointed top and had several blemishes that the Indian polishers did not remove. It weighed 186 carats and was probably not a lot larger before it was faceted. There is an unauthenticated story that it was mounted as an eye in the Peacock Throne.

The Peacock Throne became the richest and most ostentatious of all the Mogul treasures because it incorporated so many stones that were treasures in their own right. Akbar, the greatest Mogul shah, who was the son of Humayun and only thirteen years old at his coronation, also had a son who became emperor. This one named himself Jahangir (Conqueror of the World) on being enthroned. and he ruled for 23 years with little disturbance to his life of luxury and indolence.

It was he who conceived the greatest luxury of all, the Peacock Throne. Typically, he never completed it. That was done by his son, Shah Jahan (reigned 1627–1658), the most visionary of the Moguls (Figure 1–2). Jahan built what is considered the world's most beautifully proportioned and sited building, the Taj Mahal, a white marble tomb for his wife Mumtaz on the bank of the Jumna River; he had also intended to build a black marble one for himself on the other side.

Mumtaz is shown in Persian miniatures as having white skin with shoulder-length black hair. She was of Persian extraction, and her father was a high official in the Mogul Palace. She married Jahan in 1615, before he ascended the throne, and bore him fourteen children as well as accompanying him on all his campaigns. The name of the tomb, Taj Mahal, means "Elect of the Palace".

Although there were many diamonds and other gems in the treasury for setting in the Peacock Throne, the greed for more was rarely absent. Toward the end of Shah Jahan's reign, when he was ill and having trouble

Fig. 1–2 Shah Jahan. Considered the most visionary of the Moguls, (reigned 1627–1658), Jahan built the Taj Mahal and completed the construction of the Peacock Throne, the richest and most ostentatious of all the Mogul treasures. *(By courtesy of the Board of Trustees of the Victoria and Albert Museum.)*

with his sons, who were warring over the succession, he received into his court a Persian named Mir Jumla, who had been Grand Wazir (First Minister) to the King of Golconda and had become incensed with the King. While away, he left his family as hostages, which was commonly done, but attempts were made to discredit Mir Jumla and poison his son, who protested so strongly that he and the rest of the family were thrown in jail. In revenge, Mir Jumla persuaded Jahan to finance an expedition to conquer Golconda and seize its treasures.

Mir Jumla was an experienced general, a man of power, and a rich man who farmed diamond mines in Kollur and elsewhere under various names. Shah Jahan agreed to the expedition. Although the King of Golconda was about to surrender, his gunner said he could kill Jahan's son Aurangzeb, who was with the invading army. The King refused to give permission, and the general of the Mogul army was killed instead. This gave Mir Jumla an opportunity to negotiate because he still had some regard for the King. As a result, the King agreed to pay an annual tribute to the Mogul Emperor and to let his second daughter marry Aurangzeb's son, Sultan Mohammed. Jumla himself became Minister of State and Commander in Chief of Shah Jahan's armies. The Koh-i-Noor may have been presented to Shah Jahan at about this time, but there is no evidence that this was so.

Shah Jahan's sons fought each other to seize the throne when it was reported that he had died and his death was being concealed. In fact, he had become so ill after taking drugs as a cure that he had retired to the women's quarters and had not shown himself for some time. His third son, Aurangzeb, was successful in the struggle for power, killing two of his brothers and imprisoning the third.

For his own protection, Shah Jahan shut himself in the Red Fort, near Agra on the bank of the Jumna River. (It is said that the old man had a ruby with a convex surface set in a wall so that he could see a miniature mirror image of his beloved Taj Mahal down the river.) Aurangzeb continued to publish the falsehood that this father was dead and on that pretext entered Agra. Jahan ordered him back to the Deccan, where he was governor, but instead found himself virtually imprisoned in the Red Fort with his income controlled as well as some of his treasures appropriated.

In 1665, under Aurangzeb's rule (1658–1707), the remarkable French gem merchant and traveler, Jean-Baptiste Tavernier (Figure 1–3), was able to see, weigh, measure, and sketch a number of large stones in the treasury, including the Great Mogul, which some subsequent writers persuaded themselves must have been the Koh-i-Noor. It was, in fact, too large. If the Koh-i-Noor was there, it was not shown to Tavernier. It is known that Shah

Fig. 1–3 Jean-Baptiste Tavernier. The remarkable French gem merchant and traveler was able to weigh, measure, and sketch many of the precious stones he encountered during his vast travels. *(Courtesy of The Oxford University Press.)*

Jahan, who was alive and imprisoned at the time of Tavernier's visit, still owned a great number of precious stones that did not come into Aurangzeb's hands until the old Shah's death in 1666. Perhaps the Koh-i-Noor was among them.

## The Overpowering Nadir Shah

The next reference to a large diamond that certainly was the Koh-i-Noor occurs after the invasion of India by Nadir Shah (1688–1747), a shepherd boy from the northern mountains of Persia (now Iran), where they border on Afghanistan.

When Nadir first herded goats, the Persian rulers had a simple technique for avoiding the otherwise almost inevitable fratricidal battles of succession: They kept their sons in harems, where the sons developed tastes more indulgent than fighting. Unfortunately, the ultimate consequences were much the same, because a country ruled by a succession of men who had little experience outside the bedchamber became weak and vulnerable. The Afghans and the Russians, under Peter the Great, realized at about the same time that Persian rule had become decadent and that this rich country was there for the taking.

The Afghans invaded in 1721 and the Russians followed a year later; then the Turks decided there was enough plunder for them, too. In Persia, the ruling Shah tried to get his sons to organize some defense, but the first two who were persuaded out of their harems rushed back to them after a brief taste of battle. The third son made an unsuccessful attempt to raise an army, but the Shah was forced to accept an Afghan chief as Shah in his place. However, this former shepherd boy had not yet appeared upon the scene.

Nadir had left his family at the age of 15 to become one of the local governor's bodyguards, probably being given the position because of his physical strength. He was hardily built and grew to six feet, with black hair, a bushy black beard, and a stentorian voice, according to a contemporary description. Unknown to his first employer until it was too late, Nadir was also a man of exceptional cunning with an overwhelming ambition for power and wealth.

He was promoted to Captain of the Guard and then wooed and married the eldest daughter of his employer, the Governor of Khorasan. He then tried to depose the Governor but failed and was made an outlaw. Nadir became a bandit, which admirably suited his temperament, and his exploits became so notorious that the third son, who despite having no kingdom had declared himself Shah Tahmasp, appealed to him for help.

After diligently retraining what there was of a Persian army in the guerrilla tactics he had learned, Nadir created an army so successful that it managed to break the Afghans in a series of battles and throw them out of the country. His next move was very direct. He deposed the new Shah Tahmasp and appointed the Shah's eight-month-old son as Shah and himself as Regent.

He accepted so many Turks and Afghans in his army that they outnumbered the Persians. Rigid discipline held them together and induced intense loyalty, especially as Nadir was so tough he would sleep on the ground with his army, covered only by a blanket even on the coldest nights and with his saddle as a pillow. If one of his commanders gave ground when not greatly overpowered, Nadir would kill him with the battle-axe he always carried and give command to the next in rank. But although so ruthless, he was fair to the lower ranks, and because of this and his apparent invincibility in battle, they gave him their passionate loyalty.

His next move was to proclaim himself Shah and crown himself with a helmet made of gold and set with gems. By this time, the country had become poor because of the constant fighting, so Nadir resolved to plunder the riches of the Mogul Empire in India. He made his son Viceroy of Persia and declared his friendship for the Mogul Emperor but warned him that he had to pursue Afghan rebels over the Indian border.

Nadir's army rolled into the subcontinent without opposition and Muhammad, the Mogul Shah, seemingly took Nadir at this word and only realized the danger when the Persian army had crossed much of India. When the clash came in 1739, the Persian army was faced by a rambling, untrained assembly of about 80,000 Indian soldiers, 10,000 of whom were left for dead; Nadir's army suffered a loss of 2,000.

Muhammad Shah capitulated and received the victors with a cannon salute into Delhi, where Nadir Shah, occupying the palace, put down a civilian riot by a particularly bloody slaughter. Afterward he made a proclamation, "The Sultan over the Sultans of the Earth is Nadir the King of Kings, Lord of the Fortunate Conjunction." The value of the treasures he seized was unbelievable. Apparently he took a particular liking to the Peacock Throne, which must have symbolized his claim to being King of Kings. One of the Mogul's greatest belongings was, however, missing.

At least, it is assumed that the Koh-i-Noor was missing if the often repeated story of how Nadir Shah acquired it is to be believed. It also has to be assumed that Nadir knew of the diamond or saw that a large stone was missing from the Peacock Throne.

The story is that Muhammad Shah wanted to keep an item of great value that could easily be concealed as "an honorable gift" for someone who could protect or support him. So he hid the diamond in his turban. The information was passed to Nadir, who, full of guile as ever, assured the Mogul that he was restoring his Indian Empire. As a formal transfer of power, Nadir asked Muhammad to exchange turbans, which was a traditional gesture of friendship. The Persian conqueror removed his national headdress of sheepskin, and the Mogul could not refuse to offer his turban. He was not only outfought but outwitted by the Persian shepherd boy.

The story continues that on removing the big diamond from its hiding place in the folds of the puggaree, Nadir spontaneously exclaimed, "Koh-i-Noor," meaning "Mountain of light," thus naming the stone perhaps forever.

Having achieved his only objective, to seize as much wealth as possible, Nadir began the journey home after three months, but he lost many men and about a quarter of the loot when crossing a river. The Peacock Throne survived, however, and on his return, he sent a present of 200 camel loads of melons to Muhammad Shah. His Indian adventure brought about his downfall despite its apparent success. He contracted dropsy while there and gradually went mad, becoming one of the most reviled tyrants of all time. (In an uncontrollable fit of rage, Nadir had blinded his eldest son with a hot wire. Blinding became the regular way of deposing rivals for the throne. At least five of the country's would-be shahs were blinded and the others killed.) He was murdered in his own tent in 1747. At the news, unity among the different nationalities in his army was soon under strain. The Afghans began to fight the Persians, and soon the whole country was involved and in turmoil.

## The Blind Rukh Shah and the Eunuch

The Koh-i-Noor's exact whereabouts are unknown during this period. Not unnaturally, they were kept secret. One theory is that after Nadir's death, it was taken by Ahmad Shah Abdali, one of Nadir's best and most loyal generals, who had led the fleeing Afghans back to their old country. Ahmad's new fighting force managed to unify Afghanistan for the first time, and in 1749, he was able to return to Persia to help Nadir's grandson, Shah Rukh Mirza, who had been imprisoned by a rebellious Arab chief.

Rukh was still a boy and had been deposed, blinded, and restored before his present misfortune. Ahmad killed the Arab and freed Rukh but made him shah only of the impoverished Khorasan province, where Nadir had once tended goats. He annexed the rest of the territory for Afghanistan.

If Ahmad did not already possess the Koh-i-Noor, it is theorized that it was given to him in payment or as a gift by Rukh for his deliverance.

The fateful diamond was certainly taken to Afghanistan at some time, but even after it had gone, its influence was such that the most horrifying deeds in greed for it were still to come. The victim was the weak and inoffensive blind Shah Rukh Mirza.

When the Afghan Ahmad died in 1773, Rukh no longer had a protector. He was captured and held for five years by a Kurdish chief before being restored by Ahmad's son, Timur. But his succor lasted only a year because civil war broke out once more in Persia and the evil Agha Muhammad Khan seized power. Agha Muhammad was a eunuch, having been castrated at the age of five by Nadir's successor. His deficiencies were apparently sublimated by an obsessive passion for power and jewels, for which his greed and cruelty were limitless.

Blinding was still a way of life among the Persian princes. Agha Muhammad demanded 20,000 pairs of eyes from the inhabitants of a defeated city in the south of Persia and counted them himself with the point of a dagger as they were brought to him heaped on trays. He threatened the officer who had collected them with the loss of his own eyes if there were a single one missing. With his sword, he would disembowel on the spot any servant who upset him.

Agha Muhammad conquered eight of the Persian states to declare himself Shah but had not yet turned on the ineffective Shah Rukh. He had nominated a nephew to succeed him, and one of Rukh's two sons could be a threat to the succession. The two Rukh sons were of insufficient mettle to face the horrifying eunuch and fled to leave their blind father, now aged 61, to his fate while he was groping around his palace in Meshd.

Agha Muhammad managed to occupy the city by disguising his troops as pilgrims. His first objective was to seize the Crown Jewels that Rukh still owned. Torture soon elicited their various hiding places, but Agha Muhammad wanted above all the Koh-i-Noor (another report said the Timur Ruby) and would not believe Rukh's protestations that he no longer had it. Had he obtained the stone, it is unlikely that Rukh's fate would have been different because of Agha Muhammad's morbid pleasure in torture. Rukh was tied to a chair and his head shaved. A crown of thick paste was built up on his head and then Agha Muhammad personally poured a jug of molten lead into the crown in a ghoulish coronation ceremony.

So the Koh-i-Noor's baleful influence dominated the life and the death of Rukh Shah, although he probably never owned it; perhaps he had never seen it because he was blinded when young, or perhaps it was safely in the possession of Ahmad Shah, founder of the Durani Empire in Afghanistan.

Ahmad Shah was one of the strange breed of practical romantics that wars bring to the top at certain times in history — the soldier-poet, like the first Mogul, Barbur. Ahmad Shah also turned his eyes toward the riches of India, which he invaded eight times and where his main opponent was a ruler of the same name, Ahmad Shah Bahadur I. One battle Ahmad Shah could not win was against cancer of the face. In 1772, he relinquished the throne in favor of his son, Timur, who acquired the Crown Jewels, including the Koh-i-Noor. Presumably, they were kept in a treasury in Kabul.

Timur (not to be confused with the famous Timur, also known as Tamerlane) was kept too busy trying to quell rebellious tribes in his own country, Afghanistan, to have time for adventures in others. Besides, countries from farther afield were probing more and more deeply into this rich part of Asia. Both the Russians and Persians threatened invasion of Afghanistan while the British had established themselves successfully in India and the French, under Napoleon, were chafing to get back there.

Although Timur had twenty-three sons when he did die, the usual bloodbath did not occur because one son, Zaman, succeeded him and ruled for seven years before the old pattern reestablished itself. He occupied some of that time by following the example of his forebears and invading India several times. He penetrated only into the Punjab, however, not farther across the continent to Delhi.

The Punjab was inhabited mainly by Sikhs, men who had accepted the religion taught by the Sikh gurus, a form of purified Hinduism. The last of the Sikh gurus was Govind, the son of a Sikh tortured and killed for his faith by the Mogul Emperor Aurangzeb. Govind's sons were later buried alive by the same Mogul. Govind taught his followers an intense hatred of Islam, which unified the Sikhs against the Afghans and Persians as well as against the Mogul rulers in India. Nevertheless, the Sikhs still expended much of their energy fighting among themselves.

Despite their ferocity in battle, the Sikhs retreated before Zaman's army, partly because the aura of invincibility was still attached to them from the earlier invasions of Ahmad Shah. But as soon as Zaman returned to Kabul, the Sikhs would filter back to their original lands.

Around this time, a Sikh chieftain died, leaving a son of fifteen years called Ranjit Singh. When he was only seventeen, Ranjit Singh took complete control of the tribe. Although small in stature, unprepossessing in appearance, and blind in one eye, he possessed two very valuable assets — an iron sense of purpose and a natural power of command.

Ranjit Singh soon realized that with some extra mobility, he could easily win territory by moving into it after Zaman left and before the previous Sikh occupiers returned. He even took over the capital city of Lahore after Zaman had retreated from it to deal with trouble back in his own country. Moreover, Ranjit Singh had Zaman's assent for his action since presumably some deal was struck. An attempt to unseat him by an army of four Sikh tribes was abandoned after the invading army had indulged in a bout of drinking and other drug taking. So the remarkable Ranjit Singh, still only eighteen years old, proclaimed himself Rajah of Lahore. Two years later, he appointed himself the Maharajah.

In the same year as Ranjit Singh's appropriation of a kingdom, Zaman Shah discovered that the pattern of succession in his country, Afghanistan, had not changed after all. After his return, he was seized by his brother Mahmud, blinded, and confined to a room in the Palace. It appears that Zaman must have had warning of the coup, although with no chance to evade it, because he had time to bury the Crown Jewels in a hole he made in the ground with his dagger and to hide the Koh-i-Noor in a crevice in a wall, according to an account written some 44 years later by W. H. Sleeman, a lieutenant colonel in the Bengali Army.

Zaman managed to convince his brother that he had thrown all the jewels in the river, so Mahmud did not get his hands on the big diamond. In 1803, Mahmud lost the throne when another brother, Shuja, discovered a taste for power and had a big enough following to overthrow Mahmud and imprison him. Despite this seemingly decisive bid for power, Shuja was an ineffective shah by the standards of the time. In the light of future events, he seems to have prized his jewels, particularly the Koh-i-Noor, more than the exercise of power. He intended to put out Mahmud's eyes in the traditional manner, despite the appeal of their mother, until the blind former Shah Zaman backed his mother's plea for an act of mercy by offering to disclose where the Koh-i-Noor was hidden. So Mahmud escaped being blinded but remained in prison while Shuja acquired the diamond.

While shahs and their enemies came and went, the British were steadily thrusting their way into many parts of India with inducements to trading from the Honourable East India Company, diplomatic offers and pressures from the Crown, and the eventual sanction of the British army in India. The British offered Shah Shuja a treaty of friendship to gain an ally against the French, of whom they were nervous because of Napoleon's reputation for conquest, and also because of the Russians.

The envoy the British sent to negotiate the treaty, Mountstuart Elphinstone, subsequently wrote a description of the Shah that Lord Twining recorded in his *A History of the Crown Jewels of Europe* (London, 1960):

We thought at first he had on an armour of jewels, but on close inspection, we found this to be a mistake, and his real dress to consist of a green tunic, with large flowers worked in gold and precious stones, over which were a large breastplate of diamonds, shaped like two flattened fleur-di-lys, an ornament of the same kind on each thigh, large emerald bracelets on the arms (above the elbows), and many other jewels in many places. In one of the bracelets was the Koh-i-Noor, known to be one of the largest diamonds in the world.

They met in Peshawar because Shuja was unable to keep control of his own capital city, Kabul. In fact, he returned to find his brother had escaped from six years' incarceration and had gathered an army to seize power for the second time. Shuja's original act of leniency, although he was bribed by being given the diamond, cost him dearly. Once in power, Mahmud lost no time banishing his brother Zaman from the country. Shuja's harem went with him. It happened so fast that, on his way back through Sikh territory, Elphinstone passed the caravan taking Zaman and his company to safety.

To whom could the former Shah Zaman of Afghanistan turn to for help? Despite the Sikhs' hatred of Muslims, it was to the Sikh who had already shown that he could make deals with his natural enemies and in particular with Zaman himself, that Zaman turned to. He was, of course, Ranjit Singh. Is it too far-fetched to suggest that Zaman originally let Ranjit Singh take over Peshawar in return for sanctuary, should he need it?

Whatever the truth, it was a move that once more eventually led to a change in ownership of the historic stone, though it was a very reluctant gift. The Koh-i-Noor had once again returned to India, its country of origin, after nearly 75 adventurous years.

It is the will and not the gift that makes the giver.
*Gotthold E. Lessing (1729–1781)*

---

*Chapter Two*

# Symbol of Empire

SHAH Shuja managed to evade the clutches of his brother Mahmud Shah, the latest claimant to the Afghan throne, to raise an army with the aid of various local chieftains to whom he had been lenient during past uprisings. But after fluctuating battles with Mahmud Shah, he never managed to gain any territory and eventually, in 1812, three years after being deposed, Shuja was captured—but not by Mahmud. He was imprisoned in Khashmir in northern India, and his captors never knew he had with him or access to immense wealth in the form of one of the biggest diamonds known to the world.

In some way, Zaman heard the news of Shuja's capture and tried to enlist the help of his host, Ranjit Singh, in a rescue attempt. The Lion of Lahore was receptive to the idea, and he knew the price he was going to ask. After discussions with Shuja's principal wife and with her agreement, Zaman signified that, although it was not theirs to give, the Koh-i-Noor would be the fee.

By accident, or perhaps by design because self-preservation was part of his character, Ranjit Singh sent his army to invade Khashmir at the same time as an Afghan army was on its way to launch an assault on this mountain stronghold. The armies met, and their commanders agreed to join forces. Ranjit Singh, who alone knew about the diamond, agreed to take only a minor part of the spoils. The Afghans, having spent their lives in the mountains, did most of the fighting, but the Sikhs rescued Shuja from under the noses of his archenemy's troops and took him back to Lahore.

Ranjit Singh never did get his share of the loot and the Afghans obviously thought themselves very clever, but whatever anger Ranjit may have felt was tempered by the prize he had won. Shuja was churlish about his rescue when he heard of the price demanded and, because the arrangement had been made without his consent, he declared that he no longer had the stone and that it was back in Kabul, having been used as security for money to raise troops.

The Sikh was not to be put off by such feeble excuses. He made life uncomfortable for Shuja and his retinue by alternating punishment with promises. He confined them to their quarters. Later, he offered Shuja money and land. Then he cut off their food, which eventually brought the normally affable Shuja to the point of submission.

When it actually came to handing over the stone, however, Shuja could not bring himself to do so. The two sat opposite each other, cross-legged, as was the custom, for an hour, during which Shuja was unable to commit the final act until Ranjit Singh lost patience and demanded the diamond. Shuja then reluctantly handed over a small cloth bundle that the Lion accepted without a word.

After he had examined the historic stone, Ranjit Singh sent a message to Shuja stating that it was a diamond fit only for a king, and since Shuja no longer was one, Singh was keeping it for himself.

He had it set in a bracelet, as Shuja had, and on occasions wore it as a turban ornament. At one time, it was mounted on one side of his horse's bridle so that he could keep an eye on it while riding, a use of jewels much favored by the Russian czars. In the Gold Treasury in Leningrad are bridles, reins, and saddle cloths set with hundreds of emeralds and diamonds. Like the Russians, Ranjit Singh also liked to test the alcohol capacity of his visitors, and the favored ones were offered a brandy he had specially distilled for himself.

Among such guests was a party of British diplomats who presented themselves to the Lion of Lahore for talks in 1838. One of their number, William Osborne, military secretary to the British Governor General of India, subsequently wrote in his book *The Court and Camp of Rungeet Singh* (Oxford University Press, 1973) a description of the strikingly colorful spectacle that the uniforms, gold, and jewels of the court presented, adding:

> Cross-legged in a golden chair, dressed in simple white, wearing no ornament but a single string of enormous pearls around the waist and the celebrated Koh-i-Noor, or Mountain of Light, on his arm — (the jewel rivaled, if not surpassed, in brilliancy by the glare of fire which every now and then shot from his single eye as it wandered restlessly round the circle) — sat the Lion of Lahore.

Before the diplomatic party left six weeks later, Osborne was privileged by being allowed to handle the diamond, which prompted him to write:

> It certainly is a most magnificent diamond. It is about an inch and a half in length and upwards of an inch in width, and stands out from the setting about half an inch: it is in the shape of an egg, and is set in a bracelet between two very handsome diamonds about half that size. It is valued at three million sterling, and without a flaw of any kind.

Just about a year later, Ranjit Singh suffered his second heart attack in five years. It left him partly paralyzed but still in possession of his mind. Medicines having failed to cure him, he tried propitiation by giving away his riches to the priests and the poor. Osborne noted in July 1839 that "two hours before he died, he sent for all his jewels, and gave the famous diamond, called the Mountain of Light, said to be the largest in the world, to a Hindoo temple."

In fact, the priests received many of the jewels but not the Koh-i-Noor because the keeper of the jewel house, a man named Misr Beli Ram, protested to the dying Maharajah that the stone was a Crown Jewel and not a personal possession to be given away like a trinket. Misr Beli Ram must have been a brave man and a man of great principle, if the story be true. He had his way because the diamond did not go to the temple but to Ranjit Singh's successors.

## The Sikh Wars

Before this time, in an attempt to create some semblance of order in the tribal areas west of the Punjab, the British had restored the weak but resilient Shuja as Shah mainly because they suspected Russia, which had conquered Persia, of intending to advance through Afghanistan into India. Historically, this was a fundamentally wrong decision that led to the disastrous First Afghan War.

The troubles and uncertainties following Ranjit Singh's death were also of considerable concern to the British, who still maintained a treaty of friendship with the Punjab. In the inevitable battle for power, a son took the throne and was deposed in months by his own son, who was murdered and succeeded by his mother. The succession was fought over so frequently that, in the end, there was only one claimant left, the son of a water carrier and a dancer, who had been passed off as Ranjit's child by a member of his harem.

His name was Dhulip Singh. As he was a boy at the time, his mother and the man she now lived with were appointed Regents by the tribal chiefs behind them.

When the new Maharajah Dhulip Singh took over, he was still in his teens. He was not wily like Ranjit Singh and was insensitive to the balance of power that had been achieved. The Regents must have been unaware of or discounted the fact that this had been achieved by not interfering with the independent Sikh tribes south of the river Sutlej. One of their early acts was to attack the Cis-Sutlej tribes.

The British saw it as an attack upon themselves, and the result was the First Sikh War, which lasted for seven weeks over the turn of 1845 to 1846 when British soldiers and Sikh warriors faced each other in battle for the first time. Ten thousand Sikhs died but only 320 British. Slightly more than a week later, Dhulip Singh surrendered. The British appointed an agent to Lahore, and a Sikh Council of Regents was set up to advise Dhulip Singh.

The Sikhs assumed that the British would occupy the Punjab, but the British were much happier with an arrangement like that they had with Ranjit Singh. Apart from the difficulties of holding down hostile tribes and the danger of war with other would-be occupying countries, the Honourable East India Company had economic indigestion and wanted no more territories to rule, only countries to trade in.

However, that was not to be. The British were forced into the action they had been trying to avoid not by a Sikh but by the Muslim governor of the southern Punjabi province of Multan, who provoked them into laying siege to the town. After Multan had capitulated, the British moved two armies to Gujerat, where they engaged the Sikh army with much the same result as the first encounter, except that this time, the battlefield was strewn with dead and only 96 soldiers from all the British forces were killed.

On March 29, 1849, the Honorable William Elliot, emissary of the young Governor General of India, Lord Dalhousie, met members of the Sikh Regency that had been advising Dhulip Singh. Both the Regents and the Maharajah signed a document submitting to British rule.

About the occasion, Dalhousie wrote in a letter, ". . . surrendered the Koh-i-noor to the Queen of England; the British colours were hoisted on the Citadel of Lahore, and the Punjab, every inch of it, was proclaimed to be a portion of the British Empire in India."

The directors of the East India Company in Britain were far from overjoyed at the news and thought that at least they should have received the diamond to help pay for the unwelcomed gift of more territory to administer. There was an acrimonious exchange of correspondence, about which

Dalhousie commented that the directors were "ruffled at my having caused the Maharajah to cede to the Queen the Koh-i-noor. . . . " Others, he went on, censured him for "leaving even a Roman pearl to the Court."

Dalhousie was a man who made up his mind, acted, and stood by his actions. He was not even faintly apprehensive about the possibility that the British government might disapprove of his precipitous annexation because he made the remark that it was not every day an officer of the government "adds four millions of subjects to the British Empire and places the historical jewel of the Mugul Emperors in the Crown of her Sovereign." He emphasized it in a very provocative way. "If the Government sanction and approve my act (as unless they are maniacs they must do), their approval must be full and conspicuous."

## *The Journey to England*

The treaty was simple, consisting of five short statements, as Stephen Howarth wrote in his book *The Koh-i-Noor Diamond* (London, 1980), one of which related to the diamond: "The gem called Koh-i-noor which was taken from Shah Sooja-ool-Moolk by Maharajah Runjeet Singh shall be surrendered by the Maharajah of Lahore to the Queen of England."

One clause guaranteed Dhulip Singh a pension, his title, and status. As he was still underage, a Dr. Logan was made his guardian. Dr. Logan was also given charge of the treasury, which had been handed over without an inventory of any kind, so his first task was to list the contents with the help of an old man, Misr Maharaj, the keeper. The treasury contained not only great amounts of gems, gold, and silver but rooms full of Kashmeri shawls laid out and in great bundles.

Two brothers, Henry and John Lawrence, had been appointed joint governors of the Punjab, and it was to John that the diamond was entrusted when it was removed from the treasury for transfer to Britain. It appeared to have been a good choice because John Lawrence was completely untouched by greed or the value and glamour attached to the famous stone.

About six weeks later, a message came from Lord Dalhousie stating that Queen Victoria wanted the diamond to be sent to her at once. Henry Lawrence passed on the message to his brother John, who said they should retrieve it from the treasury.

"Why? *You've* got it," Henry exclaimed.

Although John was horror-stricken (according to Boswell-Smith, as quoted by Stephen Howarth), he gave no outward sign of his emotion as the meeting proceeded. He had remembered putting it in his waistcoat pocket when it was given to him and had thereafter completely forgotten it. As soon as he could slip away, he called for his bearer and asked if he had come across a small box that had been in a waistcoat pocket. With immense relief, he heard the bearer telling him that it had been put away in an old tin box. The box was retrieved and the diamond removed from its cloth wrappings. "Sahib. There is nothing but a piece of glass," said the bearer.

The first problem was to carry the diamond safely overland from Lahore to Bombay, a journey of 3,000 miles mainly by horse or carriage and often through hostile areas, to be shipped to England. It was partly solved by Lord Dalhousie offering to take the risk himself, with the assistance of his military secretary, Captain Ramsay. The diamond was doubly sewn into a belt that was not only secured around his waist but was also linked to a chain around his neck.

Dalhousie was far from impervious to the responsibility and risk despite his abounding self-confidence. "I undertook charge of it in a funk," he wrote, "and never was so happy in all my life as when I got it into the treasury in Bombay." He kept the belt on day and night except for one occasion when it was locked in a treasure check on which Captain Ramsay sat until Dalhousie returned.

Victorian writers of popular magazine and newspaper articles invented ingenious stories of the adventures of two messengers, one with the diamond and the other a decoy. Most of the stories concerned the strange religious tribe called the Thugs, who disguised themselves very successfully to gain the confidence of their intended victims and then ritually strangled them with yellow silk scarves before robbing them. They thrived in Mongol days and were still active despite British attempts to suppress them. One Thug who was caught had murdered 931 people over 40 years.

On arrival in Bombay, the diamond was placed in an iron chest, which was double locked and then placed in a larger chest similarly sealed, each key being held by different people, including Captain Ramsay. The chest was loaded aboard Her Majesty's steam sloop *Medea* whose chief officer was Commander Lockyer. It sailed on April 6, 1850.

From the start, the voyage was ill-fated. Only one day out from Bombay there was an outbreak of cholera, and two men died. Commander Lockyer decided to continue on course across the Indian Ocean and eventually put into Mauritius, the large island off the southern African coast where the French had established themselves. Stores were almost exhausted, but as the ship's flags showed she was under quarantine, the Mauritian authorities would have nothing to do with her and, after two days, threatened that she would be fired on unless she left. Commander Lockyer was unable to get any fresh provisions, only some coal and a few medicines.

That was not the end of their troubles. Before reaching the Cape, they ran into a fierce storm that took away the main rigging, much of the decking, and almost dismasted the ship, but at least, when they did reach port, provisions were available and the cholera outbreak had been controlled.

On the run from the Cape, their luck changed, and, with boilers at full steam and paddles churning, they made the passage in 40 days, breaking all previous records, to anchor off Spithead, the naval base in the Solent, on June 29, 1850.

Only four days later, the Deputy Chairman of the Honourable East India Company, no doubt firmly suppressing any disloyal thoughts that may have arisen in his mind, presented the Koh-i-Noor to Her Majesty Queen Victoria of Great Britain, who was not, however, to be Empress of India until another 26 years had passed.

The arrival of the diamond in England encouraged much comment in the newspapers and magazines and aroused considerable public interest. Queen Victoria was soon wearing it. The Duke of Wellington, who carried the Sword of State to the prorogation of Parliament in the following month, wrote that the Queen wore "the great Lahore diamond, which looked like a breastplate."

## *The Great Exhibition*

It was at a time when another matter was generating considerable heat in Parliament and among the public. Prince Albert, Consort to Queen Victoria, had become obsessed by a visionary idea to mount a Great Exhibition in Hyde Park. But he was not a popular figure, being German and rather cold and arrogant in manner, despite the obvious love that he and the Queen felt for each other and his undoubted loyalty to Britain. He was unable to raise any official enthusiasm to the scheme with Parliament refusing financial backing. However, Prince Albert was a very determined man and appealed directly to the public for subscriptions. He was closer to public opinion than the government because he succeeded.

The most imaginative part of the Great Exhibition was to house it in a vast new building in Hyde Park to be constructed entirely of iron frames and glass to the design of Sir Joseph Paxton. It was to be called the Crystal Palace and was a concept that became a source of modern building ideas.

One of the principal exhibits was the Koh-i-Noor (Figure 2–1). The diamond was associated in a leading article in *The Times* with the opening of the Great Exhibition of the Industries of All Nations on May 1, 1851, in these lyrical words, "The blazing arch of lucid glass with the hot sun flaming on its polished ribs and sides shone like the Koh-i-Noor itself."

The diamond was displayed in a cage made of gilded iron near an impressive fountain that was created at the center of the Palace. The exhibitors were Messrs. Osler, whose catalog entry was, "Her Majesty the Queen . . . proprietor. The Great Diamond called Koh-i-Noor, or the Mountain of Light . . . Main Avenue. Jewel case in Engine-centro. Style designed by L. Grover." A potted history followed. During the five and a half months, the exhibition attracted six million visitors, about a third of the population of the time, although many of the visitors were from abroad.

Most of them must have seen the diamond, but such a glorious image had been created in people's minds by the glowing words of writers who had not seen it (like, no doubt, the writer of *The Times* leader) that the reality was a disappointment. A writer in *Illustrated London News* commented, "The Koh-i-Noor is not cut in the best form for exhibiting its purity and lustre, and it will therefore disappoint many, if not all, of those who so anx-

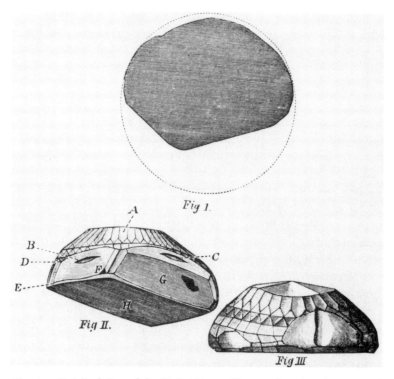

Fig. 2–1 Original Cut of the Koh-i-Noor. Figures showing the original cut of the Koh-i-Noor, before it was altered (see Fig. 2-2). It was a principal exhibit at the Great Exhibition of 1851 in Hyde Park, where six million visitors viewed it in the Crystal Palace. *(Courtesy of the Oxford University Press.)*

iously press forward to see it." After describing the stone as shaped like a pear or rather more oblong, the writer expressed the opinion that if recut by a European merchant, it would be much reduced in size but its marketable value would be increased and it would probably become one of the finest diamonds in Europe.

## Cutting the Koh-i-Noor

The appearance of the diamond had also displeased Prince Albert and, presumably, Queen Victoria. Weighing $186^1/_2$ carats, it had triangular facets over the domed part in the style known as "rose-cut." There was a large cleavage (natural split) underneath and a smaller one on the side as well as several other flaws. Although it was very large for a diamond, it undoubtedly lacked the scintillation and fire of spectrum colors that were expected. It was valued at the time at £140,000.

After it was removed from the exhibition, a decision was made at the Royal Palace to have it recut. It was a momentous decision to cause a radical transformation of appearance and weight to the most historical gem in existence for the sake of fashion because that is what it was. The decision was probably not made without careful thought, but it was certainly made with regard only to the diamond's immediate use and with no sense of history.

There does not seem to have been any strong body of opposition to the course proposed, although C. W. King, a 19th century authority on antique gems, expressed his views astringently later in his book *The Natural History of Precious Stones and of the Precious Metals* (London, 1865). "A most ill-advised proceeding, which has deprived the stone of all its historical and mineralogical value; for as a specimen of a monster diamond whose native weight and form had been as little as possible diminished by Art (for the grand object of Hindu lapidary is to preserve the weight) it was unrivaled in Europe, and giving in their stead a badly shaped shallow brilliant of inferior water but only $102^1/_4$ carats in weight."

There is no doubt that King was right. A number of years after he wrote these words, Marcel Tolkowsky calculated the best angles and proportions of cutting to provide the optimum amount of life (light returned to the eye) and fire (display of flashing color) in a diamond, a shape toward which cutters and polishers had been groping for a long time. Between this ideal cut and the original, the proportions proposed were a poor compromise and could have given little improvement while destroying much of the historical value.

Recutting was entrusted to the reputable firm of Coster in Amsterdam,

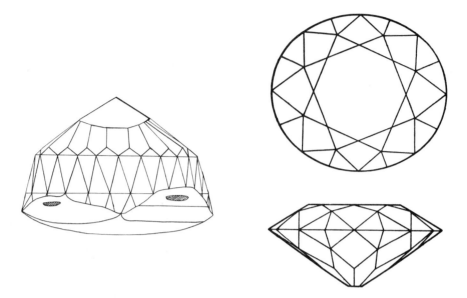

Fig. 2–2 New Cut of the Koh-i-Noor. Prince Albert and Queen Victoria had the stone recut, making a radical transformation in appearance and weight (compare old cut at *left*, with new at *right*). The diameter was actually increased by taking a sloping plane through the old stone to provide the girdle of the new one. *(Courtesy of The Oxford University Press.)*

but was actually carried out in England by an employee named Voorsanger under the supervision of James Tennant, mineralogist to the Queen, who despite his undoubted knowledge of minerals could have known little of the diamond polisher's applied crystallography, a skill learned over many centuries and not disclosed to others.

The aging Duke of Wellington was invited to watch the start of the polishing on a special scaive (horizontal grinding wheel) that had been constructed. It was driven by a "four-horse machine" because the steam engine with a crank did not come into general use until the 1880s. The Duke is supposed to have placed the first facet, but he probably held the tang (the traditional jig for holding the diamond on the scaive) for a short time. Another report credits the Prince Consort with this honor.

The work of recutting was begun on July 16, 1852, and finished on September 7, taking 38 days of 12 hours each. The cost was reported to have been £8,000. The weight was reduced to 108.9 metric carats, but the diameter was increased by taking a sloping plane through the old stone to provide the girdle of the new one, making the new stone slightly oval. The work of recutting was supervised by Garrard and Co., the Crown Jewelers, with Sebastion Garrard in charge. One of the many notable visitors asked Robert Garrard what he would do if the Koh-i-Noor flew to pieces. "Take my name plate off the door and bolt," he answered.

The "new" Koh-i-Noor (Figure 2–2) was worn by Queen Victoria set in a brooch or in a bracelet and in a small circlet made for it. She supplied a number of diamonds, including one of $17^1/_8$ carats, that had been in a stomacher given to her by the Sultan of Turkey. The circlet is now in the London Museum. On the Queen's death in 1901, the Koh-i-Noor was mounted in the center of the front cross *patté* of a new crown made for Queen Alexandra, wife of King Edward VII, for his coronation.

The crown incorporated several new features, including a frame made of platinum instead of gold and four arches instead of two. It thus became the first consort's crown to carry the Koh-i-Noor. At George V's coronation, a new crown was made for Queen Mary. Again, the Koh-i-Noor was set in the cross *patté*, and the third and fourth largest stones cut from the Cullinan were also included. Diamonds are the only gems in this beautiful crown made by Garrard, the Crown Jewelers.

The platinum frame of Queen Alexandra's crown is now in the London Museum and carries a paste (special lead glass) replica of the Koh-i-Noor. The frame of Queen Mary's crown also contains a replica of the stone but one made of rock crystal. It is on display at the Jewel House at the Tower of London. These replicas are of the diamond in its new cut. A glass reproduction of it in the original Indian cut, made for the exhibitors, was later presented for display at the Punjab Exhibition and is now in the Lahore Museum. The original Indian enameled bracelet (Color Plate 1) in which the Koh-i-Noor was set is in the London Museum.

## *A Reputation of Ill Omen*

At no time has the Koh-i-Noor been worn in the crown of a King of England, which may be by accident of history or by design. Its reputation of ill omen when worn by a man who was the owner has persisted for many years and seems to have been updated to accommodate modern history. The legend is that to own it is to rule the world, but it is dangerous for men although not for women. The corollary was no doubt added when Queen Victoria owned and wore it during a long and successful reign.

The legend makers did not attempt to associate it with the good fortune of a shepherd boy turned soldier who became fabulously wealthy, only with their inevitable deaths. Not long after Queen Victoria acquired the stone, she was attacked by a retired lieutenant of the 10th Hussary who had gone mad. The blame was laid by some on Lord Dalhousie [Private Letters of the Marquess of Dalhousie (London, 1910)] for having the stone presented, a belief that drew a spirited response from him. "Whoever was the exquisite person from whom you heard this (nobody could be so stupid except Joseph Hume) he was rather lame on both his history and tradition. . . . Nadir Shah who took it was usually reckoned well-to-do in the world throughout his life, and that Ranjit Singh has usually been thought to have prospered tolerably. . . . Shah Soojah said. . . "Its value is Good Fortune, for whoever possesses it has been superior to all his enemies."

General H. D. W. Sitwell, at one time Keeper of the Tower of London, nudged the ill-omen legend along in a lecture at the Victoria and Albert Museum about the treasures in his custody. "It came to Queen Victoria on the collapse of the Sikh Empire in the 1840s with the legend that it was bad luck for any man to wear it." He thought that if ever a precious stone dripped blood, it was the Koh-i-Noor, and in that he was right. Even as late as 1981, an Indian publication about the diamond trade revived the superstition.

In a book, *The Annexation of the Punjab and the Maharajah Duleep Singh* (London, 1882), Major Thomas Evans Bell implied that taking the Koh-i-Noor was a breach of trust. There is a curious story about Dhulip Singh, the last Indian owner of the Koh-i-Noor, being shown the stone by Queen Victoria. Dhulip Singh had been brought to London to live with Lady Login, who had taken over his guardianship after her husband had died. An arrangement had been made for him to have his portrait painted at Buckingham Palace. Lady Login always accompanied him on these occasions. One day, the Queen asked her if Dhulip Singh had ever expressed a wish to see the diamond again; the Queen had never mentioned it to him and would have felt "a certain delicacy" about wearing the gem in his presence.

Lady Login replied that although he had often mentioned the stone when they were in India and had been interested in its recutting, he had said nothing about it since they had been in England. The Queen then suggested that Lady Login find out before the next sitting what his feelings were on the subject. This was done, and the Maharajah remarked that he would not only like to see it but "would give a great deal to hold it in his hand." He was also reported as saying that he was only a child when he had surrendered it and would like himself to place it in the hands of the Queen now that he was a man.

The next day, this was reported to the Queen, and while the court painter was busy, she gave orders for the gem to be brought to the Palace from the Tower. The painting was being done on a dais at the end of a large room, and the diamond was delivered to the Queen at the other end. She advanced with it and placed it in Dhulip Singh's hands, asking if he thought that the recutting had improved it and whether he would have recognized it. He took it to the window and examined it carefully, remarking on its smaller size and greater brilliance. Then "with a low obeisance," he presented it to the Queen, saying it was with great pleasure he placed it in her hands.

That is the Login side of the story. It has been suggested that Lady Login was prompted by her worry that the diamond might not have been the state property of Lahore to be confiscated, but had been the personal property of the Maharajah to be given. Dalhousie's opinion was not in doubt. "Login's talk about the Koh-i-Noor being a present from Dhulip Singh to the Queen is arrant humbug."

According to Stephen Howarth in his book, *The Koh-i-Noor Diamond*, (London, 1980) Dhulip Singh began privately to refer to the Queen as "Mrs. Fagin" and said he had as much right to Windsor Castle as she had to the Koh-i-Noor. Some years later, he made an unsuccessful plea in letters to *The Times* for Parliament to provide him with a higher allowance and for the return of his property because of the cost of maintaining the estate he had bought at Elveden in Essex.

In 1976, President Bhutto of Pakistan claimed the return of the Koh-i-Noor. While his letter was being considered by Prime Minister James Callaghan and Buckingham Palace officials, a counterclaim arrived from India's Deputy High Commissioner in London, Natwar Singh, who said, "Mr. Bhutto can make any request he likes. There are other people interested in it." Neither Iran or Afghanistan have laid claims. Meanwhile, it reposes in the Jewel House of the Tower of London, mounted in the front of the crown of Queen Elizabeth the Queen Mother.

Suddenly, as rare things will, it vanished.
            *Robert Browning (1812–1889).*

---

*Chapter Three*

# Famous Diamonds That Vanished

 HE biggest and once most cele-
brated diamond found in India was the Great Mogul (Figure 3–1), named
after Shah Akbar (1542–1605), the greatest of all. The French jeweler and
traveler, J.-B. Tavernier, was permitted to inspect and weigh it, along with
other diamonds, in November 1665 (a month after the outbreak of the Great
Fire of London), when he was a guest of the Emperor Aurangzeb. Unfortunately, since Tavernier's visit, all traces of the diamond have vanished. It
was the size of a small hen's egg but like half an egg in shape.

The stone had been given to Shah Jahan by his Minister of State, Mir
Jumla, around 1656 or 1657. It could have passed into one of the hands of
subsequent Indian princes and still exist somewhere, although this is un-
likely. The Russian mineralogist, E. A. Fersman, believed it was the Koh-i-
Noor, then changed his mind and suggested it was the Darya-i-Noor, in the
Persian (Iranian) Crown Jewels. But it is now known that this is not so.

Dr. Valentine Ball of the Geological Survey of India, translator in 1889
of Tavernier's *Travels in India*, wrote convincingly: "Tavernier's account
of the Mogul's diamond has, I think, been fully proved . . . to be quite in-
applicable to Barbur's diamond, while all his facts and the balance of prob-
ability favour the view that in the Koh-i-Noor we are justified in recogniz-
ing the mutilated Mogul's diamond." Another explanation offered for its
disappearance is that it became the Orloff.

The Great Mogul, Koh-i-Noor, and the Orloff were of similar shape,
like half an egg, faceted over the domed area, but if the Great Mogul were
one of the other two, Tavernier must have made a mistake in his weights
and description. However, Tavernier's records have been found generally

very reliable, allowing for the state of knowledge at the time. After all, he was a diamond dealer and not likely to make mistakes in measurements affecting his livelihood and reputation. It seems unlikely that a diamond of about 280 carats (the Great Mogul) was "mutilated" to produce one of very similar shape but weighing 186 (the Koh-i-Noor) or 193 carats (the Orloff). (An "old" carat is one that was weighed before the current weighing measures, which are now uniform throughout the world.)

Tavernier was brought before Emperor Aurangzeb by a body of officers and, at the Emperor's command, the Keeper of the Jewels sent four eunuchs to bring the gems for the Frenchman's inspection. About this incident, he wrote, "The first stone that Akel Khan (Keeper of the Jewels) placed in my hands was a great diamond cut as a round rose, very high on one side. It had a small notch on one of its edges, and a flaw inside. It was of the first water. . . . " (The purest white diamonds were described as being as pure as a limpid stream, hence, the expression "the first water." Those with a tinge of color were described as "byewater.")

Tavernier declared that the Great Mogul weighed 900 ratis in the rough, "equivalent to $787^1/_2$ carats" when it was presented to Shah Jahan by Mir Jumla. But when he saw it, it had been through the hands of a cutter and polisher named Hortensio Borgio from Venice and weighed $319^1/_2$ ratis or "280 of our carats." Borgio was accused of having spoiled the stone, which should have retained more weight, and the Emperor, instead of paying him, fined him 10,000 rupees and would have taken more but that was all the Venetian possessed.

Borgio was not a very accomplished cutter, Tavernier stated, because if he had understood his trade, he could have split a large piece from the stone (by cleaving) without producing so much trouble for himself in the subsequent grinding. Although Indian cutters could cleave as well as the Europeans, their polishing left a lot to be desired, which is probably why Borgio was entrusted with the work.

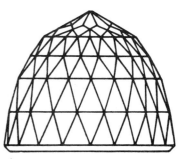

Fig. 3–1 The Great Mogul. Although all traces of the Great Mogul have vanished, it is known that it was the size of a small hen's egg but like half an egg in shape. *(Courtesy of N. A. G. Press Ltd., Ipswich.)*

## Changing Weights

Tavernier could make mistakes of memory. In the second volume of his *Travels in India*, he referred to the Great Mogul being presented to Aurangzeb instead of Shah Jahan. He also referred to the rough weight as having been 907 ratis or $793^5/_8$ carats, so the earlier figure he was given was probably rounded off. He was allowed to weigh the stone he was shown, which scaled $279^9/_{16}$ carats, agreeing with his earlier figure of 280 carats. Weights have long been a cause of confusion. The Indians used the miskat, the mangelin, and the rati. In his memoirs, the Mogul Emperor Barbur referred to the miskat being equal to 40 ratis. Tavernier calculated that the carat weight used in France was equal to seven-eighths of a rati. Diamond traders in the Kingdom of Golconda and Visapur used the mangelin, which, again according to Tavernier, was equivalent to $1^3/_8$ carats.

The European carat, too, was not standard at the time and varied from country to country. The name is derived from a tree that is quite common around the Mediterranean basin, the locust tree or *Ceratonia Siliqua*. The seeds are carried in large pods (like bean pods) and when dry vary very little in weight so that in earlier times they were used as weights for precious stones. The Biblical story of Saint John the Baptist feeding off locusts in the wilderness probably does not refer to flying insects but to the pods of the locust tree because the seeds are carried in a syruplike honey.

Another weight used in Europe was the grain, actually a grain of barley (or wheat). Variations from country to country were small in weight terms but could represent a bigger difference in value. For example, Florence in Italy had the lightest carat and Venice (and later Madras) the heaviest. There were many variations between the extremes. It was also normal until this century to give accurate weights by fractions of one-half, one-fourth, one-eighth, and so on up to one-sixty-fourth for most gems, but often only in sixty-fourths for diamonds; thus, a diamond could weight $30^8/_{64}$ carats. The grain is still used in the diamond trade today as a rough measure. "A four grainer" is a diamond weighing around a carat, so there are four grains to the carat. Until 1922, a grain was 3.1683 of a carat, and 480 grains made a Troy ounce.

The metric carat used today equals one-fifth of a gram and was not introduced internationally without overcoming considerable resistance and apathy, as was the case with metric coinage. The French led the way and adopted a metric carat in 1907, followed by Spain in 1907 and a number of other countries in subsequent years. Great Britain, Holland, Belgium, and the United States legalized the metric carat simultaneously in 1914. Other countries followed at intervals, with Czechoslovakia and Poland being

Fig. 3–2 The Orloff Diamond. One of the most superb quality diamonds ever to come from India, it has fortunately never been tampered with and retains its original Indian cut. It is one of the treasures of the Diamond Fund in the Kremlin, Moscow. *(Courtesy of De Beers Consolidated Mines.)*

among the last in 1930. Germany, it appeared, adopted it without legal·formality.

## *The Orloff Diamond*

The Orloff Diamond (Figure 3–2) is believed to be one of the most superb in quality ever to come from India. Unlike the Koh-i-Noor, it has not been tampered with and retains its original Indian cut, so it has remarkable historical value as well. It is now one of the most valuable treasures of the Diamond Fund in the Kremlin, Moscow. (Although the Orloff Diamond is not missing, it is rumored to be a smaller part of the vanished Great Mogul.)

The Orloff Diamond was the inspiration of Wilkie Collins to write his famous novel *The Moonstone,* published in 1868. In it, an English officer steals the Moonstone from the forehead of an idol in a Buddhist temple in

Seringapatam and three intrepid Brahmins (actually, they are Hindus, not Buddhists) travel to England to recover the stone. T. S. Eliot described the book as "the first, the longest, and the best of modern English detective novels."

The Orloff could have belonged to the Moguls, like other big diamonds of the time, but it is more likely that Hindus owned it until it was stolen. An early history was offered by E. W. Streeter in his book *The Great Diamonds of the World* (London, 1882), which he claimed was "generally accepted." He based his account on a story in a book, *Des Pierres Précieuses et des Pierres Fines* by Dutens, published in Florence in 1783. The diamond was one of the eyes of a statue of Brahma in a temple on the fortified island of Srirangam on the river Cauvery, two miles north of Trichinopoli in Mysore. A deserter from the French Garrison in India ingratiated himself with the priests by pretending to be converted to Hinduism and was eventually appointed guard of the temple. One day, he prized out one eye of the idol but was unable to remove the other, so he made off with the one to Madras.

There he sold the diamond for £2,000 to the captain of an English ship, who on arrival in London, found a merchant who gave him £12,000 for it. Eventually, it reached the hands of a dealer, perhaps the Persian named Khojeh Raphael, who was of Armenian extraction. A Persian traveler of the time described him as "a complete old scoundrel, who has seen a great deal of the world, and understood a number of languages." Khojeh went to Surat and then lived in Bengal, England, and Russia, settling finally in Leghorn. Another account gives the dealer's name as Laserer, an Armenian. The Court Jeweler to the Empress Catherine, who acquired the stone, was named Lasaroff, so there may have been confusion over the name and the Armenian dealer Laserer did not really exist.

At any rate, the diamond was certainly sold in Amsterdam to Prince Gregori Gregorievich Orloff, from whom it acquired its name. Orloff is said to have paid 400,000 roubles, according to one informant, and the equivalent of £90,000, an annuity of £4,000, and a patent of nobility, according to another. There are more differing reports.

A letter from The Hague dated January 2, 1776, and published in *Museum Britanicum* (London, 1791) states, "We learn from Amsterdam that Prince Orloff made but one stay in that city, where he bought a very large brilliant for the Empress, his sovereign, for which he paid the Persian merchant the sum of 400,000 florins Dutch money." This dates the purchase as at the end of 1775.

The Prince was the lover of Catherine before she became Empress

Catherine II in 1762. From 1765, however, she bestowed most of her favors on Potemkin, who retained them until he died in 1791. Orloff knew she had been offered the diamond but had turned it down on the grounds that the price was too high. So he hoped to regain favor, even perhaps to marry her, by presenting it to her. In those hopes, he was unlucky. She accepted the stone and gave him a marble palace in St. Petersburg (Leningrad) instead of her hand.

Catherine had the diamond set in an Imperial Sceptre, which was designed for her by the jeweler C. N. Troitinski in about 1784. The scepter is a burnished shaft in three sections set with eight rings of brilliant-cut diamonds, including some of about 30 carats each and fifteen weighing about 14 carats each. The Orloff is set at the top, with its domed top facing forward. Above it is a double-headed eagle with the Arms of Russia enameled on its breast.

In his exhaustive work *History of the Crown Jewels of Europe*, Lord Twining relates a story of how the big diamond fell from its setting when Agathon Fabergé was cataloging the Crown Jewels in 1914. He weighed it and forgot to make a note at the time but thought it heavier than the old recorded weight of 185 carats. Lord Twining gives the recorded weight as of 1960 as $194^3/_4$ metric carats, but the latest (published in 1981) picture cards available in Moscow state that the weight is 189.62 carats.

The original rough diamond was interesting because it was part of an octahedron. Diamond crystals formed in nature tend to be of this shape if their growth was not obstructed. It is like two four-sided pyramids base to base. A peculiarity of a diamond is that it can split by a blow in the right place parallel to any of these triangular faces. This happened to the Orloff at some time after it was formed but still probably millions of years ago. The part recovered was the largest portion of a very large rounded octahedral crystal and weighed about 300 carats. The whole crystal would have weighed about 450 carats. When the Orloff was cut, the cleaved face (that which joined it to the original crystal from which it was split) was curved, so it must have been more of a fracture than a cleavage. This was used as the base of the stone. The size is 22 millimeters high by 35 millimeters long and 31 millimeters to 32 millimeters wide (about $^7/_8$ inch by $1^3/_4$ inches by $1^1/_4$ inches) and the color is white (which is the diamond trade's name for absolutely colorless and transparent) with a faint bluish-green tint.

## The Russian Diamond Fund

Catherine contributed more gems and jewels to the Diamond Fund, where the Russian Regalia and Crown Jewels are, than anyone else. Lord

Twining estimated that through her excesses of luxury, she added about 40 per cent to what had existed. A small number of highly skilled designer-craftsmen produced extraordinary work during these times, but, unfortunately, most of what they made was broken up in the 19th century so that the raw materials could be used to produce new work, which turned out to be of inferior design.

Stones of Russian origin had a special attraction for Catherine, who added alexandrites and aquamarines among other stones to the Diamond Fund from the gem mines in the Ural Mountains and in Siberia. The Diamond Fund contains more than 25,300 carats of diamonds, including 70 with an average weight of more than 20 carats each and more than 200 weighing from 5 carats to 10 carats each. There are 1,700 carats of large sapphires and 2,600 carats of smaller ones but only 260 carats of rubies, all of which, however, are of high quality. It is also rich in fine pearls.

A start was made in 1914 on cataloging the treasures in the Fund, as mentioned earlier, by the House of Fabergé, who had become Court Jewelers. After a good start, Agathon Fabergé was beginning on the crowns when he had orders from the Czar to send the whole collection under guard to the Kremlin for safety. War broke out shortly afterwards and during the Revolution that followed, Fabergé was arrested and twice imprisoned.

On his second release, he received a message from Trotsky asking him to go to Moscow to sit on a commission that had been set up to value the Regalia and the Crown Jewels. Fabergé turned down this and a later invitation on the grounds of ill health. Then a third invitation arrived at his house—delivered by two Red Army soldiers at 3 o'clock in the morning. The letter was again from Trotsky and in friendly terms, but this time, Fabergé took the hint and joined the commission.

It took from the autumn of 1921 to the spring of 1923 to photograph, weigh, and record the measurements and details of each item, and in 1926, the jewels were put on display with a catalog in four languages, apparently as the prelude to their sale. Indeed, a syndicate did buy some and sold them through Christie's auction house in 1927. But the Russian government changed its mind and decided to keep all the items of historical value or artistic worth. Many of them can be seen today by visitors lucky enough to get passes into the Diamond Fund; but they cannot be inspected closely because a visitor who lingers in front of one of the cases is soon moved on.

An interesting suggestion was made by G. G. Waite in *Lapidary Journal* of June 1972. Pointing out that the Orloff has three facets and a groove at the back, he concluded that an attempt had been made to drill the Great

Mogul, but part had split off and the now smaller diamond had become the Orloff.

## Legend of the Moon of the Mountain

Still another diamond that has been "identified" by a few writers in the past as the Great Mogul is one listed as weighing about 126 carats and is named the Moon of the Mountains. According to E. W. Streeter, writing a century ago, it was one of the Moguls' treasures seized by Nadir Shah and taken to Afghanistan. It is also said to have been at one time among the Russian Crown Jewels, but it has seemingly vanished.

The legend is that shortly after Nadir's murder in 1747, an Afghan soldier who had served with him turned up in Basra, on the Persian Gulf, with the Moon of the Mountains, a large and magnificent emerald, and various other gemstones in his possession. He showed the stones to an Armenian merchant named Gregori Safarov Shaffras, who made an offer but declared he needed time to raise the money.

This scared the soldier, who fled to Baghdad, where he sold the diamond to a dealer for 65,000 piasters (£500 then) and two thoroughbred Arab horses. Shaffras went to Baghdad and by chance came across the soldier living in a debauched way. He heard about the sale, but the dealer refused to sell the stone to him, so, with the help of his brother, he invited both the trader and the soldier to a party, gave them poisoned drinks, and, putting their bodies in sacks, threw them into the Tigris at night. Shaffras then fell out with his brother over the division of their gains, so he killed him and disposed of his body in the same way.

With the diamond, he made his way to Constantinople and then across Europe to Amsterdam, the center of diamond trading. News of the big diamond reached the ears of Catherine, who invited Shaffras to the Russian Court. Here he was received by the Court Jeweler, W. Lasaroff, who offered him an annuity of 10,000 roubles and a patent of nobility, which he refused, demanding 50,000 roubles.

The offer was turned down, and Catherine ordered Count Pania to find out what he could about Shaffras. It was soon evident that the man was living riotously and was heavily in debt. He was told that he would not be allowed to leave Russia until all his debts were paid, hoping that this would force him to sell the diamond. Somehow, Shaffras managed to raise the money and quickly slipped away. The Tsarina was determined to have the Moon of the Mountains and ten years later, when Shaffras was in Astrakhan, he was persuaded to sell it to her on the original terms.

In *Travels through the Southern Provinces of the Russian Empire in 1793-4* published in 1812, the author, P. S. Pallas, related the story as told to him by the heirs of Gregori Safarov Shaffras in Astrakhan. In this version, their ancestor turns out to be an honest and upright man.

The Moon of the Mountains was stolen as described by an Afghan serving Nadir Shah, but after his initial offer was refused, Shaffras followed the Afghan to Baghdad and persuaded him to sell the stone for 50,000 piasters. Twelve years later, Shaffras and his brother decided that Shaffras should take the diamond to Europe to try to sell it to Catherine. He was invited to the Russian Court, and Count Pania, the Russian Minister who had helped overthrow her husband, Peter the Great, made an offer for the stone of 500,000 roubles, 100,000 roubles on demand and the rest payable in installments over ten years, plus a pension of 6,000 roubles and a patent of nobility.

Shaffras wanted a patent of nobility for his brother as well, but this was refused and the diamond returned to him. He left for Astrakhan but kept in contact with the Russians, later selling the stone, according to the descendants' account, to Count Orloff for 450,000 roubles (less 120,000 for commission and expenses) and a patent of nobility. This is where confusion occurs with the Orloff, although it is just possible that the Count, or Prince, bought two diamonds at different times and both passed into the Russian Crown Jewels.

## *The Great Table*

An unusual stone that certainly existed and was thought to be missing is usually known as the Great Table (Figure 3-3). Tavernier not only weighed it while in Golconda in 1642 but was allowed by the merchant who showed it to him to make a lead model of it to be sent to two of his friends in Surat who were interested in buying stones. It weighed $176^{1}/_{8}$ mangelins, which he calculated was $242^{5}/_{16}$ carats. The stone was named after the style of cutting, although in this case, it was unusual in tapering slightly along its length and having one corner truncated.

The merchant wanted half a million rupees, but Tavernier's friends offered 400,000 rupees if it were clean and of fine water. The sale was re-

Fig. 3–3 The Great Table Diamond. Illustration #3 among these drawings is the Great Table Diamond, unusual because of the taper and truncated corner. It has almost certainly been reduced to the Darya-i-Noor and Noor-al-Ain Diamonds. *(Courtesy of The Oxford University Press.)*

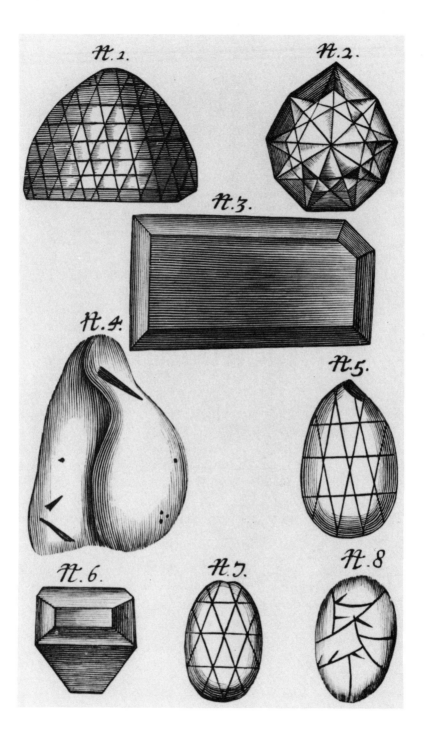

fused. Apart from the illustration in Tavernier's book, that is all that was known for a long time.

It was strange for such a diamond to be for sale in the hands of a merchant and not the King of Golconda or one of his ministers. A possible explanation is that the King, having been defeated by an army led by his ex-Prime Minister, Mir Jumla, and made to pay a heavy tribute to Aurangzeb, had been forced to sell some of his treasures.

Some researchers have surmised that the Great Table Diamond will never turn up again as itself because it has almost certainly been reduced to several smaller stones, the origin of which it would be impossible to ascertain. Another possibility was suggested by Professor S. Tolansky, who studied various technical aspects of diamonds. In 1962, he announced that the Great Table Diamond had never existed.

He pointed out that Tavernier's chapter in *Travels in India* with comments about illustrations on five plates was headed (in the translation Tolansky relied on), "Observations on the largest and fairest diamonds and rubies which the author has seen in Europe and Asia, represented according to the figures in the Plates. . . . " The Great Table was Illustration 3 on the first plate (See Figure 3–3), on which six different stones were shown, two of them twice. Illustrations 1, 2, 4, 5, and 6 were referred to as diamonds, and those numbered 3, 7, and 8 were called stones in the translation. Therefore, Tolansky inferred that these two must have been rubies and that the Great Table was a ruby.

He added that another table-cut stone was a diamond and was illustrated differently on the plate, having the pavilion (the lower part) shown attached to the top. He also maintained that the shape of the Great Table was completely anomalous as a diamond (i.e., as a rough diamond that could or would have been cut in that way). However, in Dr. Valentine Ball's translation of the passage concerned, Tavernier does later refer to the stone as a diamond.

Most researchers seem to have missed Harford Jones' report in which the author, after examining the Darya-i-Noor in 1791, stated that it is positively the Great Table illustrated by Tavernier. The Darya-i-Noor (Sea or River of Light), sister stone to the Koh-i-Noor, was looted with the rest of the Mogul treasury from Delhi by Nadir Shah in 1739 and taken to Persia. It and the Taj-e-Mah (Crown of the Moon) were set in matching armbands for the Persian monarchs to wear.

In recent times, a large polished pink diamond in the Iranian Crown Jewels called the Darya-i-Noor has been recognized as the major part of the Great Table, which was the original unpolished diamond, the Darya-i-

Noor. The identification was carried out by a team of Canadian specialists from the Royal Ontario Museum, Toronto, who were able in 1966 to gain access to the collection, which had never before been studied seriously and, indeed, had been shut away from almost all eyes except those of the Shahs and their advisers until some were put on display in December 1960. Since the revolution, they have been shut away again, but in late 1982, it was believed that Ayatollah Khomeni had secretly sold the Darya-i-Noor. The Canadians' visit was financed by a grant from the Henry Birks Family Foundation of Montreal, which owns Canada's biggest jewelry retail business.

V. B. Meen (who suggested the visit in the first place), A. D. Tushingham, and G. G. Waite found themselves with vast quantities of loose gems as well as incredibly jeweled items never before recorded. They were particularly interested in the largest and finest diamond in the collection, which was mounted in a rectangular frame set with diamonds and surmounted by a crown flanked by lions, also set with diamonds except for the ruby eyes.

The stone itself was pale pink, flawless, and "unbelievable limpid." It is of nearly rectangular shape, having a slight taper, and is tablet step-cut, being 41.4 millimeters long (1.61 inches), 29.55 millimeters (1.15 inches) across the middle, and 12.15 millimeters (0.47 inches) thick. Engraved on one of the pavilion (back) facets in Persian script is the legend "As-Sultan Sahib Qiran Fath-Ali Shah Qajar 1250," which in modern idiom means "The Sultan, Lord of the (Auspicious) Conjunction, Fath-Ali Shah, the Qajar, 1834 A.D."

Because unmounting of the stone was forbidden, it was only possible to guess the weight, but it appeared to be near the usually quoted figure of 186 old (presumably) carats. Gemologist readers might like to know that this largest known pink diamond fluoresces blue under shortwave ultraviolet light and shows anomalous double refraction (an indication of strain) between crossed polaroid filters.

There is another large pink diamond among the Iranian treasures called the Noor-ul-Ain (Light of the Eye; Color Plate 2). It is the center stone in a platinum tiara made in recent years and is set also with many large yellow, pink, and colorless diamonds. The stone is of oval, tending to pear shape, but is very shallow, measuring about 1.15 inches by 1 inch by 0.45 inches (30 millimeters by 26 millimeters by 11 millimeters) and weighs about 60 carats. The appearance and quality are the same as the Darya-i-Noor, except for an unexpected cleavage flaw known as a "butterfly" by diamond graders.

This stone, the Canadians believe, after making scale models of the Great Table and the Iranian pink diamonds and studying the crystallographic orientations, was cut from the smaller part of the Great Table. There is, however, a snag in the theory, of which the authors are aware. The combined weight of the Darya-i-Noor and the Noor-ul-Ain is much too near that of the Great Table to allow for inevitable loss of material during cutting. They think the Great Table must have been nearer 300 carats.

The person who first described the Darya-i-Noor and identified it as the Great Table was Harford Jones, later Sir Harford Jones Brydges. He visited Iran in 1791 at the secret invitation of Lutf Ali-Khan, the last of the Zand dynasty, who wanted advice on selling the diamond to finance his battles with the Qajar leader, Agha Muhammad Khan. Harford Jones, who had been in Iran in 1787, later wrote a book, *The Dynasty of the Kajars* (London 1833). In it, he described how the king threw aside his cloak to reveal himself only in his undergarment. On each arm, he wore armlets set with many superb gems, including the Darya-i-Noor and the Taj-e-Mah. The first stone was prized from its mount so that the English visitor could examine it.

Harford Jones described it as a table diamond with a slight tinge of palish pink and with perfect and brilliant water."I instantly perceived it to agree with the drawing which Tavernier, in his Travels, has given of a stone offered him at Golconda; and for which, as he says, the proprietor asked five lacs of rupees, and he offered four. It so happened that I had with me a copy of Tavernier; and I shewed the drawing and valuation, there made, to the jeweller. . . . The shape and size of the gem perfectly agreed with. . . the size of the drawing given in Tavernier."

The weight of the Darya-i-Noor was conveyed to Harford Jones as 176 carats and a small fraction. The discrepancy between this and Tavernier's weight of 242 carats worried Jones as well as the Khan. "I began to doubt whether it could be the same stone: yet a little reflection convinced me that it was not likely there should be two stones in the world of such magnitude, without it being known in whose possession they were." He recalled a Mogul edict reducing the unit of weight, the miscal, but not the number of carats in it. Thus, the carat was also reduced in weight. Taking this into account, he estimated the weights of the two stones to be 704 grains for the Darya-i-Noor and 726 grains for Tavernier's stone — an ingenious explanation.

The Canadians have a simpler one. Tavernier reported in *Travels in India* the Great Table as "weighing $176^{1}/_{8}$ mangelins, which amounted to

$242^5/_{16}$ of our carats." Harford Jones must therefore have been given the weight of 176 in mangelins, which he mistranslated as carats.

The Darya-i-Noor known today is the same shape as the broader end of the slightly wedge-shaped Great Table Diamond but has wider beveled facets and is polished. Harford Jones wrote that the diamond he saw required polishing, so it seems likely that the Great Table and Darya-i-Noor were the same unpolished stone. It would have been named the Darya-i-Noor after it had passed into Persian hands. How then did the polished Darya-i-Noor become reduced in size?

After Harford Jones saw the original stone, it changed hands four times between 1795 and 1797 as the result of fighting. Fath-Ali Shah wore it in an armband early in his reign, which was from 1797 to 1834, but the inscription on it gives the date 1834, when he died. It is possible that the stone was damaged by a blow that cleaved it into two pieces at about that time, and the inscription was made when the larger part was polished, to become the largest polished pink diamond in the world.

## The Mirror of Portugal

The Mirror of Portugal was another table-cut diamond but much smaller, weighing 30 carats. It vanished after the bizarre robbery of the French Crown Jewels to be described in Chapter Four. The earliest owner recorded was Dom Antonio de Castro, Prior of Crato, an illegitimate nephew of King Manuel of Portugal, who reigned well over half a century earlier. When the old and feebleminded Cardinal Prince Henry died in 1578 after only a year on the throne, Dom Antonio proclaimed himself King and marched into Lisbon with a makeshift army, but he did not hold power for very long.

Philip II of Spain sent his army into Portugal because he had a stronger claim. Taking the throne, he declared that Portugal would remain a separate kingdom, a promise later broken. Dom Antonio fled to France and then on to England, hoping that Queen Elizabeth would support him. He took for payment a collection of jewels, including the Mirror of Portugal. (In his own country, he was sentenced to death on several charges, including theft of the Crown Jewels.)

Elizabeth accepted the jewels and promised aid. What might have been the Mirror was listed in the 1605 inventory (recorded in Lord Twining's book, *A History of the Crown Jewels of Europe* [London, 1960] of James I: "A flower (pendant) with a very large table diamond set in gold called "The Mirror." That same year, James issued an edict that the Imperial Crown and certain Crown Jewels be "forever annexed to the Kingdom of this realm." He did not reckon with his successor, Charles I.

Many years earlier, when he was Prince of Wales, Charles became very familiar with the Mirror because he wore it with other jewelry from the Tower of London (selected by the Royal Jeweler, Heriot) when trying to make an impression on the Spanish Royal family, and particularly on the Infanta, whom his father hoped he would marry. Suspended from the diamond, as it was worn, was the Cobham Pearl. In his hat, Charles displayed the Mirror of France (described by King James as a fellow of the Mirror of Portugal). He also wore the great Lorraine cross of diamonds and four other

Fig. 3–4 The Mancini Pearls. Each earring is composed of a large teardrop pearl with diamond-set leafage cap, supported by a pear-shaped diamond trefoil and surmounted by three circular-cut diamond collets. The drops are detachable and weigh more than 400 grains. *(Courtesy of Christie's, New York.)*

crosses. The array still did not win him a Spanish bride. He instead married a French woman.

In the first year of his reign, 1625, Charles sold various items from the Crown Jewels and some plate in Holland. His Queen, Henrietta Maria of Bourbon, sold or pawned more, including some of her own jewelry early in 1642 to raise money for weapons and powder. (Among Henrietta Maria's personal jewelry were the Mancini Pearls (Figure 3-4), which had acquired their name when Louis XIV presented them to Maria Mancini (1640–1715), the niece of Cardinal Mazarin, hoping to win her favor. In 1661, Maria married Prince Colonna, and the earrings with the Mancini Pearls remained in the Colonna family until one of the princesses married into the Rospigliosi family. They were later acquired by an anonymous collector, who consigned the earrings to Christie's as the highlight of the Geneva jewel sale in October 1969. Charles was in conflict with Parliament, which led to the Civil War in October of that year. In 1644, a year before Charles was defeated at Naseby, Henrietta Maria was back in France, still selling or pawning jewels for funds to support the Royalist army and herself. However, she resisted selling her cherished earrings until, as an impoverished widow living in exile, she sold them for 78,000 livres to her nephew, Louis XIV, King of France.

One of the ruby collars that had belonged to Henry VIII she gave as security for a substantial loan from the Duke of Epernon, but he wanted more collateral, so Henrietta Maria handed over the Sancy Diamond as well as the Mirror of Portugal. As she had no cash to redeem them, the Duke sold them to Cardinal Mazarin. There is a picture by van Dyke in The Hermitage, Leningrad, of Henrietta Maria wearing the Mirror of Portugal.

The Puritans, then in power, decided to sell the plate and jewels that remained in England but later came to the conclusion that to do so would be immoral. So they decided to convert all the metal into coins and to sell the gemstones and robes separately. The clerk in charge of the Jewel House, however, refused to cooperate, so the Jewel House was broken into and all the Regalia "totally broken and defaced." This was in 1649, the year that Charles I was beheaded. Cardinal Mazarin bequeathed his collection of diamonds to Louis XIV of France, and it remained part of the Crown Jewels until they were stolen from the Garde Meuble after the French Revoltuion. The Mirror of Portugal was among them and is still missing to this day.

## The Missing Pigot

Another missing diamond is the Pigot (or Pigott), an oval-shaped stone of fine quality believed to have weighed 49 carats. It acquired its name

Fig. 3–5 The Nawab of Arcot. Queen Charlotte was given five big Indian diamonds by the Nawab of Arcot, two of which are shown above with a circular diamond from the crown of George IV in the center. *(Courtesy of the Twining Collection; copyright by The Worshipful Company of Goldsmiths, Goldsmith's Hall, London.)*

from the Governor of Madras, who held office twice in the second half of the 18th century. He had received it as a gift from an Indian prince, possibly the Rajah of Tangore, his friend, or the Nawab of Arcot (Figure 3–5), from whom he admitted having received gifts "of a trifling nature."

Pigot's indecision is supposed to have been partly responsible for the Black Hole of Calcutta, the prison into which 146 foreigners were jammed after an army led by an illiterate 18-year-old Indian prince had seized all English property in the city. Three-quarters of the prisoners died during the night because Pigot had dithered about sending help even after the local governor had fled ignominiously. Eventually, Colonel Clive, who was to become known as "Clive of India" was dispatched with a small force to recover Calcutta, which he did; but Pigot, in the meantime, had neglected to protect Madras from the French.

Nevertheless, when he returned to England in 1776, Pigot was made an Irish peer. He brought the diamond with him and left it in his will to a member of the family. The family parted with it and some time later, in ~~1891~~ [handwritten: 1800], the Pigot appeared as the prize in a lottery (Fig. 3-6). The young winner sold it for much less than it fetched later in the same year, £30,000.

At some stage, Rundell and Bridge, the principal jewelers of the time, bought and sold it at the same sum to Ali Pasha, who ruled Albania. Ali Pasha always wore the Pigot on a green silk purse attached to his girdle, according to an observer.

In 1822, Ali Pasha found himself in conflict with the Sultan of Turkey, who was his overlord. As a result, he was assassinated in his own palace and, mortally wounded, was helped back to his divan. From there, according to an article in the *Journal of the Royal Society of Arts*, he ordered that his wife Vasilika be poisoned. He gave the diamond to a faithful soldier, Captain D'Angals, and instructed him to crush it in his presence.

The story ends, "Vasilika still lives, but the model of the diamond alone remains. The too obedient officer bitterly regretted his folly; and the destroyed diamond haunted him in his dreams for months afterwards." There is no evidence that the Pigot was actually destroyed, as it could have been with a hammer. But there has been no trace of it since, although the model cast from it in England is said still to exist. It is just possible that a

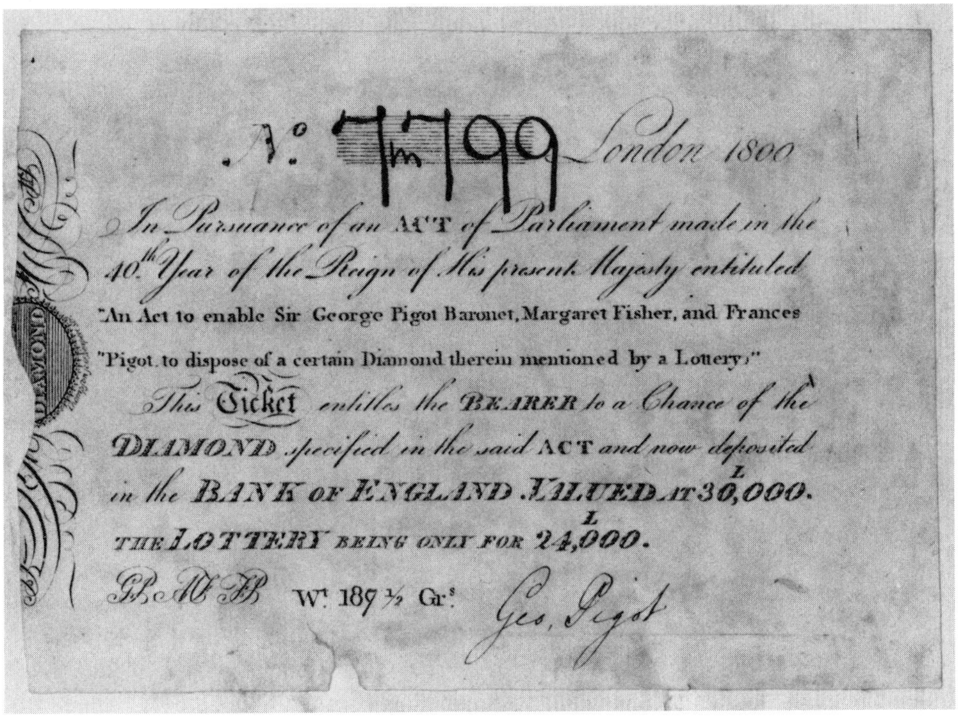

Fig. 3–6 Lottery Ticket for the Pigot Diamond. This is the only lottery ticket for the Pigot Diamond known to exist. The diamond is now missing. *(Exclusive and first publication from a private collection in London.)*

pear-shaped diamond of 85.8 carats called the Spoonmaker in the Topkapi Museum in Istanbul may be the Pigot, the weight of which has been variously recorded from 47 carats to nearly 90 carats. The Spoonmaker Diamond is supposed to have been found in a rubbish dump by a Turkish fisherman, who exchanged it for three spoons from a spoonmaker.

The famous yellow Florentine, which is also missing is described with other colored diamonds in Chapter Six.

Men at some time are masters of their fates; The fault, dear Brutus, is not in our stars, But in ourselves, that we are underlings.
*William Shakespeare (1564–1616). Julius Caesar.*

---

*Chapter Four*

# The Great Blue Diamond

**D**URING the last century, a unique blue diamond attracted more legends of dire fate than any other gem. Blue diamonds are very rare. Dark blue ones are very much rarer, and large dark blue ones are so rare that only two are known for certain to exist. One was the Tavernier Blue. When first polished, it was called the French Blue or the Blue Diamond of the Crown (Figure 4–1), part of which may be the Hope Diamond. The other is the Wittelsbach. (The story of the still extant deep blue, the Wittelsbach, will be told in Chapter Six along with other famous colored diamonds.)

That indefatigable traveler and diamond merchant, J.-B. Tavernier, bought a magnificent blue diamond almost the color of sapphire in India about 1642. It is believed to have been found in the Kollur mine, and it weighed $112^1/_4$ old carats. Tavernier's plate in his book of 1675 *(Nouvelle Relation de l'interieur du Serrail du Grand Seigneur)* shows it in three views as a flatish stone with a few irregular facets. It was, however, described as "cleane of a faire violet" in a reproduction of this plate in an article published in London two years before the book.

On his return to France, Tavernier was summoned by Louis XIV to bring his collection to the Royal Court. The King was delighted with the gems and bought forty-four large diamonds, including the Blue as well as 1,122 smaller ones. As well as the money, Tavernier benefited by being raised to the nobility, which enabled him to buy the Barony of Aubonne in Switzerland.

The Blue Diamond cost Louis 220,000 livres, but he was unhappy with

Fig. 4–1 Queen Maria Luisa. A portrait by Goya of Maria Luisa wearing the Blue Diamond of the Crown. It is now believed that the Hope Diamond may be part of the Blue Diamond. *(Courtesy of the Taft Museum.)*

the Indian cutting, in which facets were used to remove flaws, leaving an irregular stone without much brilliance. In 1673, he ordered it to be recut by Sieur Pitau, who produced a triangular stone with convex sides following approximately the shape of the rough.

Weighing $67^{1}/_{2}$ carats in its new form, it was set in a gold mount and named "The Blue Diamond of the Crown." Louis wore several hundred diamonds in his frock coat, set in buttons and elsewhere, and in his hat, garters, and shoe buckles. The Blue Diamond was sometimes hung on a ribbon around his neck, but he wore it in several other ways. (Louis XIV was interested enough in diamonds to have many of those in the King's Wardrobe recut from their old Indian rose and table shapes to a more modern form with more facets. The work was done in Amsterdam and Antwerp, to the chagrin of French jewelers, it was reported.)

The insignia of the French orders of chivalry up to this time were made in gold or silver and sometimes decorated with colored enamel, but during the reign of Louis XIV, designers began to incorporate gemstones. In 1749, the next King, his great grandson, Louis XV (Color Plate 15), instructed the Crown Jeweler, Jacquemin, to design a new insignia for the Order of the Golden Fleece for the King's use and to have set in it the Blue Diamond and another famous French Crown Jewel, the Côte de Bretagne. Also incorporated was a diamond of $31^{3}/_{4}$ carats cut in hexagonal shape.

At the time, the Côte de Bretagne, a "balas ruby" now called by its correct mineralogical name of red spinel, was of irregular shape and weighed 206 carats. With two other large "balas rubies" it had survived from the old Crown Jewels of 1530. The others were the Roman A, weighing 121 carats and the Oeuf de Naples, biggest of the three at 241 carats. In Jacquemin's design, the spinel became a dragon cleverly shaped to eliminate three disfiguring holes. He gave it to Jacques Guay, the gem carver, who carved the body and head in what has been described as one of the finest examples of the art of gem carving; but, unfortunately, the weight was reduced to 105 carats.

The dragon's tail was set with small brilliant-cut diamonds and curled around the hexagonal diamond above the dragon, which was mounted head down. The dragon's wings were set with brilliants, which decorated the palms around the beast. Flames of topaz and gold issued from the dragon's mouth, partly enveloping the Blue Diamond, below which hung the Golden Fleece.

This priceless insignia was for the King's use alone, as it was for his grandson successor, Louis XVI, who wore it with a special set of jewels known as the "colored set", which included an epaulette and a sword set with diamonds. There was also a "white set" of jewelry with another Golden Fleece insignia in gold and white diamonds. The Order was founded by Philippe the Good of Burgundy in 1429 and restricted to thirty-one knights. It became the first Order of Austria and of Spain and was instituted in England as well as in France and elsewhere.

Eight years after the Côte de Bretagne became a dragon, the other two big spinels came into the hands of Jacquemin, but there was not the same excuse for cutting the Roman A as he instructed. He seems to have regarded it simply as raw material and not as a historic jewel. The Oeuf de Naples was fashioned to the shape of a dove, and the Roman A suffered the ignominious fate of being cut into pieces to form flames around the dove. The whole was mounted on a rather ugly star-shaped frame with fleur-de-lis points set with brilliant-cut diamonds of several colors to make a new insignia for the Order of Saint Esprit.

## The Tragic Louis XVI and Marie Antoinette

Louis XV was succeeded in 1774 by his 20-year-old grandson Louis, who had been married to Archduchess Marie Antoinette at the age of 16 and who became the weak, ineffective, and tragic Louis XVI. The new King was more interested in hunting than in the people of France or even in flaunting the extravagances of the Court in the same way as his two predecessors. By modern standards, his extravagance of dress was still extreme. In this, he was more than matched by his wife.

The history of jewelry shows swings to two extremes, emphasis on the mounts, usually made of gold, or emphasis on the stones set in the mounts. Marie Antoinette's taste swung the pendulum away from gems toward mounts. She had even famous stones like the Regent and the Sancy Diamonds and some of the Mazarin Diamonds set simply to decorate mounts representing flowers and feathers instead of being used for their own sakes. Her personal gems became so mixed up with the Queen's ornaments belonging to the Crown that in 1788 she persuaded the King to make a decree assigning her all the jewels she wore.

The Blue Diamond, however, remained in the insignia of the Golden Fleece, although it was the practice to break up insignia to make fresh designs and retain only the lead castings of old designs made by jewelers before remaking them in gold.

Marie Antoinette was involved in an unsavory scandal in 1785 that became known as "the affair of the Queen's necklace." In the hope of selling it to the Queen, Boehmer and Bassenge, the Crown Jewelers, made a fabulous necklace (Figure 4–2) at huge cost incorporating the finest diamond

*Fig.* 4–2 Marie Antoinette's Necklace. This is an accurate reproduction of the notorious necklace, involved in an unsavory scandal that became known as "the affair of the Queen's necklace." *(Property of BASZANGER Jewellers in Geneva.)*

Fig. 4-3 Cardinal Rohan. Widely believed to have been deliberately discredited by Marie Antoinette, Cardinal Rohan was arrested while in his pontifical vestments and surrounded by priests, but later was cleared of all charges. *(Courtesy of the Museum of The Louvre.)*

available at the time. But the Queen refused to buy it on the several occasions when it was offered to her. At this time, the French Ambassador in Vienna, Cardinal Rohan, (Figure 4–3) had upset Maria Antoinette and her mother, the Empress Maria Thèrésa, by adverse comments on the French Queen's behavior.

When Cardinal Rohan returned to Paris, he had hopes of becoming Prime Minister but knew that the appointment would be obstructed by the Queen. He happened to meet a woman who was a descendant of one of Henry II's bastards and who called herself the Countess de la Motte. She persuaded both the Cardinal and the Crown Jewelers that she had considerable influence with Marie Antoinette and later announced that the Queen would buy the necklace after all and would leave the negotiations to a high-ranking person.

Cardinal Rohan produced for the Crown Jewelers what appeared to be an authority from the Queen agreeing to buy the necklace and pay 1.6 million livres for it in installments. The necklace was handed over and given by the Cardinal to a man who purported to be one of the Royal valets. When approached by Boehmer for payment, the Queen expressed her astonishment and declared she had never ordered the necklace. Boehmer then told her about the negotiations that led to his request.

In August of 1785, the presence of King Louis XVI and Queen Marie Antoinette was awaited in the Salle des Glaces by members of the Court in their finery, along with Cardinal Rohan in his pontifical vestments and surrounded by priests. They were startled when the Minister of Marine appeared in the doorway and shouted to the Captain of Marines, "Arrest Monsieur the Cardinal Rohan." After a trial, the Cardinal was exonerated, but the Countess de la Motte was sentenced to be incarcerated in the Saltpetrière and to be whipped and branded. The Countess was more than equal to the process of the law. She not only escaped, but she took the necklace with her to England, where it was broken up and the gems sold.

Although the Queen and probably Cardinal Rohan were blameless in this affair, that did not prevent talk of her complicity in a plot to discredit Rohan, which added to the unpopularity of the Crown. In 1789, the Constituent Assembly, apprehensive about the decree awarding jewels to the Queen and fearing that more might pass into the private possession of the monarch, passed a law that made the Crown Jewels available for the use only of the reigning monarch.

That was the year when feelings of French citizens erupted over the injustices of their rulers and the bankruptcy of the nation. They stormed the Bastille on July 14, 1789. The King was so out of touch with the outbreak of revolution that the made only one entry in his diary for that day — *Rien*. The Royal family became virtual prisoners of the mob. Louis was intrigued with foreign powers but still dithered about what action to take until June 1781, when he took the wrong one. With the Queen and some jewels, he made an attempt to flee the country. They were caught in Vincennes the next day and brought back to Paris, where they were put under guard and the jewels sent to the Garde Meuble, which served as a museum and furniture storeroom. The main collection of the Crown Jewels was also kept there under the supervision of the Ministry of the Interior.

## *The Stolen Crown Jewels*

The Garde Meuble was an obvious target for a revolutionary mob or a band of criminals because it was open to visitors. It was not a strongroom and had no boundary or internal protection except for the National Guards on duty. In it were not only the Crown Jewels but the arms and armor of Kings, Cardinal Richelieu's church plate, and a remarkable collection of tapestries among the furniture.

The curator, whose name was Thierry, was well aware of the vulnerability of the place and had often protested to the authorities but without avail. After the Royal couple's attempted escape, a new inventory of the contents was made and the future of the jewels was considered by the National Assembly, which decided not to sell or alter them for the time being and, apparently blind to security, to leave them in the Garde Meuble.

Thierry had the jewels distributed among eight boxes, one of which contained the Regent and Sancy diamonds, pearls, and other stones; the others held many unset diamonds. Another famous diamond, the Mirror of Portugal, was also in the collection. The boxes were placed in the strong drawers of a marquetry commode, which had a secret lock. The commode was not big enough to hold the King's decorations as well, so these, presumably including the insignia of the Order of the Golden Fleece with the Blue Diamond and the Côte Bretagne, as well as many diamond buttons, were locked in a walnut casket that was placed in the middle of a table in the middle of the room where the jewels were kept.

On August 16, 1792, the Minister of the Interior, Cambon, made a proposal to the National Assembly that all the Crown Jewels be sold and the proceeds (foreign currency) be used to back French paper money — a familiar tactic of present-day bankrupt governments that sell assets for credit. The National Assembly delayed making a decision, which cost them dearly, for, on the morning of September 17, 1792, it was discovered that thieves had broken into the Garde Meuble and had stolen all the Crown

Jewels from the eleven cabinets to which they had been moved by Thierry's successor, Sergent. The intruders had climbed a collonade and broken through a window facing the Place Louis XV.

The jewels they had taken were valued at 30 million francs. All they left were diamonds and pearls worth about 5,500 francs strewn on the floor with burglars' implements and the cabinets with their broken seals.

It happened at a time when law and order had broken down in the chaos after the massacres of September 2, 1792, when Thierry was one of the victims of the mob. Convicts of every description, from pickpockets to highwaymen, from thugs to assassins, had been released from jail, and Paris was in the hands of the gangs and looters, many purporting to be revolutionaries but really intent on stealing from houses and shops and robbing honest citizens or murdering them for gain or revenge.

Naturally, the blame for the theft of the Crown Jewels was accorded indiscriminately by the politicians and officials regardless of any evidence or lack of it, and it never entered their heads that they were to blame. Accusing fingers were pointed at Sergent, the new curator, as well as at the guards, the aristocrats, even the government, which it was said needed the money to bribe the King of Prussia for some reason. The Public Prosecutor was quite sure that Marie Antoinette was responsible.

According to G. Bapst in his *Histoire des Joyaux de la Couronne de France* (Paris, 1889), a burglar called Paul Miette devised the plan to rob the Garde Meuble while he was in prison. With his chief accomplice, Cadet Guillot from Rouen, he recruited a large number of thieves from all over France and formed them into bands. Members of one band first penetrated the building through a window on September 11, 1792. They closed all doors leading to a staircase to the first floor, where the jewels were housed. Every door was taped and an "official" seal attached to it to dissuade anyone from entering. To be doubly sure, every door was also wedged.

On this first raid, the gang took a number of items that had been on show to the public along with the walnut casket that probably contained the Blue Diamond and the Côte de Bretagne. On September 13, another gang made an entry and escaped with the boxes containing the diamonds, including the Regent, Sancy, and the Mirror of Portugal. When, again, no alarm was raised, an even bigger gang made a third raid on September 15, 1792.

Members of the third gang afterward quarreled about the spoils, and one of them sold a box of diamonds to a passerby on the bank of the Seine. This casual purchaser took the stones to a pawnbroker who became suspicious and reported the circumstances to the police the next day. The police checked the Garde Meuble but, finding all the doors to the room where the Crown Jewels were kept officially sealed, took no further action.

On September 16, 1792, about 50 thieves and their women entered the building, some of the men masquerading as National Guards. The real National Guards were so slack, it was reported, that those on duty would often leave before their reliefs arrived. The thieves were so confident, they took food and wine with them to have a party. When the robbery was discovered the next day, there were still some thieves on the premises, who were arrested. (There was an attempt in 1848 to steal the French Crown Jewels that had been recovered. It ended in a much worse orgy, as told in Chapter Five.)

On the day that the robbery was discovered, Sergent, the curator, who was assisted by two Commissioners of the Commune, was arrested. According to reports, he announced that he had a special magnet that would locate the stolen jewels. The authorities were so credulous that he was believed and proved his point by asking to be taken to a place called the Allée des Veuves (now Avenue Montaigne), where he was blindfolded. He pointed to the foot of a tree, where diggers found a substantial part of the stolen gems.

The most legendary gems were missing, however: the Regent, the Sancy, the Mirror of Portugal, the French Blue Diamond, and the Côte de Bretagne spinel. The Regent was found later, and the Sancy was traced in 1835, to be related in Chapter Five. The Côte de Bretagne turned up later in the possession of someone named Cadet, who allowed another man, Lancry, to take it to Hamburg, probably to be offered to the French government in return for a reward. He was unsuccessful. The gem did find its way back to France in the end, but it is not known by what means. Today, it is displayed in The Louvre.

The Mirror of Portugal completely vanished and nothing has been heard of it to this day. The Blue Diamond also vanished, but nearly 40 years later, in 1830, a London banker and gem collector, Henry Thomas Hope, bought for £18,000 a diamond that was dark blue like the French Blue but only 44.53 carats in weight. It became known as the Hope.

## The Hope Diamond

It is possible that the Blue Diamond was, unfortunately, cut into three pieces with the intention of disguising its origin and theft. It came somehow into the hands of a trader, Wilhelm Fals of Amsterdam, who is said to have given instructions for it to be cleaved into three pieces. The largest of these when polished weighed $44^{1}/_{4}$ old carats. This stone is said to be the

Hope. The second largest, of 13³/₄ carats, was bought in Geneva in 1874 from the estate of the Duke of Brunswick by Ochs Brothers of Paris. The smallest stone, of 1¹/₄ carats, was bought in Vienna by Hertz and Co. of Paris, who sold it in about 1876 to then well-known Bond Street, London, jeweler and writer about gems, Edwin W. Streeter, for £300. He had it mounted in a butterfly ornament made up of diamonds of every known color.

Streeter claimed in the second edition of his book *The Great Diamonds of the World* (London, 1882) that he examined the Brunswick Blue Drop "in juxtaposition with the Hope diamond. It is identical in *colour* and *quality*." He came to the conclusion that they were cut from the same original stone because the triangular-shaped Brunswick stone "once formed the triangular salient gibbosity" that was a characteristic of the French Blue. It fitted to the flattened side of the Hope in the rough stone.

Streeter stated that the three diamonds were the only ones known in Europe that could be termed blue. One cannot know now whether he was referring to the tint or the hue of the stones because the hue or intrinsic color would be the same but not the tint or depth of color. It was well known to diamond cutters and graders, long before scientists called it "color saturation," that the color of a stone becomes lighter as it is reduced in size. Streeter was plausible, but Herbert Tillander, the Finnish jeweler and gemologist, made quartz models of the Tavernier Blue, the French Blue, and the Hope and declared in 1975 that Streeter was wrong to claim that cutting the French Blue would produce one or more smaller stones. A replica of the French Blue was made for Napoleon III about the time it was on shown at the Paris Exhibition.

Another gem dealer and author, John Mawe of 149 The Strand, London, in his *Treatise on Diamond and Precious Stones* of 1813, referred to a superlatively fine blue diamond of above 44 carats being owned by someone in London. In the second edition (1823), he named him as Mr. (Daniel) Eliason, a diamond merchant, and added (wrongly) that the stone was "now said to be in the possession of our most gracious sovereign." This was the Hope. Mawe described the stone as being undervalued at £30,000 and of a "deep sapphire blue."

He also mentioned a fine *light* blue brilliant that weighed 67¹/₂ carats with an estimated value of £100,000, which was in the Crown Jewels of France. This was the French Blue, which in fact had been stolen in 1792 and could not have been light blue.

A British gemologist, Kenneth Parkinson, writing in 1957 to the author of this book (who had not then seen the Hope), described it in these words after viewing it at the International Diamond Exhibition in Amsterdam: "I saw it for the first time though I was very disappointed in the colour which to me was very like a steel blue spinel — so much so that few people would take it to be a diamond by appearances — it was by no means so blue as I had been led to think by the various descriptions in textbooks and of course the many copies which are on the market in the set of famous diamonds." An article on precious stones in *The Edinburgh Review* of July 1866 also described it as "of a decided, but rather steel-like blue."

In truth, most of the many people who have seen the Hope on exhibition in Washington, D.C., or on the few occasions when it has been shown elsewhere have looked at it with eyes tinted by its lurid history so that it becomes a "tiny fragment of midnight sky," as a journalist on the *Washington Post* picturesquely described it.

It was after the major portion of the Blue Diamond became the Hope and was bought by Mrs. Evalyn McLean, (who described herself as always wanting to do outlandish things so that people stared at her and her possessions) that it acquired its legend of bad omen. This was conveniently stretched back to encompass any ill fate suffered by past owners, such as Tavernier, who lost his fortune at the age of 80. He was supposed to have stolen it from a Hindu idol in a temple built by worshipers of Rama, an ancient Indian king who was a reincarnation of Vishnu, the preserver of all life. It was, according to the legend, set in an eye socket or as the third eye in the forehead. The god is supposed to have placed a curse on Tavernier and all subsequent owners of the diamond. The belief also illustrated a profound Western ignorance of the Hindu faith.

Henry Philip Hope was a member of a family of Dutch extraction that had founded a prominent merchant bank in 1762. Hope and Co. made loans to many countries, including Russia and Spain, and also advanced money in association with another merchant bank, Baring and Co., to the new United States of America for the Louisiana Purchase. He was a rich man, having sold out to the Barings with other heirs some years before buying the blue diamond.

Hope's hobbies were collecting Dutch and Flemish paintings and gems, particularly colored diamonds. His gems were kept in a mahogany cabinet with sixteen numbered drawers, which had glass covers and engraved ivory labels giving the weight and catalog number of the contents. A catalog of the collection had been prepared by Bram Hertz and published in 1839 in two parts, one with descriptions and the other sketches. The description of the Hope reads:

This matchless gem combines the beautiful colour of the sapphire with the prismatic fire and brilliancy of the diamond, and, on account of its extraordinary colour, great size, and other fine qualities, it certainly may be called unique; as we may presume there exists no cabinet, nor any collection of crown jewels in the world, which can boast of the possession of so curious and fine a gem as the one we are now describing; and we expect to be borne out in our opinion by our readers, since there are extant historical records and treatises on the precious gems, which give us descriptions of all the extraordinary diamonds in the possession of the crowned heads of Europe, as well as of the princes of Eastern countries. But in vain do we search for any record of a gem which can, in point of curiosity, beauty, and perfection, be compared with this blue brilliant.

The stone was "most tastefully mounted as a medallion with a border . . . of small rose diamonds, surrounded by 20 brilliants of equal size, shape, and cutting, and of the finest water, and averaging four grains each . . . " (about a carat each). The collection also contained the Hope Pearl, one of the largest ever found.

One of Henry Philip Hope's two brothers, Thomas, was a talented writer with a London house and one in Surrey called "Deepdene," which is curious because there is a Deepdene Diamond (see Chapter 11), but the house was named after an American family's estate.

When Henry Philip Hope died a bachelor, he left fortunes to his three nephews. The eldest, Henry Thomas Hope, and became the Member of Parliament for Gloucester. He acquired Deepdene from his father and the Hope Diamond from his uncle. He lent the diamond for display in the Crystal Palace at the Great Exhibition of 1851, where the Koh-i-Noor was the principal exhibit.

When Henry Thomas Hope died at the age of 54, he left the diamond, with other property, to his widow, who in turn left it to her second son when he was 21 years old. This one became the notorious Lord Francis Hope, who fell in love with an American singer and actress, Mary (May) Augusta Yohe, and married her secretly in Hempstead in 1894. The next year, he was bankrupt in spite of having a life interest in a great collection of paintings, the sale of which his brother and three sisters had successfully opposed in court.

Later Lord Hope managed to get permission for the sale of the collection, but his spending was running much higher than the interest from the proceeds, which went into a trust. So he petitioned the court for permission to sell the Hope Diamond, claiming that because it was permanently in Parr's Bank, it gave neither pleasure nor utility to anyone. His wife May had worn it only twice.

The diamond was valued at £18,115 by Edwin W. Streeter, but other valuers' estimates differed widely which was understandable because the value of anything is the highest a willing buyer will pay for it, and there was no precedent for such a unique diamond. The court and subsequently the appeal court refused permission for it to be sold.

Other troubles were in store for Lord Hope. In 1900, he took his wife to the United States where they met Captain Putnam Strong, son of a former mayor of New York, who had a magnetic attraction for women. At once, May was under his spell. In March, Hope sued for divorce and, in April, May left him to travel to Japan as the "wife" of Captain Strong. At about the same time, permission was at last granted for the Hope Diamond to be sold, but again the proceeds went into the trust fund, from which Lord Hope received interest.

A year later, the divorce was granted and Hope married another divorcee, who died eight years after their marriage. May Hope eventually married Captain Strong in Japan, but every venture they tried went wrong and the marriage was stormy. She tried to resume her stage career in London in a show called "Little Christopher Columbus," where she wore a replica of the Hope Diamond. This was the year that Hope's second wife died, but he is said to have been at the premiere. May divorced Captain Strong, and in 1914, she married Captain John Smuts, a cousin of General Jan Smuts.

The blue diamond called the Hope (Color Plate 10) was bought in London by Simon Frankel, who took it to New York on the liner *Kronprinz Wilhelm* in November 1901. According to Susanne Steinem Patch, who wrote the history for the current owners, the Smithsonian Institution, Washington, D.C., the invoice value was $141,032, on which a duty of 10 per cent was paid. The firm of Joseph Frankel's Sons, who were diamond merchants, reputedly sold it in Paris in 1908 to a keen collector called Habib, and when the Habib Collection went up for sale a year later, it passed into the hands of the diamond merchants, Auroc and Rosenau.

## The Hope's Tragedy

Cartiers bought the Hope Diamond next and sold it to Evalyn Walsh McLean, on whom most of the tragedy of the legend centers. Her father found the rich Camp Bird gold mines in Colorado and thereafter spent most of his time squandering the revenue from them. Money was lavished on his daughter, who had a coach and horses with a uniformed coachman to take her to school. The first tragedy occurred when she was a teenager and was involved in an accident with her younger brother. He was killed, and she was left with a short leg.

At the age of 22, Evalyn married Edward McLean, son of the proprietor of the *Washington Post*. Before their wedding, she and Edward visited Cartiers to choose a wedding present from her father. Cartiers offered a platinum and diamond necklace with loops of diamonds and a pendant of three stones—a large pearl weighing $32^1/_4$ grains, a $34^1/_2$-carat emerald, and a magnificent pear-shaped diamond of nearly 95 carats. The large diamond was the Star of the East, which had been found in India and was said to have belonged to Abdul Hamid II of Turkey. The price was about $120,000 and, according to Mrs. McLean, "We signed a receipt and Cartier allowed us children to walk out with the Star of the East." The two of them managed to go through an additional $200,000 in Europe in less than four months.

On a visit to Paris in 1910, the McLeans were shown the Hope Diamond by Pierre Cartier, who brought it to their hotel. It could have been he who started the legend because he told Evalyn it would bring bad luck to anyone who wore or even touched it. He knew of Mrs. McLean's belief that articles of ill-omen for others were lucky for her. But she refused the Hope because she did not like the setting. A few months later, Pierre Cartier turned up in New York with the diamond in a new setting. This time, she bought it for $180,000, which was paid in monthly installments over many years.

At first, Mrs. McLean would not let anyone else touch it, and she was superstitious enough to have it blessed by a priest. Thereafter, she wore it constantly, sometimes as a head ornament but mainly as the pendant of a diamond necklace. She was so ostentatious that she often wore the necklace with the Star of the East pendant at the same time.

There is a true story that Mrs. McLean put the necklace with the Hope around the neck of her dog, a Great Dane, like a collar to impress guests. The necklace was also in pawn on several occasions because even the richest spendthrifts run out of money from time to time.

The bad fortune that began with her brother's death and her disability continued with the death of her son at the age of nine in a car accident. Her husband became obsessed with another woman, which led to his dypsomania and eventual insanity. Her daughter died by taking an overdose of sleeping pills at the age of 25, which led to Mrs. McLean's own death shortly afterward. But the bad luck did not necessarily seem to attend the hundreds of other people who touched the stone, although they included many soldier casualties of the First World War she had let play with it when she visited them.

After her death, the New York diamond merchant Harry Winston bought it. He was a showman by nature and used it to raise money for charity. Winston offered it to the Smithsonian Institution to encourage others to give famous stones to found a national collection because the United States has no Crown Jewels like the old monarchies. The Smithsonian already had a fine collection of minerals, of which George S. Switzer was the curator. On November 10, 1958, Winston sent the Hope Diamond to Washington, D.C., by ordinary registered mail with an insurance cover for $1 million.

Harry Winston had no fears of evil from the diamond; neither had his wife. There is a fascinating tale of his traveling in Africa by air when his neighbor on the plane, hearing who he was, refused to travel further with him and caught the next plane. The nervous man then explained to his new neighbor how the previous flight had been at risk. She did not tell him that she was Mrs. Winston, traveling separately from her husband so that if there were an accident, one parent would survive to take care of the children. She also didn't mention that she, not her husband, was carrying the Hope.

## From Legend to Scientific Marvel

The Hope is unique in a scientific sense as well as in legend. Diamonds are divided into two main types known as Type I and Type II. The first are the kind normally found in jewelry, being white to yellowish in color. They are about a thousand times more plentiful than Type II, although most diamonds are a mixture of the two. Each group is further divided into two, known as *a* and *b*. Type IIa are about a thousand times more plentiful than Type IIb.

All diamonds in Type IIb are blue or grayish blue in color and most of them today come from the Premier mine in South Africa, where the giant Cullinan Diamond was found. They are unique in the diamond world not just because of their color but because they are semiconductors of electricity, like the doped silicon and germanium used in transistors, which are similar in crystal structure to diamond. Blue diamonds have very special applications in science.

It has been known since the 1950s that a white or whitish diamond (i.e., Type I) can be colored blue (although not the dark blue of the Hope) by bombarding it with electrons. An artificially colored stone, being Type I, is an excellent insulator of electricity, whereas a natural blue one will pass some current.

The late Robert Webster of the London Gem Testing Laboratory, then in Hatton Garden, demonstrated this in a highly dramatic manner to the author about 30 years ago when he placed two blue diamonds on an insulated metal plate and connected the plate to the neutral side of the electric mains supply. He touched first one stone and then the other with an insulated probe attached to the supply side of the mains. Nothing happened to the first, which was artificially colored. The other, a few seconds after having current applied to it, began to glow and was soon at red heat. It was a natural blue, and its electrical resistance was causing it to glow like the bar of an electric fire. The electrical resistance of a blue diamond drops as the temperature goes up, which makes its temperature rise even more rapidly; had the probe been left in contact for a little longer, the diamond would have reverted to graphite, caught fire, and burned away.

The Hope has left the Smithsonian twice, in 1962 for a showing at The Louvre in Paris during the exhibition "Ten Centuries of French Jewellery" and in 1965 to be displayed at the Rand Easter Show in South Africa. While there, it was examined by the Diamond Research Laboratory in Johannesburg. The Hope was exposed in the dark to ultraviolet light (of less than 350 nanometers wavelength). Many diamonds will glow with a blue, mauve, yellow, or greenish yellow fluorescence in these circumstances. If the ultraviolet light is turned off, some diamonds will continue for a time to glow in the dark with the same or another color. The color of this phosphorescence is normally blue for Type IIb diamonds. But the phosphorescence of the Hope is a strong red, which surprised the scientists, who were unable to account for it.

The stone also has some extra facets on the girdle, which is uncommon. They were probably added, perhaps by Cartiers, as suggested by Herbert Tillander, because there was a reflection from the girdle in the table of the stone.

Love is an ocean of emotions, entirely surrounded by expenses.
*Lord Thomas Dewar, the distiller (1864–1930)*

*Chapter Five*

# A Lover's Diamond and a Lost Reputation

HE Sancy Diamond (Color Plate 16) was called "the very Sphynx of diamonds" by one of its earlier historians, Edwin W. Streeter, because its beginnings were wrapped in a dense cloud of mystery, but it is likely that the mystery was created by another writer attempting to flatter King Louis XV of France. It is one of the most legendary of all diamonds. Almond-shaped and faceted on both sides, like a large bead, The Sancy is of fine quality and weighs 55 carats. The form of faceting suggests an Indian origin and is known as "double rose."

An unknown writer declared that the Great Sancy, as the stone was also called, was lost on the battlefield by Charles the Bold of Burgundy in 1477 and picked up by a soldier. If the event is true, the stone lost by Charles could have been another double rose-cut stone, the Florentine, but not the Sancy because of its history. On the other hand, the story could be a fabrication.

The first known fact about the Sancy is that it was bought in Constantinople (Istanbul) by Nicholas Harlay, Seigneur de Sancy, an avid collector of jewels. Harlay was French Ambassador at the Ottoman Court in Turkey for Henry III of France, and the first account of his ownership appeared in 1593, although it has been surmised that he bought the stone about 1570.

## The Woes of Henry III

The thoroughly debauched Henry III at 26 became entirely bald and used to cover his head with a toque or turban on the front of which was fas-

Fig. 5-1 Henri III. The thoroughly debauched Henri III was bald by age 26 and covered his head with a toque or turban, on the front of which was fastened a very large diamond. (*Courtesy of the Museum of The Louvre.*)

tened a very large diamond (Figure 5–1). This glittered "when he was engaged in combing lap dogs, fondling his monkeys, stringing death's heads (skulls), playing with his ivory cup and ball, or caressing his detestable dwarfs and minions, his cheeks plastered with white and rouge, his lips, eyes, and ears smeared with unguents and cosmetics, while the streets of Paris ran with the blood of his bravest subjects, and his realm was brought to the verge of ruin by the feuds and intrigues of lawless passion and religious animosity," as Streeter wrote in *The Great Diamonds of the World* (London, 1882).

Whether or not Streeter's imaginative description was near the truth, Henry III, who had been crowned King of Poland a year before succeeding to the French crown, tried to deal with a few problems but so unwisely and ineffectively that the country was soon in financial chaos. Security was threatened by mercenary troops in the country, controlled by Count Palatine, who refused to move them until he was paid eight million livres.

Henry did not possess such a sum and to reduce the threat gave the Count the Crown Jewels as security. The Count displayed them to the French people on a specially converted wagon. The King stole precious stones out of reliquaries and sold or pawned every other gem he could lay his hands on. He even persuaded Henry of Lorraine to send him jewels from the ducal crown of Lorraine and the cross of Lorraine on the security of a large forest. As the debt was never repaid, Henry of Lorraine cut down the forest.

Another of Henry III's problems was the Duke of Guise, an ardent Catholic who had formed the Holy League to exterminate the Huguenots, put the King in a monastery, and help himself to the throne. Henry was also concerned with producing an heir, at which he and his wife seemed particularly inept. The Duke was assassinated by Swiss mercenary soldiers in 1588, which solved that problem. The Swiss Cantons had provided troops since the early 16th century to serve the French Crown in return for regular payments to the soldiers.

By this time, Henry had sold or pawned all the Crown Jewels, few of which were recovered in later times. The expert at raising money on the security of gems was Nicholas Harlay, Seigneur de Sancy, a financier who understood diamonds and their values as well as being a soldier. In 1589, he offered diamonds and jewels of his own for pledging to raise an army of Swiss troops. The warrant refers to a great flawless diamond, facet cut, weighing 37 carats to 38 carats. This was probably a stone now known as the little Sancy, the weight of which was later given as $34^{1}/_{2}$ carats. It was bought by Henry of Orange in 1647 and became part of the Prussian Crown Jewels.

The King was only required to pay the price for which the gems were pledged if that was below 24,000 ecus. Sancy became Colonel General of the 12,000 Swiss mercenaries that were hired. Henry was assassinated by a Dominican Friar and died, as he had feared, without an heir, so on his deathbed, he named Henry of Navarre as the new king, King Henry VI. It was Sancy's army that made sure of the succession.

There was no money in the treasury, the Crown Jewels were sold or in pawn, and some had been stolen by the Holy League, so the new King had to wear a gilded silver crown at his coronation. But he had the financial genius, Sancy, by his side, some of whose complex deals have never been unraveled. It was mainly he who managed to recover some of the state's property and to bring a measure of order to its finances. There is no doubt that the loan of his personal collection of precious stones to the unsavory spendthrift, Henry III, was masterly in its timing.

## *The Sancy Disappears*

If Sancy did ever pawn the Sancy Diamond on anyone's behalf, he must have regained possession of it. There is a story, probably apocryphal, of his lending it to Henry of Navarre to raise troops before Henry became King of France. The messenger taking it to Henry disappeared, it is related, and Sancy assumed he must have been abducted or murdered because he was loyal. After a long search, the messenger's body was found in a forest. The body was opened, and the famous diamond was in his stomach. Much more likely is the story that Henry wanted to buy it but could not afford it.

In England, when James I succeeded the last of the Tudors, Elizabeth I, the French Ambassador in London was the brother of Nicholas Harlay de Sancy. He sold the Sancy Diamond to the new Jacobite King in 1604 for 60,000 ecus, to be paid in three equal installments over a year. Nicholas de Sancy was still alive at the time; he died in 1627.

An inventory of the jewels in the Tower of London (as recorded in the book by Martin Holmes and H. D. W. Sitwell, *The English Regalia* [London, 1972]) dated March 22, 1605, described the Mirror of Great Britain, which contained "one verie fayre table dyamonde, one verie fayre table rubye, twoe other lardge dyamondes, cut lozengwyse, the one of them called the 'Stone of the letter H' of Scotlande, garnyshed with smalle dyamondes, twoe round perles, fixed, and one fayre dyamonde, cutt in fawcettis, bought of Sauncey.

The "Stone of the letter H" was a diamond known as the Great Harry, brought by James to England from the Scottish Crown Jewels. The "fayre dyamonde, cutt in fawcettis" was the Great Sancy, which is generally known now as the Sancy.

The Sancy did not remain in the British Crown Jewels for very long. It was among the many pieces stolen by Charles I and his Queen, Henrietta Maria, to be sold or pawned to try to save his tottering throne. On a visit to the Netherlands in 1644, Henrietta Maria raised 1,006,275 livres and 11 sols in Dutch currency through her agent, M. Cletstex at the Rotterdam branch of the Bank of Lombardy, who acted as a pawnbroker.

Because there was no money to redeem them, the Sancy and the Mirror of Portugal were eventually sold to Cardinal Mazarin, who had great influence with the French monarchs. Mazarin paid 360,000 livres for the two stones, which became the finest in his collection. He had also bought some personal jewels from Henrietta Maria, Charles I of England, and Queen Christina of Sweden. In his will, he left a collection of eighteen fine diamonds, headed by the Sancy and the Mirror of Portugal, to the French Crown with the understanding that they should be known as the "Mazarin Diamonds" (Color Plate 17). He died in 1661, and the King's great-grandson wore the Sancy on two occasions in his hat, with the Regent Diamond on a knot of pearls and diamonds as a shoulder ornament, before he became Louis XV in 1715.

Ten years later, Louis XV married the Polish princess Marie Leczinska, and afterward, she often wore the Sancy as a pendant and the Regent as a hair ornament. The Dauphin (her eldest son) displayed the Sancy in his hat when he married Marie Thérèse of Spain, but the Queen recovered it afterward and wore it on most special occasions. Marie Antoinette, wife of Louis XVI, had the Sancy, the Regent, and the Mazarin diamonds set at random in jewelry representing feathers and flowers with drops of water on them.

The Sancy was one of the state treasures stolen from the Garde Meuble in the year that the First Republic was established, as related in Chapter Four. It was one of the famous stones that was not recovered when the hiding place of others was disclosed. It came back to the French treasury in a way unknown because when the French Adjutant-General pledged a number of diamonds to the Marquess of Iranda in Madrid to raise a million francs to help finance Napoleon's armies, one unidentified diamond was never returned. It weighed 54³/₄ carats and must have been the Sancy. It passed into the hands of the Spanish Bourbons, but about 1828, it is believed to have been sold by a French dealer to the Demidoff family.

A few years later, M. Levrat, Director of the Society of the Mines and

Plate 1 Indian Armlet. A replica of the Koh-i-Noor is set in this Indian enameled bracelet, whose owner is reputed to be destined to rule the world. *(©British Crown copyright; reproduced with permission of the Controller of Her Britannic Majesty's Stationery Office.)*

Plate 2 Farah Tiara. The fabulous Noor-ul-Aim (Light of the Eye) is a large pink diamond. It is the center stone in this platinum tiara made by Harry Winston; it is surrounded by many large yellow, pink, and colorless diamonds. *(Courtesy of the Royal Ontario Museum, Toronto, Canada; photo by Varouj Yazejian, Photo Vahe, Tehran).*

Plate 3 The Golconda Stones. Tavernier's magnificent stones, including the Taj-i-mah *(lower left).(Courtesy of the Royal Ontario Museum, Toronto, Canada.)*

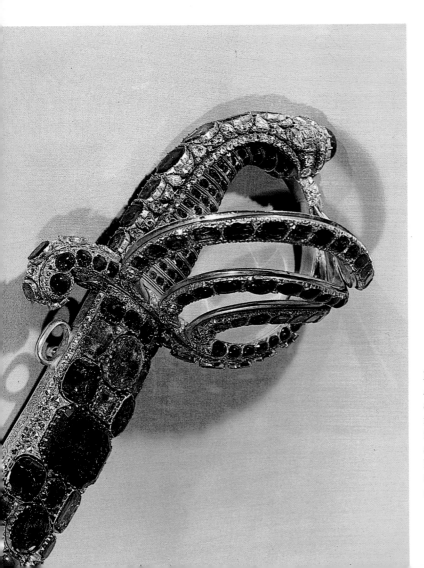

Plate 4 The Imperial Sword. A spectacular emerald of about 100 carats is set, with many other large gemstones, in the hilt of this sword, among the Crown Jewels of Iran. *(Courtesy of the Royal Ontario Museum, Toronto, Canada.)*

Plate 5 The Canning Triton Jewel. One of the most famous baroque pearls forms the torso; the arms and face are in white enamel with gold hair and beard. The tail is enameled in bright green and set with graduated diamonds and a large carved ruby. The mask of Medusa's head holds a ruby in its mouth. This pendant is believed to have been made in southern Germany in the late 16th century, a present from one of the Medici Dukes of Tuscany to one of the Mogul Emperors. *(By courtesy of the Board of Trustees of the Victoria and Albert Museum.)*

Plate 6 Côte de Bretagne Spinel in the Order of the Golden Fleece. A "balas ruby," now called by its correct mineralogical name of red spinel. In Jacquemin's design, the spinel became a dragon cleverly shaped to eliminate three disfiguring holes; Jacques Buay carved the body and head for what is considered one of the finest examples of the art of gem carving. *(Courtesy of the Museum of The Louvre.)*

Plate 7 Amethyst in Austrian Crown. Emperor Leopold received the amethyst from Charles II of Spain; the Vienna Treasury now houses the huge, pear-shaped amethyst, hung as a pendant from a gold crown set with emeralds. *(Courtesy of Kunsthistorisches Museum, Austria.)*

Plate 8 Head of the Royal Sceptre and Cross. The sceptre is part of the British Crown Jewels, housed today in the Tower of London. *(© British Crown copyright; reproduced with permission of the Controller of Her Britannic Majesty's Stationery Office.)*

Plate 9 British Imperial State Crown. The back of the famous crown, studded with diamonds, pearls, and other quality gems. (© *British Crown copyright; reproduced with permission of the Controller of Her Britannic Majesty's Stationery Office.*)

Plate 10 The Hope Diamond. A major portion of the legendary Blue Diamond became the Hope, whose history has been fraught with rumors of evil omen. *(Courtesy of the Smithsonian Institution, Photo No. 78-8853A.)*

Plate 12 The Black Orloff. More accurately described as gunmetal in color, and weighing perhaps 195 carats in the rough, it was reduced to 67.50 carats when cut into cushion shape. *(Courtesy of the Gemological Institute of America.)*

Plate 11 White Rose Jewel. White enameled petals surround the large balas ruby. *(Copyright the Historical Museum in Basel, Switzerland.)*

Plate 13 Abraham Lincoln. James and Harry Kazanjian of New York commissioned heads of American presidents in sapphire. Lincoln was carved by Norman Maness from a 2,302 carat stone. The color is mostly black, but there are patches of deep blue. The carving, completed in 1951, took 1,800 hours. *(Courtesy of the Smithsonian Institution, Photo No. 77-14887.)*

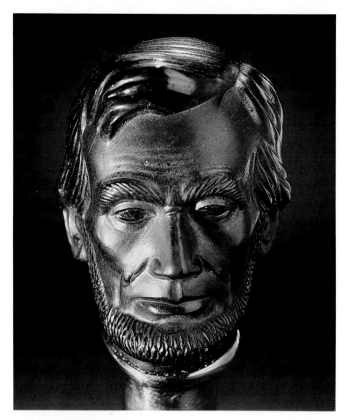

Plate 14 The De Beers Diamond. One of the biggest yellow diamonds known, weighing 234.65 metric carats, the De Beers was found at Kimberley in 1890. *(Courtesy of Sotheby's, London, England.)*

Plate 15 Louis XV Crown. Louis instructed the Crown Jeweler, Jacquemin, to design a new insignia for the Order of the Golden Fleece; it was set with the Blue Diamond and another famous French Crown Jewel, the Côte de Bretagne. *(Courtesy of the Museum of The Louvre.)*

Plate 16 The Sancy Diamond. One of the most legendary of all diamonds, the Sancy is almond-shaped and faceted on both sides like a large bead. The form of faceting suggests an Indian origin and is known as "double rose." *(Courtesy of the Museum of The Louvre.)*

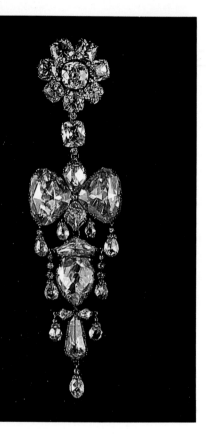

Plate 17 Mazarin Diamonds Set in Brooch Reliquaire. Cardinal Mazarin left eighteen fine diamonds, including the Sancy and the Mirror of Portugal, to the French Crown. *(Courtesy of the Museum of The Louvre.)*

Plate 18 The Three Brethren. Best known of the Tudor jewels is this pendant, named for the three large rectangular balas rubies of almost exactly the same size and color. They are spaced by three very large pearls, with another hanging below. In the center is a pont-cut or pyramid-cut diamond. *(Copyright the Historical Museum in Basel, Switzerland.)*

Plate 19 Emerald Belt. Made of woven golden wire, with a clasp in which a huge heart-shaped emerald of about 175 carats was mounted, the belt was worn by Nasir-ul-Aim Shah and his successors. *(Courtesy, the Royal Ontario Museum, Toronto, Canada.)*

Plate 20 Emerald Mine, Chivor, Colombia. The finest emeralds were, and still are, found in South America, in mines such as this. *(Courtesy of the Gemological Institute of America.)*

Plate 21 Nadir Throne. There have been descriptions of many Peacock Thrones through the years, some of which, like the Nadir, probably incorporated parts of others. The true Peacock Throne was, in all likelihood, destroyed after Nadir Shah was murdered. *(Courtesy of the Royal Ontario Museum, Toronto, Canada.)*

Plate 22 Ruby Mine, Thailand. Large spinel rubies, almost certainly including the Black Prince's Ruby, come from mines such as this one in Burma and Siam (Thailand), long the sole sources of such stones. *(Courtesy of the Gemological Institute of America.)*

Plate 23 Sapphire Mining, Thailand. Sorting rough at Chantaburi, where mining is still a hand operation. *(Courtesy of the Gemological Institute of America.)*

Forges of the Grisons in Switzerland, agreed to pay Prince Demidoff 600,000 francs for the stone but then complained that it had been recut in modern brilliant style with considerable loss in weight and was not worth a third of the amount he had agreed to pay. What it weighed originally is not known today, but it is surprising that Levrat made the agreement without, it is implied, seeing the stone. The Prince reduced the price to 145,800 francs to be paid in three installments over 18 months, and Levrat gave him entitlement to 200 shares in the Swiss company as security but did not pay even the first installment. In 1832, the Prince sued him and won back the diamond, Levrat having to pay costs.

It seems that the Demidoff family gave up trying to sell the stone after this experience until 1865, when a London merchant bought it on behalf of Sir Jamsetjee Jeejeebhoy of Bombay. For some reason, the Indian prince did not keep it for long because it was shown at the Universal Exhibition in Paris in 1867 by the French Crown Jewelers, Messrs. Bapst, who were asking a million francs for it.

After this, the Sancy disappeared once more from the public eye until 1906, when bought by William Waldorf Astor, who became the first Viscount Astor. It went once more on public view in 1962 in the "Ten Centuries of French Jewellery Exhibition" in The Louvre.

## Romancing the Regent Diamond

More is known of the remarkable history of the Regent Diamond (Figure 5–2), which was associated with the Sancy in the French Crown Jewels. They were in the same box when these were stolen after the Terror of 1792. Some diamond specialists insist that it is the finest and most brilliant of all large diamonds. The story of its discovery sounds like romance, but it is more likely to have an element of truth in it than many other legends attached to gems.

An Indian slave working in the Partial mines on the River Kristna, near Golconda, found the 410-carat stone in 1701. He decided not to hand it in but to escape with it. He inflicted a wound in one of his calves to enclose the stone under a bandage. (It must have been a substantial wound to enclose a diamond the size of a box of matches.) When he reached the coast, he confided in an English sea captain to whom he offered a share in return for passage to a country where he would remain free. His trust was misplaced. On the journey, the captain stole the diamond and tossed the slave overboard.

The captain sold the stone to the biggest diamond merchant in the East, Jamchund, for what was said to have been £1,000. It was bought from

Fig. 5–2 The Regent Diamond. Considered by some diamond specialists to be the finest and most brilliant of all large diamonds, the Regent has a colorful and sometimes sordid history. *(Courtesy of the Museum of The Louvre.)*

the merchant by Thomas Pitt, President of Fort Madras, for about £24,000 and became known as the Pitt.

## The Pitt's Predicament

News of the stone got around when Pitt sent it to England to be recut and polished, and a rumor spread that he had cheated an Indian to get hold of it. The allegation was published in the news sheets, and Alexander Pope, the poet and satirist, joined the pack by writing, in *Moral Essays*, these lines:

Asleep and naked as an Indian lay,
An honest factor stole a gem away;
He pledg'd it to the Knight, the Knight had wit,
So he kept the diamond, and the rogue was bit.

It was hinted that Pope had originally written another last line:

So robbed the robber and was rich as P—.

By a strange twist of fate, Pitt's successor as Governor of Madras was the brother of Pope's contemporary essayist, Joseph Addison, and a report had been submitted to him that Pitt had gained possession of the big diamond unfairly. Diamonds were often used as a means of remittance to England in those times, and many had been sent by Pitt, so he was experienced at bargaining and also undertook commissions.

Pitt was, of course, incensed. He was in Bergen in Norway when he heard of the accusation and at once wrote a letter to the editor of the *European Magazine* setting out the facts. It was published in October 1710. It is difficult to get rid of a smearing slander, and 17 years after Pitt's death, the same rumors were recirculated, which led to his descendants persuading the editor of the *Daily Post* to republish in his issue of November 3, 1742, a certified copy of the long letter of denial.

In this, Pitt referred to "the unparalleled villany of William Fraser, Thomas Frederic and Sampa," who had falsely accused him before Governor Addison. It went on:

About three years after my arrival in Madras, which was in July, 1698, I heard there were large diamonds in the country to be sold, which I encouraged to be brought down, promising to be their chaperon, if they would be reasonable therein, upon which Jamchund, one of the most eminent diamond merchants in these parts, came down about December 1701, and brought with him a large rough stone, about 305 *mangelins*, and some small ones, which myself and others bought. But he, asking a very extravagant price for the great one, I did not think of meddling with it; when he left it with me for some days, and then came back and took it away again, and did so several times, insisting on not less than 200,000 *pagodas*, and as I best remember, I did not bid him more than 30,000 and had little thoughts of buying it for that. I considered there were many and great risks to be run, not only in cutting it, but whether it would prove foul or clean, or the water good.

Pitt explained that in the following February, Jamchund returned with another Indian who pressed him to know whether he would buy it if the price came down to 100,000 pagodas. After a great deal of talk, the stone was offered for 55,000 pagodas. On a later visit, Jamchund said he would rather sell it to Pitt than anyone else and reduced the price to 50,000 pagodas. After more bargaining, it came down to 49,000 pagodas, and Pitt finally agreed to pay 49,000 pagodas. "So I closed with him for that sum, when he delivered me the stone, as by my books doth appear."

Pitt did not know what Jamchund paid for the diamond, and although he may have appeared to have struck a hard bargain, it was typical of dealing in the East, as anyone who has done so will recognize. Presumably, he did not know the story of the slave either, which leaves that in some doubt. The stone was shipped to London in the merchant ship *Bedford*, where it was valued on the bill of lading at 6,500 pagodas. (Another report said it was sent on the *Loyall Cooke*.) It was addressed to three people: Pitt's son, Sir Stephen Evance, and Alvaro da Fonseca.

The diamond was cut and polished by Joseph Cope in London, which reduced the weight from 410 carats to 400.50 carats. The charge for this was reported to have been £5,000, a large sum in the early 18th century. Apparently one small speck (inclusion) remained but in a position where it could be concealed by a setting. Messrs. Bapst, the French Crown Jewelers, reported later that there were two almost invisible cleavages (cracks) within the stone.

It took about two years to reshape and polish the diamond, mainly because it was sawn instead of being cleaved. Cleaving takes a moment once the true direction has been found, but it can result in a very awkward-shaped stone because of the very limited directions in which cleaving is possible. Sawing is possible in certain other directions; but at the time, it had to be done using a bow with a wire "string" on which olive oil with diamond dust in it had been rubbed. Even today, using special high-speed revolving cutting discs, it takes a day to saw through a one carat diamond. It is not surprising that it took way more than a year to saw tediously through the Pitt with the primitive Indian bow.

The parts that were removed were very valuable, of course, and, in fact, were sold for between £7,000 and £8,000, much more than the cost of sawing and polishing. They were made into a number of smaller stones, of which Peter the Great of Russia bought some rose cuts.

Selling the stone proved to be difficult. The price was outside the range of almost everyone, but, at last in 1717, it was sold for £135,000 to Isaac Abendana, Duke of Orleans, who was Regent of France while Louis XV was coming of age, and that is how it acquired its new name, the Regent Diamond. The cost of selling it was £5,000, but Pitt still made a handsome profit.

There was much popular interest in the stone at the time, expressed in the press, and many people tried to see it. Pitt became almost paranoic about the possibility of its being stolen and always kept it on his person, never sleeping more than two nights in the same place. He would never announce where he was going next or when he would arrive or depart, and he often used disguises. The sale must have been a great relief to him. A model of the stone made in lead to help sell it was later sent to the British Museum.

The sale to the Regent was not easy because the French treasury was short of funds, and the £5,000 fee for negotiating the sale went to a Scottish banker named John Law, who had tried to help the French government out of its financial difficulties, helped by the Duke of St. Simon. They succeeded by flattery and the help of the model. It is ironical that the sale of the stone to the French Crown restored the fortunes of the Pitt family, whose descendant, William Pitt the Younger, played such an important part in the downfall of Napoleon, who financed himself with the help of the diamond. It was William Pitt, the "Elder Pitt," who gave his name to Pittsburgh, Pennsylvania.

The Regent was mounted in the crown of Louis XV for his coronation in 1772, but after the reign of his ill-fated successor and the revolution, it was stolen in 1792 with the rest of the Crown Jewels. When many were recovered buried under a tree, the Regent was not among them. Other missing jewels had come into various private hands and were handed back, but again, the Regent was not among them, or the Sancy, the Mirror of Portugal, most of the Mazarin diamonds, or the Côte de Bretagne red spinel (Color Plate 6).

The Regent was found about 15 months later in a hole in the timberwork of a garret in Paris. It was returned to the Public Treasury, which contained many other jewels, including those confiscated from private owners and the King of Sardinia's jewels, redeemed from the coffers of a Dutch firm when the French invaded the Netherlands. All of these became, in effect, the new State Jewels.

## In Napoleon's Sword

During the Directory, after Napoleon had overthrown the National Convention and appointed himself Consul in 1799, the State Diamonds were used as security for various complex transactions to raise loans. In one, Parceval, the Adjutant-General, pledged a number of diamonds, including the Regent, to Trescow, a Berlin banker, for four million francs. At the same time, he managed to raise a loan of a million francs from the Marquess of Iranda in Madrid with other diamonds.

After being redeemed from Berlin, the Regent was sent to the Netherlands as security against a loan from a financier named Vandenberg, who became popular for displaying it at the many receptions that he held. After returning the diamond, he confessed that he had always shown a model of the stone and that the real one had been worn by his wife all the time on a necklace underneath her bodice.

Napoleon Bonaparte's conquering army was in Italy during the Directory, and a treaty placed most of the costs of this on the Pope, so much of the wealth of the churches there, including vast amounts of precious metals and gems, along with the great emerald from the Papal tiara, were carried off to Paris. The French Treasury was rich again, and Napoleon and his finance minister redeemed most of the diamonds in pawn. These had raised the huge amounts of money needed to keep fourteen armies in the field, and the proceeds that resulted paid the bills and redeemed the diamonds.

Napoleon had a sword made with the Regent Diamond mounted in the guard. It also held two other brilliant-cut diamonds of about $16\frac{1}{2}$ carats each that had been confiscated from someone who had escaped the Terror of 1792. Josephine, the widow he married in 1796, wanted to wear some of the State Jewels, and this was agreed, but for the sake of form, 254,196 francs had to be paid by the Consulate into the Treasury. When Napoleon proclaimed himself Emperor in 1804, the State Jewels were placed at his disposal.

He anticipated his coronation by entering Notre-Dame already wearing a crown and carrying a scepter. He had refused to wear the original French coronation regalia, some of which was missing and the remainder incomplete and needing repair. He had a new crown made—the Crown of Charlemagne, and also an orb, although such an ornament had never before been part of the French regalia.

Before the ceremony, Napoleon had insisted to the Pope that he crown himself, quoting Charlemagne as saying that he "would never have entered it [St. Peter's for his coronation] had he known the Pope had the intention of crowning him, since he was not willing to seem to owe the Holy See a crown which he held only by his sword." The Pope gave in and also agreed that Napoleon should present a crown to Josephine.

After the Napoleonic Wars that gave him control of most of Europe, Napoleon divorced Josephine and married Marie-Louise. Huge purchases of jewels were made for the wedding for both the Emperor and his bride. During the following year, the Consular Sword in which the Regent was set was broken up and a new one made. This hung from a band set with rose-cut diamonds and also bore the Regent and other diamonds.

Disaster overtook Napoleon in the retreat from Moscow, and Paris was threatened by Cossacks. In 1814, Marie-Louise and her son, whom Napoleon had appointed King of Rome, left for Blois by a train laden with baggage containing everything she could lay her hands on from the State Jewels and elsewhere.

In case the train might be looted, she wore as many jewels as possible, assuming that even Cossacks would not search her personally. (It was possible to rely to some extent on chivalry in those days). Because the Consular Sword was difficult to conceal, she asked a M. Meneval, one of her entourage, to take it to pieces. He lacked the tools to do this so snapped off the blade and hid the hilt bearing the Regent under his cloak.

From his palace at Fontainbleu, Napoleon ordered the jewels taken by Marie-Louise to be returned to the safe custody of the state, but the provisional government that had been set up thought otherwise and sent an official to remove all the baggage wagons. Marie-Louise had been so thorough in her own form of looting that, apart from the jewels, she had articles of silver plate worth three million francs and gold and silver coinage worth 10 million francs. The official did not possess the chivalry she had expected. He ordered her to hand over the necklace she was wearing. It was a present from Napoleon for which half a million francs had been paid.

The State Jewels enriched by Napoleon became Crown Jewels again on the restoration of Louis XVIII, but he only had time to have the N removed from some pieces and others remodeled, before Napoleon returned from the Isle of Elba, to which he had retreated after renouncing the thrones of France and Italy. Napoleon marched on Paris and Louis fled, naturally taking the Crown Jewels with him.

The Bourbon Kings were again restored after Napoleon's defeat at Waterloo in 1815, and a later monarch, Charles X, had the Regent set in a diamond crown that had originally been made for Louis XVIII by Frederic Bapst.

After taking such a battering, the Crown Jewels had a relatively uneventful time for nearly 40 years until 1848, when they might have been stolen again in a drinking orgy. A new revolution had broken out, and Louis Philippe had abdicated. A mob broke into the Tuileries, but, warned by a workman, the National Guard had removed the jewels and other valuables on a stretcher. The mob instead came upon 10,000 bottles of wine in the cellars of the Commandant of the Guard, and the orgy that followed became so wild that a dozen bodies were found in pools of wine among piles of broken bottles the following morning.

The Second Republic was proclaimed in that year and lasted until 1852, during which the treasures remained undisturbed; but when the Second Empire began in the following year and Napoleon III married the Empress Eugenie, the State Jewels were removed to be remodeled. This was done to such an extent that Messrs. Bapst, Crown Jewelers once more, had to ask help from many other jewelers. One new piece, a Greek diadem, was designed with a socket to take the Regent when it was not being used in another piece.

There was more violence before the Third Republic came into being, and this time, the State or Crown Jewels reassumed their ancient role of providing emergency finance. A state of siege had been declared in Paris, and the Regent, with other jewels, was sealed in a box and taken from the Tuileries to the Bank of France, where the box, curiously, was labeled "Special projectiles." From there, it went by train to Brest and was loaded onto a ship. Instructions were given that in an emergency, it should be transferred to a frigate and taken to Saigon.

A number of the revolutionaries searched the Treasury for the jewels but found only models. The Commune ordered the Bank of France to hand them over, and bank officials had considerable difficulty in persuading leaders of the Commune that they no longer had the gems. Eventually, in 1872, they were returned and certain deputies, notably Benjamin Raspail, began advocating that they should be sold or destroyed, as his father had done during a previous revolutionary government. There was considerable argument about what should be done with the money.

At last, in 1886, there was agreement. Jewels of special merit for historic, scientific, or artistic reasons would be saved and passed to the Natural History Museum, the School of Mines, and The Louvre. The rest would be sold by public auction and government stock bought with the proceeds.

There were two exceptions, however. For emotional reasons, the Imperial Crown and the swords of Louis XVIII and the Dauphin were to be broken up. Because he associated the Imperial Crown with Napoleon III, of whom he had an obsessional hatred, Raspail insisted on smashing it himself. But fate took a hand as Raspail managed to smash his leg instead in an

Fig. 5–3 The Hortensia Diamond. Along with the Regent Diamond, the most famous remaining gems from France's Crown Jewels. Both are currently in the Galerie d'Apollon in The Louvre, Paris. *(Courtesy of the Museum of The Louvre.)*

accident before the day. In consolation, he was presented with the hammer used by someone else to do the deed.

Jewelers from all over the world bid against each other for the gems and other treasures of France at the sale in 1883, which lasted from May 12 to 23.

The Regent Diamond at one time represented two-thirds of the value of all France's Crown Jewels. It was not in the sale, and, with the Hortensia Diamond (Figure 5–3) is one of the two most famous gems of what remains of a great collection. They are on show today in the Galerie d'Apollon in The Louvre, Paris. During the Second World War, just before the fall of Paris in 1940, the Regent was taken to the Château Chambord on the Loire and hidden behind a stone panel. It was returned to The Louvre in 1945. In January 1962 in The Louvre exhibition, "Ten Centuries of French Jewellery," the Regent, the Sancy, and the French Blue (Hope) came together for the first time since they had been stolen from the Garde Meuble 170 years earlier.

*The purest and most thoughtful minds are those which love color the most.*
*John Ruskin (1819–1900)*

---

## Chapter Six

# Diamonds of Many Colors

**D**IAMONDS occur in many colors, the most common being tints of yellow or brown. White or, more accurately, transparent stones are those most highly regarded as gems unless a color is particularly attractive; then it is labeled in the diamond trade as a "fancy." In fact, a white stone is at the top of a group of stones categorized as the Yellow Series. Most diamonds used in jewelry have a yellowish tinge to some degree, although this may only be seen by an expert grader and not at all when the stone is set in jewelry. White stones are of the same group, but a peculiarity of their atomic structure is that any yellowness is completely absorbed, leaving them transparent. Brown Series tones are also used as gems when the tint is very light. There are no white stones at the top of this group. Many stones comprise a mixture of the two types of diamond.

Fancies include a different yellow from that of the Yellow Series, known as "canary" because of its brightness. Most stones with a brownish tinge are not very pleasant to the eye, but occasionally a big stone is acceptable for its size if the tint is very light. The most attractive in this group are the golden browns and the cinnamons. Definitely, red stones are rare and only small ones are known, but there are several large and famous pink gems. Mauve is another color that seems to occur only in small stones.

Blue is particularly beautiful in diamonds because even a hint of it seems to add to the purity, although darker blues can have a steely appearance. A blue diamond is *not* what is often described as a "blue-white." That term is reminiscent of laundry detergent ads and that is nearer to diamonds than might be guessed. To laundry detergent is added an ingredient that causes a blue fluorescence in daylight that produces the illusion of "whiter than white." Many diamonds fluoresce with a bluish glow in light that contains some ultraviolet, such as daylight from the south in the northern hemisphere.

Although this may not be evident to most people, it can mask some yellowness in the body of the stone and make it appear whiter. That is why the term "blue-white" has been banned by professional gemological and trade organizations in a number of countries. They insist that the word "blue" must refer only to the body color of the stone and not to its fluorescence; if there is no tinge of blue in the body, the word "blue" must not be part of the description. There are some stones in which the blue fluorescence is so strong that the stone seems to glow bluish all the time, although it is not blue at all. They are called "over-blues" in the trade.

Green diamonds fall into another category of diamond because the apple green of the natural green diamond is quite different from the bottle green color produced artificially by bombarding the diamond with neutrons in an atomic pile or exposing it to certain isotopes. Nevertheless, it is surmised that most naturally green diamonds, if not all, have been exposed to radioactive elements such as uranium at some time during their history, probably many millions of years ago. Unlike neutrons, the charged particles from radioactive rocks will not penetrate deeply and will only color a patch in the stone or the outside to a certain depth, forming a colored "skin."

The green skin is soon removed by polishing it away to reveal, perhaps, a fine white stone underneath. This is one of the speculations indulged in by some diamond buyers, who will accept a stone with a "dirty green" skin on a hunch that it contains a superb white inside. A color patch in a stone will suffuse the whole stone, especially when it is polished, and any patchiness of color will be almost impossible to see without using some gemological technique to do so.

An uncharged particle, the neutron, is needed during artificial coloration to penetrate and color the diamond right through. Such radiation does not occur naturally, so only very small stones are likely to be colored right through by charged particles; but a long passage of time, over millennia, obviously allows deeper irradiation and coloring and perhaps also explains the yellowish bias of naturally green stones and bluish bias of those artificially treated by man.

Most diamond mines produce a proportion of stones with a greenish tint. Some are of gem quality and are used with the whiter and slightly yellow tinged stones in jewelry if the tint is faint. Many are insufficiently pure and are consumed as abrasive in industry.

The deeper yellows are the most common of the fancies, but there are many more shades of color in diamonds than even many jewelers realize, unless they have seen the colored collection assembled by De Beers Consolidated Mines, put on exhibition from time to time.

## The Florentine: A Tangled History

Most historic of the big yellow diamonds is the Florentine, a double-rose-cut stone of pear-shaped outline with 126 facets and nine sides. Double-rose means that it is faceted all over on both sides. We know its shape because J.-B. Tavernier not only referred to it but provided an illustration in Volume Two of his *Travels in India* of 1676. He called it the Grand Duke of Tuscany's diamond and added that the duke (one of the Medicis, Ferdinando II, 1610–1670) "had the goodness to show me [it] upon more than one occasion." It is also known as the Austrian Yellow, and according to Tavernier, it was in his time the second biggest polished diamond in the world after the Great Mogul. He calculated its weight as $139^1/_2$ Florentine carats, which would be equivalent to 137.25 metric carats.

Tavernier wrote that it was "clear, and of good form, cut on all sides into facettes . . . " but was not very complimentary about the color, commenting " . . . it is unfortunate that its water tends towards the colour of citron." If, indeed, it was lemon yellow, it could have been attractive, and models made from his description deliberately support this view.

The history of the Florentine is tangled and uncertain, but one established fact, at least, is that it cannot be associated for certain with any diamond known today.

The story is often told that the diamond belonged to Charles the Bold, Duke of Burgundy (1433–1477), and was "one of the largest in Christendom." He lost it with all his large jewels and baggage at the Battle of Morat or the Battle of Granson in 1476 or the Battle of Nancy in 1477 (where he died), according to different chroniclers. In the rout that followed the battle, a Swiss soldier found it with a fine pearl in a box. He recognized the pearl for what it was but threw away the "piece of glass"; then, on second thoughts, he recovered it from under a wagon, where it had fallen.

A priest in Montigny bought it for a florin from the soldier and passed it on to the authorities in Berne for three francs. Next, it went to a wealthy Bernese merchant, Bartholomew May, for 5,000 florins, to a Goanese dealer, and to the Milanese Regent for 10,000 florins. Pope Julius II then bought it for 20,000 ducats when the Milanese treasures were dispersed.

That is the story. On the other hand, J. J. Fugger, of the once-famous Nuremberg family, wrote in 1555 that his great-uncle, Jacob Fugger, bought the yellow diamond and other jewels as well as the Cap of Maintenance from the Duke of Burgundy for 47,000 florins. That seems more likely. He described the Duke's diamond as shaped like a pyramid five-eighths of an inch square at the base with the apices cut into a four-rayed star in relief, each star coinciding with the middle of each face of the pyramid. (This is not very clear, but presumably each of the four sides was polished with four facets to form a star, with a fifth one at the apex). The stone was the centerpiece of a diamond, ruby, and pearl pendant that belonged to the Fugger family for some years until J. J. Fugger sold it to King Henry VIII of England in 1547, not long before Henry died.

Henry's daughter Mary, when on the throne, presented it in 1554 to her husband, Philip II, who was a fourth generation descendant of Charles the Bold.

However satisfying the story, from Fugger's description of the cut, this was certainly not the stone that Tavernier saw. Robert de Berquen wrote that the famous 15th century diamond polisher, his uncle, Louis de Berquen, cut and polished three diamonds for Charles the Bold in 1476. One was triangular shaped and was presented to Louis XI of France; another was thin and presented to Pope Sixtus IV; and the third was thickly cut and set in a ring. In no way could the large Florentine Diamond have been mounted in a wearable ring, so the third stone was not the Florentine, meaning the Florentine is not likely to have belonged to Charles the Bold.

Unfortunately, the false history was perpetuated in an official publication *Catalogue of the Objects Contained in the Treasury of the Imperial and Royal House of Austria* (1880) that stated, "The 'Florentine' also called the 'Great Florentine diamond,' actually forming part of a hat button, is known to be one of the largest diamonds in the world. It weighs $138^1/_3$ carats of Vienna, but is rather yellow. The stone is cut in nine surfaces covered with facets forming a star with nine rays. This jewel was once the property of Charles the Bold. . . "

The real Florentine undoubtedly came from India to Europe by way of one of the established trade routes (overland to Constantinople and then on to Rome or to Alexandria and then by sea to Venice) and into the possession of the Medici family, which ruled for a long time in Tuscany. When the Medici reign came to an end with the death of the last Duke, under the Treaty of Vienna, the European powers arranged for Tuscany to come under the influence of the Dukes of Lorraine. Francis Stephen, successor to both Dukedoms, had married the Empress Maria Theresa, one of the Austrian Hapsburgs, two years earlier in 1736. After he was crowned as Emperor Francis I of Austria in 1745, the Florentine was set with other diamonds in a hat. Tavernier saw it sometime around mid-17th century when Ferdinand II was Grand Duke of Tuscany.

During the Second World War, the Nazis took the Austrian Crown Jewels and hid them in a salt mine near Salzburg, but after the war, the jewels were recovered by the American occupying forces and returned to the state by General Mark Clark at a public ceremony. The Florentine was not among them, although there was a large brilliant-cut yellow diamond.

So what happened to the Florentine after it was cataloged in 1880? It is certainly one of the great diamonds of world, despite the doubts expressed about its color. Was it recut into the form of a brilliant? And where is it now?

## Kimberley's Revelations

If it does still exist in its original form, the Florentine would not be the second biggest diamond today and not even the biggest yellow diamond. The De Beers Diamond (Color Plate 14) weighs 234.65 metric carats, the Red Cross (Figure 6–1) 205.07 metric carats, the Moon 183 metric carats, and the Iranian A 152.16 metric carats. All are bigger and yellow.

The De Beers Diamond was found in the De Beers mine in Kimberley in 1890. The annual report of De Beers Consolidated Mines for that year states that a $428\frac{1}{2}$ carat rough, 1.78 inches long, was found in the De Beers mine by a native whose "brother" gave information that led to its recovery

Fig. 6–1 The Red Cross Diamond. A fancy yellow diamond despite its name, the Red Cross is a square-cut African stone. The London Diamond Syndicate gave it to the British Red Cross Society and the Order of St. John of Jerusalem. *(Courtesy of Christie's in Geneva; photography by A. C. Cooper Ltd.)*

while being taken from the mine. It was cut and exhibited at the Paris Exhibition of 1889.

One yellow stone, the Shah of Persia, cushion-shaped and weighing 99.52 carats is believed to have been one of the Moguls' treasures taken to Persia by Nadir Shah after he had sacked Delhi in 1739. It is supposed to have been given by the Persian government to a General V. D. Starosselky, a military expert loaned to them by the Czar about the time of the First World War. He took it to the United States, where it was sold to a Los Angeles jeweler. It was bought in 1957 by the diamantaire, Harry Winston of New York. At that time, it was mounted in a pendant/brooch with 178 small rose-cut diamonds and 72 brilliants.

A diamond of 287.42 carats in the rough and described as golden in color, was found at the Kimberley mine in 1878. This mine, which closed in 1914, was once the biggest man-made hole in the world (Figure 6–2). It is now part of the Open Mine Museum, with many of Kimberley's old houses, shops, bars, booths, and other buildings reerected around it. The polished stone is cushion-shaped with 90 facets, the extra ones over the standard 58 facets providing extra life and fire because of the size. It was cut in Paris and belongs to Tiffany and Co., the New York jewelers, who named it the Tiffany (Figure 6–3).

More recently in Kimberley, Andrew Moraldi was an attendant on the crusher plant at the Dutoitspan mine, where blue ground (Kimberlite rock) is crushed into small lumps before being delivered by a conveyor belt to the diamond recovery plant. One day in 1973, he plucked a huge yellow diamond of octahedron shape from under the crusher box. It weighed 223.6 carats and would undoubtedly have been smashed into small pieces had it gone through the crusher. Indeed, it was part of Moraldi's job to remove any big stones he spotted, but most attendants worked for a lifetime without seeing one. He was rewarded, of course, and the stone was bought by Sidney Barnett, head of the Stern group of retail jewelry shops in South Africa. It was cut by Kagan of New York, and the largest stone obtained is known as the Sterns Star, weighing 85.93 carats. Barnett takes his friends to the vaults of a bank in Johannesburg to show off the Sterns Star.

Another fine Kimberley stone is described as champagne-colored.It is 55.09 carats in weight in its polished emerald-cut form and was another large stone found in the old Kimberley mine. Somehow it came into the possession of the Czars of Russia, where it was described as a large, flat stone. It was recut in 1921 into a 70 carat stone, also of emerald shape (i.e., rectangular shape with beveled corners), which was still somewhat lifeless because it was still too flat. Baumgold Bros. of New York bought it and re-

Fig. 6–2 The Big Hole. The Kimberley Mine in South Africa, which closed in 1914, was once the biggest man-made hole in the world. It is now part of the Open Mine Museum. *(Courtesy of De Beers Consolidated Mines.)*

Fig. 6–3 The Tiffany Diamond. The largest and finest canary diamond in the world, it is unique among yellow diamonds not only
because of its purity and size but also because it retains its fabulous color even under artificial light. Cut from its rough weight of
287.42 carats to 128.51 metric carats in order to contain the un-
usually large number of 90 facets, it is now on view at Tiffany's
in New York. *(Courtesy of Tiffany & Co.)*

cut it to its current weight, with more scientific proportions to increase its
brilliancy. From a plaything of the Czars, this flawless stone has become a
favorite prop of fashion show organizers and film producers. They own another champagne-colored diamond, the Transvaal, which is pear-shaped,
has 116 facets, and weighs 67.89 carats. The ninth largest rough diamond is
a fine complete octahedron known as the Kimberley Octahedron or the
"616" (Figure 6–4). It was found in the Dutoitspan mine as recently as 1974
by an African worker, Abel Maretela. It is yellow, like many of the larger
stones from this mine. The "616" is the largest ever found in Kimberley
and is on permanent show at the Open Mine Museum there. It has not been
cut, perhaps because the weight, 616 carats, is the same as De Beers' area
code number.

Fig. 6–4 The Kimberley "616." A closeup of the 616-carat diamond found at Dutoitspan Mine in Kimberley, South Africa, in 1974. It is the largest octahedron in the world and the ninth largest stone ever found. The small stone on the left is a one carat diamond. *(Courtesy of De Beers Consolidated Mines.)*

## No Match for the Wittelsbach

The most famous blue diamond, the Hope, and the two smaller stones that some believe to have been part of the French Blue have been discussed in Chapter Four. There is only one other blue stone that has a legendary history, the Wittelsbach, an oval-shaped brilliant-cut stone of Indian origin.

The difficulty of describing a color exactly is well known in the diamond trade, and various descriptive scales have developed at the mines and trading centers over the years to identify the fine graduations from colorless to faint tinges of yellowness. With fancies, it is difficult to describe a color, as J. Konkommer of Antwerp, the last diamantaire to handle the

Wittelsbach, pointed out: "Even if there were a hundred words to describe a hundred hues of blue, I could not find the one that is right. So I shall try a negative approach. The stone is not what we call 'blue-white' and it is certainly not 'over-blue.' Neither is it sapphire blue, nor is it ink blue. And to put an end to this game: if you were to grade pale blue as 1 and dark blue as 100, then the colour of the stone might be somewhere around 50."

The Wittelsbach is an Indian stone without doubt, although its early history is unknown. It was first heard of in Spain when it was part of the wedding dowry of Margaret Theresa, daughter of Philip IV, on her marriage to Leopold I of Austria in 1667. She died only six years later and Leopold's second wife only lived until 1696, so the blue diamond was passed on by Leopold to his third wife, with all the jewelry he had inherited from his previous wives. On the death of this wife, Eleanora Magdalena, the stone was left to the youngest of the two archduchesses, Maria Amelia, who married Charles Albert of the Bavarian Wittelsbach family.

She did not keep the diamond for long. Her father-in-law, the Elector of Bavaria, who was deeply in debt, took it and pawned it to a man named Oppenheimer. (Could he have been an ancestor of Sir Ernest Oppenheimer, who played such a vital role in the South African diamond industry?) After Charles Albert became Elector, the diamond, together with a gold service, was redeemed from Oppenheimer for the sum of 434,377 florins.

Before the stone came to Munich in Bavaria, it was known by the cumbersome title of the Great Blue Thick Diamond. As the Wittelsbach, it was passed in 1761 from the private treasury of the Elector to the national exchequer, where it was described as "of such exceptional beauty, purity and colour, that there is no other to match it. Value 300,000 florins. Weight 36 carats." The weight in metric carats is 35.56. In 1918, after the First World War, all the possessions of the Bavarian Crown were transferred to a special fund, but the blue diamond belonged to or was associated with the Wittelsbach family from 1722 to 1931, when the Munich newspaper *Munchener Zeitung* announced that it was to be auctioned in London. There was some mystery about the seller, and, thereafter, it appeared to vanish.

Then in 1961, one of the top diamond merchants in Antwerp sought the advice of J. Konkommer about an "old miner," as early cut stones are called. "What do you think would be the best way to cut this stone—pear shape, emerald-cut or oval?" Konkommer was shocked because it was a blue diamond of obvious historical significance that he held in his hand and to recut it would be sacrilege. The color was deep blue and uniform, and the cutting pattern was one he had never seen before. He decided he would like to buy it himself, so he told the dealer and added that he could not then be both buyer and adviser. The dealer and his son, along with the three experts they had with them, were pleased to give him an option.

This meant that, in the universal custom of the diamond trade, the stone was returned to its briefca, a specially folded piece of paper, and Konkommer put his seal on it. The seller now has to keep the sealed briefca until the transaction is settled. No one would be allowed to see the stone, not even the seller himself, until the seal was broken, and that could only be done by the buyer. Konkommer hurried back to his office and told his son about the stone. They had a copy of the *Diamond Dictionary* published by the Gemological Institute of America, but going through it page by page was too slow, so the son went out to buy another so that he could start from the back. Soon he alighted upon the entry for the Wittlesbach, which ended, "Present whereabouts unknown."

It was, indeed, the missing Wittelsbach, and Konkommer organized a syndicate to buy it. It was sold in 1964 to a private collector in West Germany.

At one time, the Wittelsbach was mounted in the center of the insignia of the Order of the Golden Fleece (Figure 6–5), the highest honor of the House of Hapsburg, and there are paintings of at least two Electors wearing it.

By far the biggest blue diamond, described as being of intense blue, was almost certainly found in South Africa. It was cut and polished in Amsterdam in 1904. Cushion-shaped, it weighed 136.25 carats, which ranked it 18th in a list of the largest polished diamonds of the world. The Dutch firm of F. Friedman owned it for many years and exhibited it at the Paris Exhibition of Arts and Industry in 1925. It came into the hands of a Parisian jeweler, who sold it to an Indian maharajah, and that is about all that is known about it.

## The Dresden Green

Green gemstones of any kind, size, and quality are very rare. There is none in the list of 127 of the world's biggest polished gem diamonds of 50 carats or over in weight, compiled by the author with the help of N. W. Ayer and Sons Inc., New York, and the honorable Iain Balfour.

In some cultures, green is an unlucky color, but ill-fortune could hardly be associated with the Dresden Green, which has a long but uneventful history compared with most historic diamonds. It was named after the capital of Saxony, a country that, under Augustus the Strong—Frederic Augustus I (reigned 1694–1733)—became one of the cultural centers of Europe.

Fig. 6–5 The Wittelsbach Diamond in the Order of the Golden Fleece. The Wittelsbach Blue was set in the Order of the Golden Fleece while part of the Austrian Crown Jewels. It was removed and offered at auction in 1931. The Order, now in the Schatzkammer of the Residenz in Munich, is set with a glass imitation. *(Courtesy of the Residenz Museum of Munich Collection.)*

Fig. 6–6 Jewel Chamber of the Green Vault. In 1932 in Dresden, the Jewel Chamber of the Green Vault housed three legendary diamonds: the Dresden Green, the Dresden Yellow, and the Dresden White. *(Courtesy of the Twining Collection, copyright of the Worshipful Company of Goldsmiths, Goldsmith's Hall, London.)*

During his rule, many magnificently baroque buildings were erected in Dresden to house great collections of sculptures, paintings, and other objets d'art. For the jewels and other especially valuable articles, Augustus the Strong built a series of eight rooms in the west wing of Dresden Castle, which were decorated by selected French interior designers and named the Green Vault (Figure 6–6). The eighth room was kept for the Crown Jewels.

The next Elector, his son Frederic Augustus II (reigned 1733-1763), bought a large green diamond at Leipzig Fair. This was one of Europe's oldest trading events, having started as Easter and Christmas markets in 1458. In 1497, it became an Imperial Fair. (There was even a book fair in Saxony from 1545). He paid a Dutch merchant 200,000 thalers for the stone in 1742. It is brilliant-cut in pear, otherwise known as pendeloque, shape with 58 facets, and weighs 40.7 carats. Frederic Augustus II deposited it in the Green Vault, and there it remained for more than two centuries except for the occasions when it was worn or was in the hands of jewelers. The Dresden Green Diamond was not named after the Green Vault, but perhaps the name of the vault influenced its purchase.

At first, the Dresden Green was set in the Order of the Golden Fleece, but in 1746, instructions were given for it to be removed: the insignia was to be remodeled by the jeweler J. F. Dillinger and the Dresden White set in its place. The Dresden White was already in the treasury, having been bought by Augustus the Strong for what was, at the time, a record price per carat. It is colorless, square-cut, and weighs 49.71 carats. A few years later, the Dresden Green was mounted by a jeweler named Diessbach with two white diamonds weighing about 40 carats, along with many smaller ones in a hat clasp. The Dresden White was also eventually removed from the Insignia of the Order of the Golden Fleece and, in the 18th century, became the main stone, with nineteen other large diamonds and 216 smaller ones, in a shoulder knot. There is also a Dresden Yellow, a brilliant-cut stone of 38 carats.

The Dresden Green is often stated to have been of Indian origin, but there is no evidence for this. One diamond historian, Iain Balfour, has suggested that as the Elector bought it from a Dutch merchant, it came from Brazil. Brazil replaced India as the main source of diamonds after the 1720s. Amsterdam's zenith as a diamond cutting center was in the 17th century, known as the Golden Century in Holland, but the Brazilian discoveries had caused a revival of the industry because the Dutch consul in Rio de Janeiro had made arrangements for supplies of rough diamonds to be sent to Amsterdam. The rival industry was in Antwerp, which is now the world's biggest. Balfour's suggestion seems a strong possibility. At any rate, the Dresden Green must have been an impressive stone in the rough because it must have weighed about 100 carats.

When the Second World War broke out, the jewels in the Green Vault were removed from display and in 1942 taken for safety to Konigstein, a Saxon castle on the River Elbe, so they escaped the Allied Forces' bombing raid of February 13, 1945, which destroyed most of the beautiful city of Dresden.

The Russians had a military body, the Soviet Trophies Organization, to deal with such treasures. It was conveniently located outside the city, in Pillnitz Castle, and it removed all the contents of museums, including what had been in the Green Vault. Among the jewels taken to Moscow were the three Dresden diamonds. In 1958, after Dresden became part of East Germany, the treasures were returned and have since been put on view again in the restored Green Vault.

Confused at one time with the Dresden White was another stone first called the Dresden Drop and later just the Dresden. It is now universally known as the English Dresden because it was once owned by an Englishman named Dresden. The rough stone of 119.5 carats from the Bagagem mines in Minas Gerais, Brazil, in 1857, was bought for a London merchant, E. H. Dresden, by his agent in Rio de Janeiro. Cut to 76.50 carats, it became a flawless stone of the highest purity. Dresden once remarked that the Koh-i-Noor looked yellowish beside it.

In 1864, it was bought by a Bombay cotton merchant who had made a fortune quickly and unexpectedly because the Civil War in America had caused a cotton shortage. Dresden was tricked in the sale because the cotton merchant's agent obtained £40,000 for it but persuaded Dresden that the highest offer was £32,000 and so pocketed the difference as well as his commission. The cotton merchant died soon after, and the stone was sold to the Gaekwar of Baroda.

## *Brazil's Star of the South*

E. H. Dresden also acted as agent for the sale of another great diamond, the first Brazilian stone to become famous. It was found by a woman, a slave at the same mines in Minas Gerais, a huge stone weighing 261.9 carats in the rough. The woman was given her freedom and a pension, but even the slave master was unaware of the true value of the stone and sold it to a dealer who resold it for five times as much.

After changing hands a number of times, it was cut and polished in Amsterdam by Coster, who had manufactured (that is the word used in the diamond trade) the English Dresden and recut the Koh-i-Noor. It became an oval brilliant of 128.80 carats "with a decided inner rose tint" and became known as the Star of the South. Through Dresden, it was also sold to the Gaekwar of Baroda, who had it and the English Dresden mounted in a necklace worn by members of his family.

A stone of a very decided pink hue is the 20 carat Hortensia Diamond, which has a very long history, being one of the stones bought by Tavernier in India and sold to the French King Louis XIV in 1669. It has also been described as peach-colored and earned its name from Hortense de Beauharnaise, Queen of Holland (1783–1837), daughter of Empress Josephine, Napoleon's first wife.

It was one of the French Crown Jewels stolen from the Garde Meuble in 1792 and was not recovered until some time later, apparently from a hiding place in a garret in Les Halles district, where the fruit and vegetable market once was. The diamond is now in the Gallerie Apollon, or Gallery of Apollo, in The Louvre, Paris, and was one of the legendary diamonds shown at the Ten Centuries of French Jewellery Exhibition in 1962.

Among the Iranian Crown Jewels, of which there is talk of selling from time to time by some of the revolutionaries of the Ayatollah regime, is a much bigger pink diamond weighing 60 carats. Called the Noor-ul-Din (Light of the Eye), this large stone was set centrally in a truly dramatic tiara, surrounded by 324 diamonds, some of them very large by ordinary standards.

Other large pink diamonds have been reported, such as the 72-carat Nepal Pink, which is said to have a soft rosy hue and to be cut in the old Indian style. There is a pear-shaped white diamond called the Nepal, believed to have come from the old Golconda mining area. It was shown at the Ageless Diamond Exhibition in London in 1959. An oval pink diamond of 81.83 carats was sold in London in 1972 but had not been given a name at the time.

Perhaps the best-known pink or, more accurately, rose-colored diamond in the United Kingdom is the Williamson, found in the huge Tanzanian diamond mine at Mwadui discovered and owned until his death by Dr. John T. Williamson (Figure 6–7). It was cut and polished by Briefel and Lemer in London, where the 54.5 carat rough had to be reduced to 23.60 carats to produce what has been described as one of the finest diamonds in the world because of its unusual coloring and its fine quality. It was mount-

Fig. 6–7 Dr. John T. Williamson. Discoverer and owner of the Williamson Diamond, perhaps the best-known rose-colored diamond in the United Kingdom. It was found in the huge Tanzanian diamond mine at Mwadui. *(Courtesy of N. A. G. Press Ltd., Ipswich.)*

ed as the center of a flower brooch (Figure 6–8) with the petals made up of other diamonds from Mwadui and was presented by Dr. Williamson to Princess Elizabeth before she was Queen and when she married Prince Philip in 1946, which was also the year when the diamond was discovered, or so it was said.

The biggest and most legendary rose colored diamond of all is the Darya-i-Noor, described in Chapter Three. Among the known polished diamonds of 50 carats and more, this was the only one described as rose, although the last gemologist to examine it called it pink. Five others are labeled pink, but because no single person has seen more than very few of these stones, it has not been possible, and never will be, to compare them.

## The Color List

By far, the biggest group in the color list is the yellow one, numbering thirty-four stones. As well, there are two canary-colored, which are brighter than the usual yellow, two labeled golden, one honey, and one amber. Some unusual colors are peach (rather than pink), bronze, and gunmetal; two other stones are listed as black. The only blue stone of 50 carats or more is surprisingly large, the Queen of Holland at 136.50 carats. Even more curious is that of the two stones listed as bluish, the larger, an unnamed stone sold in London in 1960, is almost the same size, at 136.32 carats.

White stones in the list number fifty-four. Browns are not numerous among large gem diamonds, although they are much more so among rough stones because the brown tinge is not attractive enough to be called "fancy." The smaller a stone is cut, the lighter it appears to become, and "fine light brown" diamonds are popular for low-priced diamond engagement rings in the United Kingdom in particular, one of the biggest markets for lower qualities. Five stones are described as champagne-colored. Some of the brownish ones may have been given names suggesting they are yellowish. In the color list are eleven large diamonds of which the color has never been stated, which may imply they are colorless, or what is generally called "white."

## The Black Dilemma

Black is something of a misnomer in a list of colored gem diamonds. Firstly, black is not a color but the absence of color; secondly, the blackness is not inherent in the diamond itself; and, thirdly, a black diamond is not a gemstone by definition.

One of the principal requirements for a gem diamond is that it must be

Fig. 6–8 Flower Brooch Containing the Williamson Diamond. The rose-colored stone was mounted as the center of a flower brooch; the petals are made up of other diamonds from the same Tanzanian mine. The brooch was presented by Dr. Williamson to Princess Elizabeth when she married Prince Philip in 1946. *(Copyright reserved to Her Majesty Queen Elizabeth II.)*

colorless or almost so and have few if any inclusions (i.e., tiny crystals of other minerals, tiny cleavages, cracks, or clouds of submicroscopic particles or bubbles inside it). A black diamond is filled with extremely small or submicroscopic inclusions. They absorb all the light falling on it so that it appears to be black. Black diamonds are rarely attractive. Some have surfaces covered with black pock marks; only a very few have a good luster; and there are only a very few big ones worthy enough to achieve fame. In other words, it is the paradox value that results in big black rough diamonds being cut and polished.

The biggest known black, exhibited in Tokyo in 1971, weights 202 carats and is called the Black Star of Africa. The second biggest is the Black Orloff (Color Plate 12), which is described more accurately as gunmetal in color. It is believed to be of Indian origin, and the story is that it came from a temple in Pondicherry, where it was known as the Eye of Brahma (although it seems unlikely that Brahma had a black eye). Weighing perhaps 195 carats in the rough, it was reduced to 67.50 carats when cut into cushion shape. It acquired its current name when it belonged to Princess Orloff, It was bought in this century by Harry Winston of New York and was exhibited at the Diamond Pavilion in Johannesburg in 1967.

The most recent black diamond on the way to becoming famous arrived in Amsterdam as a rough stone in a parcel of mine boarts from South Africa. Boarts are diamonds with so many impurities and other imperfections that they are only fit for crushing for use as an abrasive in industry. It weighed 55.85 carats and was valued at between $5 and $6 a carat. D. Drukker & Zn N.V. tried to cleave it to produce industrial diamonds for tool tips and discovered that it was of the deepest black color all through and without transparency. They decided it was unique, so polished it during a very laborious process taking from October 1972 to January 1973 into a pear-shaped gem of 33.74 carats with 145 facets, including extra facets polished on the girdle.

Even under the strongest light, the diamond is opaque yet of deep black, which might make it appear odd that it has been described as gunmetal in color, but that is due to the lack of transparency combined with the particular luster of diamond. It was named the Amsterdam (Figure 6–9) and was first exhibited on the 700th anniversary of the City of Amsterdam in 1965. The only black diamond cut to modern proportions, it is 23.96 millimeters long by 17 millimeters wide by 12.30 millimeters thick and is mounted in a pendant surrounded by white diamonds.

Prominent diamantaires have long declared that there are no black diamonds — that they exist only in detective stories. The origin of this belief

Fig. 6-9 The Amsterdam Black Diamond. A unique gem of the deepest black color, without transparency. Prominent diamantaires have long declared that there are no real black diamonds, but the Amsterdam has been certified as a truly black one. *(Courtesy of D. Drukker & Zn N.V.)*

may be that some so-called black ones are actually dark brown with so many specks of dark mineral inclusions that they only appear black. Drukker submitted its stone to an international gemologist, Dr. P. C. Zwaan, Director of the Netherlands Institute for Scientific Testing of Gemstones and Pearls, established in the Rijksmuseum van Geologie en Mineralogie in Leiden. He certified the Amsterdam as a natural diamond.

One thing is certain about famous colored diamonds: the descriptions of their hues have to be regarded cautiously because of the different commentators and their different times, as well as the enormous difficulties of checking and comparison.

*Chapter Seven*

# The Greatest Gem of All Time

Oᴺᴱ of the most dramatic moments in the history of gemstones occurred not in the bloodthirsty times of the Moguls and the shahs but in the quiet period at sunset when most of the workers in a mine in the Transvaal had returned to their huts. It was January 25, 1905, at the end of a summer's day, when Frederick G. S. Wells, the surface manager of the Premier mine, about 24 miles east of Pretoria, was walking along the edge of the open pit when he saw something glint in the rays of the dying sun. It was near enough to the top for him to clamber down and dig it out with the help of his pocketknife. It was a lump of transparent crystal almost the size of half a brick. He could not believe his eyes. Surely, it could not be a diamond . . . no diamond even a fraction of this size had ever been seen before.

But it *was* a diamond, and it weighed 3,106 metric carats or about one-and-a-half *pounds* (680 grams). It was more than three times bigger than the biggest diamond ever seen, the Excelsior, also found in South Africa in 1893. That night, the stone was put in the mine's safe and the find reported to the company chairman, Thomas Cullinan. During the later celebrations, "Daddy" Wells, as he was known to his staff, was presented with a check for £2,000.

As well as producing this entirely exceptional stone, the mine itself was an exception for the time because all the other pipe mines were in the Kimberley area. A pipe mine is an original source, where diamonds were brought to the surface from deep down in the earth, where they were formed. Diamonds found in all other places were carried there perhaps millions of years ago and as far as thousands of miles by ancient rivers.

Many were deposited in gravels now lying many feet under the surface of dry land. They were also carried into the sea and thrown back on the beaches, where they are trapped under up to 15 meters of sand. Some remain in potholes in the sea bed. All these types of alluvial deposits are mined today.

The old miners called deposits on land either "dry diggings," if the old river had long vanished, or "wet diggings" if they were in or on the banks of a still active river. In those days, they never suspected that diamonds could be found in the sea.

Percival White Tracey was one of the old diggers who worked a claim in the De Beers mine in Kimberley, which Cecil Rhodes used as his first steppingstone to controlling the diamond industry. His claim did not produce enough to keep him there, so he decided to move to Johannesburg, where gold prospectors were discovering the outcrops of gold reef along the Witwatersrand, not then knowing they were on the edge of an enormous dried-up inland sea with a bed of gold. While washing dirt in a stream for traces of gold, Tracey recognized patches of ground similar to what he had seen in Kimberley.

He paddled upstream to trace the source of the ground and found himself on the land of a farm called Elandsfontein, where there was a small hill or kopji like those he had seen around Kimberley. A kopji or a pan (a depression sometimes holding water) could be the top of a diamondiferous pipe going like a gigantic carrot deep into the earth.

Tracey got no further because the farmer, Joachim Prinsloo, was a Boer with very fixed ideas about prospectors. He hated them, all of them, and would happily have shot any who nosed about his farm. He had owned a farm at Madderfontein when the gold rush occurred there in 1886. Selling out, he moved to Kaalfontein, where diamonds were found. So he moved to Elandsfontein, and prospectors were still bothering him.

Tracey retreated, and Prinsloo carried on with his primitive farming on the wild tract of poor land, renting parts of it to local blacks. Tracey, wondering what to do next to follow up his hunch, remembered that Thomas M. Cullinan, a prominent Johannesburg building contractor, had expressed his belief that the Transvaal could be a diamond producing state. Cullinan was also well known for his skill in negotiating property sales. There is another story that Cullinan was himself prospecting in the area when he met Tracey, who showed him a three-carat diamond he had picked up at Elandsfontein. Whatever the preliminaries, the two men managed to visit Prinsloo on some pretext.

Cullinan asked for an option on the property for three months so that they could prospect and if he was then satisfied that there was mineral wealth on the farm, he would buy. It seems that Prinsloo not only did not want prospectors on his land but that he had little faith in their finding anything because he would only sell outright for £25,000. He had paid £500 for the farm.

Neither would budge; then came the Boer War (1899–1902) between the British Empire and the two Boer republics, the Transvaal and the Orange Free State, and communications were suspended. After the war, Cullinan renewed his offer, but Prinsloo had hardened his attitude and now demanded £50,000 for the farm as an outright sale without an option to prospect it first. In the end, the Boer farmer won and, with extra expenses, Cullinan had to pay £52,000 to act on his hunch. The deal was sealed in October 1902, and prospecting began at once. The first hole produced only garnets and olivines, which are usually found with diamonds and have more recently been named "sputnics" by the Russians because they are found in a rough circle around diamond deposits. The second bore hole delivered eleven diamonds, one of which weighed 16 carats.

The Premier (Transvaal) Diamond Mining Company was formed in 1903. The word "Transvaal" was included because there was already a mine named the Premier in Kimberley, now known as the Wesselton. In the first two years or so, the mine produced four diamonds of more than 400 carats each, two between 200 carats and 300 carats each and sixteen between 100 carats and 200 carats. But even that did not prepare the owners for the monster stone of the year 1905 that became known as the Cullinan (Figure 7–1).

Cullinan's property far away from Kimberley caused a lot of heartburning in the empire of Cecil Rhodes. The Elandsfontein pipe was so large that Rhodes's partner, Alfred Beit, nearly had a heart attack when he learned of the extent of the pipe and what it was producing. It was, indeed, severe competition, especially when the market for selling such a huge output had not been established. (The diamond engagement ring tradition came out of the discoveries; it had not existed before then.)

Selling a stone the size of the Cullinan posed enormous problems. There was no one rich enough in the world to pay what it was worth as a big stone. It could have been cut into a great number of smaller stones that were saleable, but that would have destroyed its uniqueness. And it was well known that it had taken the Kimberley syndicate many years to sell the Excelsior, which will be related later in this chapter.

The Cullinan was found at a more fortunate time, however, because the Boer War was now over, and the Boer Generals, Botha and Smuts, now

7–1 The Cullinan Diamond. The biggest and most precious diamond ever found, it was discovered in 1905 by the surface manager of the Premier Mine in South Africa. *(Courtesy of the Royal Asscher Diamond Company, Ltd.)*

South African leaders, were working to gain the British support they needed for the new Union of South Africa. General Botha, the Prime Minister, moved a resolution before the Transvaal Legislative Assembly to present the diamond to King Edward VII on this 66th birthday on November 9, 1907.

The offer, surprisingly, was not immediately accepted. The British government was of two minds because the Britons in South Africa were unenthusiastic, being suspicious of the Boer Generals' attempt to bypass them. In the end, the government shilly-shallied and asked the King to make the decision. He said the diamond should be accepted. So it was sold to the Transvaal government for the nominal sum of £175,000.

There was much deliberation on getting the stone from South Africa to England. Detectives were sent from London to guard it, and it was also insured for a large sum. News was leaked that a certain steamer was carrying it, and the presence of the detectives confirmed this. In fact, the package

Fig. 7-2 Joseph Asscher Cleaving the Cullinan. In February 1908, authorized experts gathered at the factory of the Asscher Diamond Co. in Amsterdam to witness the destiny of the Cullinan under the blow of the cleaving hammer. As a result of the manipulation of the Cullinan, a royal collection of diamonds of remarkable purity was obtained. *(Courtesy of the Royal Asscher Diamond Company Ltd.)*

they accompanied contained a fake stone. The real one was sent in an ordinary unregistered parcel — such was the well-justified faith in the Royal Mail in the early 20th century.

## Cleaving the Cullinan

Asschers of Amsterdam were the most trusted cutters of the time and had cut the Excelsior a few years earlier. It was announced in the newspapers that the diamond was being posted to Amsterdam, but this was another bluff. Joseph Asscher (Figure 7–2) came to London to see it and took it back to the works in his pocket, traveling by train and steamboat. The Asscher brothers studied the stone for six months, building up their knowledge of it before deciding how to cut it.

In diamantaire's language, cutting means cleaving, although used loosely, it means other processes, too. Every diamond has four directions in which it will split if the right knowledge and skills are used. The diamond cleaver learns how to identify these directions by experience in what he calls "finding the grain." There is a rough similarity to splitting wood, which is easy along the grain but impossible across it. The grain is very easy to distinguish in wood, but in a diamond of irregular shape, it is sometimes difficult. Also, like knots in wood, there are often "naats" in diamonds that can cause cleaving, sawing, grinding, and polishing problems.

The problem hardly existed with the Cullinan, however, because it had already been cleaved by the forces of nature at some time during its history, and if one cleavage plane is identified, the others are always at certain angles to it. The problem was where to cleave the giant stone in order to reduce waste to a minimum and yet produce the largest possible number of stones of modern cut, which have precise angles to produce the maximum brilliance. The Asschers marked the stone with Indian ink to indicate where it was going to be cleaved and then made a notch, using another diamond, along one of these lines. This is normal practice, but for the Cullinan, specially large cleaving tools had to be made.

Imagine the tension when the moment came. The greatest and most priceless diamond the world had ever known was going to be split into two with a single blow. If it split wrongly, it could not produce the finest and biggest polished stones. A steel blade with blunt edge and polished sides, to act like a wedge, was placed in the notch, the diamond having been cemented into a holder fastened to the end of a bench. Joseph Asscher stood, with a white overall covering his suit and stiff collar, with his left hand steadying the holder. With his right hand, he raised a special mallet in the shape of a rod and brought it down sharply on the top of the blade. The diamond split perfectly into two parts of about 2,000 carats and 1,000 carats each (Figure 7–3). The day was February 10,1907.

Further cleaving and sawing produced nine major gems (Figure 7–4) and ninety-six smaller brilliants as well as about ten carats of "ends," which were not polished. The total weight of the polished stones was 1,063 carats, giving a recovery of 34.25 per cent of the rough. Even with a rough diamond of perfect octahedral shape, on which the brilliant cut is based, it is impossible to get much more than 50 per cent recovery; usually, it is very much less. Considerable improvements in the ratio can be made by sawing across the grain, but the process is very slow, indeed, and the sawing machine is a relatively modern innovation.

It emphasizes the size of the rough Cullinan when it is realized that from it came the *two* largest polished diamonds in the world. Cullinan I is a pear-shaped stone with 74 facets, weighing 530.20 carats, and Cullinan II is cushion-shaped and weights 312.40 carats. These and the seven other larg-

Fig. 7-3 The Cullinan Diamond After Cleaving. The Cullinans I and II were considered worthy to be added to the Regalia of the British Crown. I is a pear-shaped diamond, while II is a four-cornered stone. The Cullinans I and II are currently in the Tower of London. *(Courtesy of the Royal Asscher Diamond Company Ltd.)*

Fig. 7-4 Nine Polished Stones from the Cullinan. Further cleaving and sawing of the Cullinans I and II produced nine major gems and ninety-six smaller brilliants, as well as about ten carats of "ends," which were not polished. Seven of the largest stones are in the British Crown Jewels or in the personal possession of the Royal family. *(Courtesy of De Beers Consolidated Mines.)*

est stones that came from the rough stone are in the British Crown Jewels or in the personal possession of the Royal family. The King ordered that the largest stone be known as the Star of South Africa and be added to the scepter. The second largest was set in the brow of the State Crown after the Stuart Sapphire, the place of which it occupied, was moved to the back.

The rough stone had a natural "skin" on one side only and a small blemish that influenced where it was going to be cleaved. When the blemish was removed, the resulting stones were of the greatest perfection in every way.

Asschers were allowed to keep the "ends" in return for their services, except for a small proportion that went to Arthur and Alexander Levi, who acted as supervisors. King Edward presented a silver cup to the Asschers as a souvenir, and when the Nazi, Marshal Goering, called on the factory during the occupation of the Second World War, he declared that he wanted to take it, obviously knowing of its existence. Somehow, it had vanished, but it reappeared in the boardroom after the liberation and is still there today.

The fact that the Cullinan had a natural cleavage face has led to many speculations that, large as it was, it was only part of a diamond that could have been more than twice as big, a super monster weighing more than three pounds. Sir Williams Crookes, a top scientist of the time and President of the Royal Society, who had made a special study of diamonds, thought it was "probably less than one half of the octahedral diamond." There was the story of Johannes Paulus, who had worked at the Premier mine. He, it was said, had found another huge diamond within two years of the Cullinan's appearance. Although there was undoubtedly a piece missing from the Cullinan, it may not have been as big as once supposed because it is now known that large stones do not always form as octahedra, on which the size of the missing part was calculated.

## The Wonders of the Excelsior

Until the Cullinan came to light, the greatest rough diamond was the Excelsior, just as big a wonder in 1893, when it was found, because it weighed 995.2 carats or about seven ounces in the rough. It came from an open pit mine on the farm Jagersfontein, a few miles from Fauresmith near Kimberley. The farm foreman had picked up the rudiments of diamond digging from the Vaal River prospectors who had passed through and decided to try his own luck on the farm. He dug down several feet to reach several layers of gravels of what was once a riverbed. Using a tank of water and an old garden sieve to wash away the dirt and get rid of small stones, he found a 50 carat diamond.

His find attracted some diggers, but Miss Visser, the farm owner, charged what was then considered the excessive fee of £2 a month for working a claim, so not many persisted. Those who did found they were gradually working in toward each other, and it became evident to those who had seen pipes that here was another original source. Many claims were bought out and a mining company formed because it is impossible to work separate claims that are vertical rather than horizontal in a haphazard way.

The company made an agreement with Werner, Beit and Co., associates of Cecil Rhodes, to sell all the diamonds found between July 1892 and midnight on June 30, 1893. The agreement specified a low average price per carat because Werner, Beit were taking all the production. There was nothing in it about a special price for exceptional diamonds found because none of the mines around Kimberley had produced any that were particularly noteworthy.

Late on June 30, the day that the agreement ran out, a young overseer happened to notice an African working slightly apart from the others in his gang. The man would stop from time to time, take a pinch of snuff from a tin, and turn around slowly as if studying the layout of the area. The overseer moved to a position where he could watch the man more closely. Then, when the overseer's attention was distracted for a moment, the man vanished, although it was not the end of the working day. The overseer rushed to the spot and questioned other workers. All denied knowing or noticing anything, and most became frightened because there were high penalties for stealing diamonds, and they did not want to become involved. The entire area was searched, but there was no trace of the missing worker.

Just half an hour before midnight, when the agreement expired, the man reappeared as suddenly as he had vanished and gave himself up to the mine superintendent. He explained that he had found a huge diamond and was going to give it up and claim the reward offered by the company for such finds, but the overseer's suspicious behavior had frightened him and made him suspect that the stone might be taken from him and he would be robbed of his reward. So he hid until he could contact the most senior official at the mine.

No one will know where the truth lies, but the superintendent seemed to have believed him because he was escorted from the mine, given £500, a horse, and some equipment. His contract was cancelled, and he was sent home to his kraal. The escort was probably to save him from jealous fellow workers. If he *had* been trying to steal the stone and the young overseer had caught him, the rewards would have gone to the overseer, and the worker would have spent most of the rest of his life in jail.

The diamond was handed over to Werner, Beit in accordance with the contract. It was valued then at £50,000 and was not only the biggest diamond ever found at that time but of the highest quality.

It weighed 995.2 carats and was flat on one side and humped on the other rather like a very rough small loaf. The color was described at the time as "blue-white," which is now regarded as a misnomer. The body of the stone is actually colorless, as with all the finest white diamonds, but it

has a slight bluish fluorescence in daylight or any light containing some ultraviolet, giving it a faintly bluish "whiter than whiteness." This is now
known to be typical of many stones from the Jagersfontein mine, which are
called "Jagers" in the diamond trade.

## Cleaving the Excelsior

Despite their luck in acquiring the world's biggest and finest diamond,
Werner, Beit had a problem. No one had enough of what we now call "dis-
posable income" to buy it. The Shah of Persia was interested and began negotiations, which were inconclusive, and two Indian princes were thinking separately of buying it as a present for their prospective brides, but in
neither case was there a marriage or a sale, it seems. For 33 years, the diamond remained in the safe awaiting a buyer. In 1903, the owners decided
that it could not be sold as a rough stone and decided to have it cut and polished by the Amsterdam firm of Asschers.

They entrusted Henry Koe with the task. He marked the stone with India ink after many discussions had taken place and it was divided to yield
six pear-shaped stones of 69.80 carats, 47.15 carats, 47.03 carats, 34.97 carats, 18.00 carats, and 16.81 carats, four marquises (boat-shaped stones) of
40.36 carats, 28.55 carats, 26.37 carats, and 24.38 carats, and eleven circular brilliants that together weighed 20.33 carats. All the polished stones to-
taled 373.75 carats in weight, a yield of about 37.6 per cent.

So the Excelsior never provided a famous big polished stone because
there was no one to buy one. Who bought the stones has never been disclosed. Tiffany's, the New York jewelers, handled a number of them and,
in 1903, sold the largest pear-shaped stone, which Sir Richard Tate is
known to have owned at one time. De Beers showed one of the marquise-
cut stones at the New York World's Fair in 1938.

It is interesting to speculate on what would have been the biggest polished diamond in the world had the Excelsior been sold for a nominal price
and cut into the largest gems possible, like the Cullinan. As it is, the largest
of the Excelsior stones ranks 80th among the world's polished diamonds,
whereas those from the Cullinan rank 1st, 2nd, 54th, and 88th.

## The Mystery of the Nizam

The third listed large polished diamond, the Great Mogul, is missing
or, according to some gem historians, did not exist and is in fact the Orloff,
ranking ninth. The fourth largest is the Nizam, which is supposed to be one
of the last stones of any note to come from the Kollur mines in the Kingdom

of Golconda in 1835, much more than a century after the mine's most productive period. It is another mystery stone.

E. W. Streeter quotes this in his book, *The Great Diamonds of the World* (London, 1882): "The King of Golconda possessed a magnificent stone in the rough state. It is known by the name of the Nizam and weighs 340 carats and is valued at 5,000,000 francs." The Kings of Golconda became known later as the Nizams of Hyderabad, who were lineal descendants of the former Mogul Viceroys of Hyderabad. Another story gives the weight of the rough diamond as 440 carats or 340 carats and its weight when cut to a dome-shaped stone with irregular facets as 277 carats. The loss in weight for Indian cuts is much less than for more modern ones, but only the most modern cuts give optimum fire and brilliance. Other reports declare it is still uncut and was broken mysteriously in 1857, the year of the Indian Mutiny.

The last Nizam to live in Hyderabad, who was reputed to be the richest man in the world with about 500 million pounds' worth of tangible assets, died in 1967. The present Nizam, Prince Mir Barkat Ali Khan, lives in Australia. The jewelry collection from Hyderabad was deposited in the vaults of the Merchantile Bank in Bombay and administered by the Jubilee Trust, which, after examination of the one hundred or so treasures, decided to release thirty-seven for auction.

These jewels were sold to two buyers, Harry Winston of New York, who paid $8 million for some pieces, and the Antwerp Diamond Co., which paid $5 million for the rest. The items were nearly all emeralds and diamonds. Before delivery, an heir lodged a complaint that the prices paid were too low, and this was upheld in a law court. Then it became known that another buyer had been allowed to see the items and had made an offer of $25 million for the thirty-seven pieces.

The first buyers strongly protested that since the sale to them had been concluded, the stones should not have been shown to anyone else, let alone their sale renegotiated. So the Supreme Court at Delhi organized a completely new sale in October, although some thought a fairer action would have been to let the original sale stand.

The Indian government required would-be buyers to deposit a surety of about £11 million before even being allowed to see the jewelry. The original buyers understandably dropped out, receiving their monies back. There were only two new potential buyers, the Greek shipowner, Stavros Niarchos, and a Dubai businessman, Abdul Wahah Al Adhari, who sent his wife, Badria Galadhari, to bid (she was actually representing a very

Fig. 7–5 The Jubilee Diamond. When found in the Jagersfontein Mine, the Jubilee was an irregular octahedron. After it was cut to a cushion-shaped gem that was perfect in every way, it was renamed in honor of Queen Victoria's jubilee in 1897. It was last on public show in the De Beers Pavilion in Johannesburg in 1966. *(Courtesy of De Beers Consolidated Mines.)*

wealthy oil sheik). But when the two parties sat at opposite ends of a jury in the New Delhi Supreme Court buildings, a Sotheby's official representing Niarchos announced that he would only be interested provided that the jewels could be exported. Mrs. Galadhari made a similar statement. So the sale was suspended, to the relief of lovers of Indian art, who had been pressing the government not to sell any of the Nizam's jewelry. The Nizam Diamond was not among the gems up for sale and it has not been possible to ascertain if it is among the remaining treasures.

Next in size of polished stones is the Jubilee (Figure 7–5), which is definitely extant and was on public show last in the De Beers Pavilion in Jo-

Fig. 7–6 The Star of Sierra Leone. Found in Sierra Leone, West Africa, in 1972, the Star is the third-largest diamond found: weight, 968.9 carats. This photograph illustrates well how irregular a large rough may be. *(Courtesy of the Institute of Geological Sciences.)*

hannesburg in 1966. It was lent earlier, near the end of 1961, by its present Parisian owner to the Smithsonian in Washington, D.C., for exhibition. Like the Excelsior, it was found in the Jagersfontein mine, but two years later, as a 650.8-carat irregular octahedron. It was first named the Reitz, after the President of the Orange Free State, but after it was cut to a cushion-shaped gem that was perfect in every way, it was renamed the Jubilee because of Queen Victoria's jubilee in 1897.

Returning to the top sizes, after the Cullinan and the Excelsior, the largest rough came from Sierra Leone, one of two from this country among the five biggest. It is the Star of Sierra Leone (Figure 7–6), weighing 968.9

carats. It was spotted in 1972 by a Sierra Leonean, E. O. Williams, engineer in charge of the separator house, where a concentrate of heavy minerals, including diamond, is separated from the rest of the sand and gravels. The place was the Diminco mine at Yengema, 300 miles north of Freetown.

The time was St. Valentine's Day, February 14, and there, as a special gift stuck on the grease belt while streams of water flushed much smaller pebbles in the concentrate, was a diamond as big as a man's palm. How it missed being broken or rejected by previous treatments is amazing. Diamonds will stick to grease while other stones can be flushed over it by water, so a greased belt moving across the stream of water and concentrate will take any diamonds to one side while every other mineral is swept across the belt and eventually carried to the tailings dump.

The stone was offered to cutters at a million pounds and bought for an undisclosed sum by Harry Winston of New York, who cut it into eleven fine white gems, the largest of which was an emerald-cut stone of 143.20 carats. There were many small marks in the stone and, near the tip, an orange-colored spot that gemologists hoped might be a very rare ruby inclusion, but, unfortunately, it was a common iron stain.

A curious story attaches to models of the rough diamond made in the United Kingdom. The author was asked if he knew anybody who could make a number of models at low cost for publicity purposes. Fine models could have been ordered but were much too expensive. The previous week, his Fiberglas-bodied car had been run into by an employee of a small firm that specialized in Fiberglas vehicles and that also made special plastics models. They got the job.

The Great Mogul, if it existed, was the fourth largest of the rough diamonds and the only one from India in the first twenty-six, although India has supplied most of the really legendary diamonds. The fifth, the Woyie River from Sierra Leone, weighed 770 carats. It was named after the river in whose gravels it was found in 1945 and was the largest diamond from an alluvial source until the Star of Sierra Leone turned up. Two other large stones, of 532 carats and 249.5 carats, have been found in this rich diamond river. It is surprising to think that they had been carried hundreds of miles from their original and still unknown pipe sources over millions of years by turbulent waters. The Woyie River was cut in London by Briefel and Lemer but yielded no very large gems. Largest of the thirty weighed 31.35 carats.

The Vargas, or President Vargas, of 726 carats is the only large rough diamond in the first nineteen to have come from Brazil. The twentieth, which also did, weighed 455 carats. The Vargas came from an alluvial deposit, too, in the San Antonio River in Minas Gerais, an area of Brazil that abounds with gems of many kinds.

## The Lesotho

One of the unlikely places to find diamonds was high in the mountains of Lesotho, formerly Basutoland and now a landlocked country somewhere near the middle of South Africa. In the 1960s, some hundreds of Lesothos, many wearing colorful blankets over their shoulders, made the laborious climb to about 10,000 feet (3,000 meters) to dig holes in the ground in sandy areas where diamonds had been found. Often the diggers were families. Diamond buyers took small bare offices from time to time in Maseru, the capital, and kept in touch with the diggings by runners, who could make the journey in a couple of days on donkeyback.

One day in 1965, a Lesotho woman, Mrs. Ernestine Ramoboa, was working in one of the hundreds of pits at Letseng-La-Terai, where diggers' pits had created a kind of moonscape, when she unearthed a huge diamond that was found to weigh 601.3 carats. The claim was owned by four members of the family, the principal one being her father-in-law, Petrus Ramoboa, who at the time had only about £2 to his name. Often the women would wrap any stones found in a twist of newspaper and take them to a buyer's office and do the negotiating. This time, Petrus himself hitchhiked donkey rides over the 110 miles of tracks to Maseru.

News of the find spread rapidly and the government took a hand to safeguard the Ramoboas' interests by providing a three-man committee to accept sealed bids. The highest bidder at 216,360 rands was a well-known Blomfontein diamond buyer, Eugene Serafini, who sold the stone to a Dutch colleague, J. W. Vermey.

The next buyer was Harry Winston of New York, who commented, when the stone was shown briefly in Geneva, "If an agent [of mine] had been there [at the mine], he [Ramoboa] would have sold it for $20,000 on the spot. I bought a stone once for $300,000 from a dealer who had bought it from a digger for $20,000." He did not disclose what he had paid, but the figure of $604,800 has been quoted as what either he or the previous buyer, Vermey, had to find. But he did estimate that polished diamonds from the rough should fetch about a million dollars. The price paid to Ramoboa was more than $200,000. The stone had a pale brown hue and was first called the Lesotho Brown, but later the word "Brown" was dropped (Figure 7–7). It was cut into a number of smaller stones to reduce the brownish tint.

Ramoboa and his partners were transformed from poor to rich within weeks by the find, and he made a trip to America at Harry Winston's invita-

Fig. 7-7 The Lesotho Diamond. High in the mountains of Lesotho in the middle of South Africa, a huge diamond was unearthed that had a pale brown hue. The stone was later cut into a number of smaller gems to reduce the unwanted brownish tint. *(Courtesy of De Beers Consolidated Mines.)*

tion. With the help of one of De Beers's officials in Johannesburg, Michael Grantham, who, although not involved in the deal took a personal interest in the family's welfare, Ramoboa bought a suit and some shirts. Grantham arranged for someone to travel with him because the native Lesothoian knew little of the world outside the rough diggings in the mountains of Lesotho.

The diggings turned out to be the mouth of a diamond pipe, which became the highest mine of any kind in the world. The government awarded the mining rights to Rio Tinto Zinc, who carried out some extensive sampling and decided not to continue. De Beers was then offered the contract, which they accepted. After further sampling, they decided that the mine would be economic only if what their geologists suspected were true — that Letseng-La-Terai (Figure 7–8) could supply more huge diamonds than any other mine in history. The man whose vision this was, Keith Whitelock, started prospecting in the mountains for diamonds with Colonel Jack Scott in the early 1960s. He joined Rio Tinto Zinc as their field geologist then went as general manager to De Beers. Although the mine was the smallest operated by the company, a number of large diamonds have been found since mining began. Unlike other recovery plants, the one at Letseng is geared to trap giant diamonds, but the big bonanza of future legendary gems is still to come, if the gamble pays off. Meanwhile, in 1982, the mine was closed because of the world recession.

Fig. 7–8 Letseng-La-Terai. The diggings at Letseng-La-Terai, high in the Maluti mountains of South Africa, encompass approximately 50 acres. Before being taken over first by Rio Tinto Zinc and then by De Beers Consolidated Mines, the area had been worked by individual miners. *(Courtesy of De Beers Consolidated Mines.)*

## *Jonker in the Rough*

The last stone to be discussed in this chapter, the Jonker, brings us back to the beginning because it was found on the Elandsfontein farm long after part of the farm had become the great Premier mine that gave up the Cullinan, the greatest diamond of all. Not only that, the Jonker, which was the size of an egg, was found only three miles from the spot where the Cullinan had been spotted 29 years earlier. The Jonker ranks seventh among the world's largest rough diamonds.

The farm belonged to Jacobus Jonker, a 60-year-old digger, who had been working riverbed claims most of his life with little to show as the result of his diamond fever. Then in January 1934, one of his workers, Johannes Mokane, found a 726-carat rough crystal that was flawless and of the first water. It was so pure and colorless that some diamantaires reckon it to be the finest in quality ever to have been discovered. It had a cleavage face, indicating that it had been bigger at some time in its history.

It was bought by the Diamond Corporation, who sold it to Harry Winston for a reputed $700,000. He cut it into twelve perfect gems, the largest of which was emerald-cut with 58 facets, weighed 142.90 carats, and was called the Jonker. Later, it was recut to 125.65 carats. King Farouk of Egypt bought it when it was valued at a million dollars, and after he lost his throne, it was sold to the Queen of Nepal in the Himalayas.

There were ten more emerald-cut stones and one marquise, and all twelve weighed 358 carats, a high yield of 49.3 per cent. It is not realized by the layman that if a large rough diamond weighs, say, 100 carats and costs $200,000, when it is cut and polished into several gems, they may weigh only 40 carats but those 40 carats cost $200,000 in raw material alone, so the basic value per carat has gone up from $2,000 to $5,000, or 150 per cent, without any profit. The "ends" left over are largely used up in cutting and paying for it; if any are left, they will not materially affect the calculation.

The blood of man should never be shed but to redeem the blood of man. . . .
The rest is vanity, the rest is crime.
*Edmund Burke (1729–1787)*

---

*Chapter Eight*

# Bloodstained Rubies and Star Sapphires

IN 1836, Maharajah Ranjit Singh, The Lion of Lahore and owner of the Koh-i-Noor, was visited by Baron Charles von Hugel. The Baron noticed that a large ruby about two square inches (5 centimeters) in area was set in the pommel of the Maharajah's saddle. It had some writing engraved on its surface. It was the celebrated Timur Ruby that had belonged to Tamerlane, conqueror of India in 1398-1399. Part of its history was spent decorating the fabulously enriched Peacock Throne.

It is not, in fact, a real ruby but what is today recognized as a red spinel and commonly called in earlier days a "balas ruby." It weighs 352.2 carats and was formerly known as the Khiraj-i-Alam or Tribute of the World. It is unique in carrying its own history engraved on the surface, in the Persian language but with Arabic script.

The main inscription can be translated as "This is the ruby from the twenty-five thousand genuine jewels of the King of Kings, the Sultan Sahib Qiran which in the year 1153 from the jewels of Hindustan reached this place." The date corresponds to our year of 1740. Nadir Shah stole Delhi's treasures in 1739 and, after a hazardous journey, returned to Isfahan, where the "ruby" was engraved. "This place" in the inscription is Isfahan.

There are five other inscriptions giving the names of former owners and their dates:

Akbar Shah: 1021 (1612 A.D.)
Jahangir Shah
Sahib Qiran Sani: 1038 (1628 A.D.)
Alamgir Shah: 1070 (1659 A.D.)
Bagshah Ghazi Muhamad Farukh Siyar: 1125 (1713 A.D.)
Ahmad Shah Dur-i-Duran: 1168 (1754 A.D.)

Nadir Shah had the long inscription engraved. Sultan Sahib Qiran is the name by which Timur was known to the Muslims. He was a Mongol who lived from c. 1336 to 1405 and who seized the throne of Samarkand in Tartary (now Turkestan in the U.S.S.R.). He tried to unite the empire of Ghengis Khan. Timur is also known as Tamerlane, meaning Timur-i-Leng or Timur the lame.

On his death, the "ruby" came into the possession of his successor, Mir Shah Rukh (not to be confused with the blind Shah Rukh, who was tortured to death about two-and-a-half centuries later for the Koh-i-Noor, which he did not possess or, some say, for the Timur Ruby). Mir Shah Rukh reigned for nearly 40 years and was succeeded by his son, the celebrated astronomer, Mirza Ulugh Begh (1394-1449), who published the first substantial star catalog since Hipparchus. He ruled only for two years before he was murdered by his son. The "ruby" was passed on, but, alas, Tartar astronomy ceased forever.

The Timur Ruby no doubt changed hands a number of times as the power of the Timur dynasty dwindled and eventually came to Shah Abbas Safari, members of whose family held power for a number of years. His own rule lasted from 1587 to 1629.

The names of these three owners — Mir Shah Rukh, Mirza Ulugh Begh, and Shah Abbas Safari — were engraved on the stone at one time and were probably removed on the instruction of Jahangir or a later Mogul emperor. Jahangir received the "ruby" as a gift from Shah Abbas Safari and had his own name engraved on it as well as that of his father, Akbar Shah, although Akbar never owned it. It seemed uncharacteristic of him to have removed the name of the man who gave it to him, if, indeed, he did.

A mid-19th century travel book about Khashmir and the Pubjab quotes Jahangir as saying after Nurjahan had complained about the damage to the stone caused by the engraving, "This jewel will assuredly hand down my name to posterity more than any written history. The house of Timur may fall, but as long as there is a King, this jewel will have its price."

Jahangir died in 1569, and his successor, Shah Jahan, had the stone mounted in the Peacock Throne. He awarded himself the title Sahib

Quiran Sani, meaning Second Lord of the Conjunction. The first Lord of the Conjunction was the Sultan Qiran Sani (Timur) of the inscription on the stone. The reference is to a conjunction of planets that occurred and was thought very significant at the time.

Alamgir Shah, the next name inscribed, was that of Jahangir's third son, better known today by his earlier name of Aurangzeb, meaning Ornament of the Throne. For some reason, the next two Mogul emperors did not have their names engraved, although two later owners did.

After the Mogul treasures arrived in Persia, the "ruby" was described as "upwards of three fingers in breadth and two in length." On Nadir Shah's violent death in 1747, it passed to Ahmad Shah Durani, known then as Taimur Shah. The last of the Persians to own it was Shah Shuja. When Ranjit Singh freed Shuja from imprisonment in Khasmir and held him in Lahore, the Timur Ruby came into the Sikh's possession with the Koh-i-Noor and other stones. Finally, the British acquired it from his successor, Dhulip Singh, after the Sikh Revolt, as related in Chapter Two.

In England, all attention was directed toward the Koh-i-Noor, and other gems, including this great "ruby," were overshadowed and almost ignored. While the famous diamond merited special security arrangements, armed guards, and transport in one of Her Majesty's ships, the Timur Ruby went to London by ordinary transport. And while other stones were put on show with the Koh-i-Noor in the Crystal Palace at the Great Exhibition of 1851, the historic Timur Ruby was not even recognized in the catalog.

The entry stated: "Short necklace with four very large spinele rubies." In fact, the Timur Ruby, almost triangular in shape, was the center stone of three in the middle of this necklace, and the fourth was much smaller and mounted in the snap at the back. The necklace had been presented to Queen Victoria by the Honourable East India Company in 1851 after they took it from the Treasury of Lahore.

There is a close historical association between the famous diamond and the great "ruby" because, although they have been fought over and presented for services rendered, they have remained in common ownership in the five centuries since 1612.

The Timur is the most historic of the old balas rubies and has remained uncut, but it is not the largest. That distinction goes to one, also a red spinel, mounted on the top of the Russian Imperial Crown, which weighs 414.3 metric carats and is also uncut. Peter the Great of Russia, who killed his son, suspecting him of opposition, broke Russian tradition by announcing that he was going to crown Catherine as Empress. An Imperial Crown was made for the ceremony in 1724, and a contemporary report declared, "In the whole crown there was but one coloured stone, a ruby or spinel of peerless beauty and of greater size than a pigeon's egg. It certainly was the most remarkable ruby known at the time. The stone was placed on top of the diadem in the middle of the crown and was surmounted by a cross with brilliants." The other gems were diamonds and pearls.

J.-B. Tavernier in *Travels in India* wrote about and illustrated a stone sold as a ruby for 95,000 rupees to Ja'fan Khan, who presented it to his nephew, Emperor Aurangzeb. At the birthday ceremony, when the Mogul Emperor was weighed, an old Indian in the court, who had previously been chief jeweler but had been dismissed, handled the stone and declared it was not a balas ruby and was not worth 500 rupees.

The Emperor heard about this and summoned the Indian, as well as all the jewelers who took the opposite point of view. As no one was more knowledgeable about precious stones than Shah Jahan, who was a prisoner in the fortress at Agra, the stone was sent to him. Shah Jahan confirmed the opinion of the old Indian, so Aurangzeb compelled the merchant who had sold the stone to take it back and refund the money.

In the same part of his book, *Travels in India*, Tavernier remarked that on his last visit, he had never seen Aurangzeb wear any other jewel than a large topaz weighing $157^{1}/_{4}$ carats, bought for 181,000 rupees. He illustrated it as octagonal with its beveled sides of slightly different lengths and with many smaller facets around the octagonal table.

Henry VIII of England had two great collars set with balas rubies. There were thirteen of them in the larger collar, some square, some oval, and all large and linked by foliated gold ornaments, each set with sixteen pearls.

## The Three Brethren of the Tudors

Best known among the Tudor jewels was a pendant called The Three Brethren (Color Plate 18) after the three large rectangular balas rubies of almost exactly the same size and color set in it. They are spaced by three very large pearls, with another hanging below. In the center is a point-cut or pyramid-cut diamond, which follows the shape of a rough octahedral crystal as a four-sided pyramid. It was made by the best-known cutter of the time, Louis de Berquen, and is said to have been the first diamond cut in this form; but this is unlikely, and the claim by one of his descendants that he was the first to use diamond powder for faceting diamonds is definitely untrue. Point-cut diamonds and table-cut diamonds (Figure 8–1) and other stones, which were four-sided with a flat top, were popular in Tudor times.

De Berquen was under the patronage of Jacques Coeur (1395–1456), a financier and diamond merchant from Bourges, who made the wearing of diamonds popular for women at a time when they were almost entirely worn by men. Jacques Coeur presented diamond jewelery to Agnès Sorel (Figure 8–2), mistress of King Charles VII of France, and followed it with gifts of more diamond jewelry and buckles. He also helped to finance the King's battles against the English.

In turn, Agnès persuaded the King to make Coeur his financial adviser and later the Master of the Royal Mint, which was ironic because Jacques Coeur, when young, was a coinmaker and had been exiled for competing with the Royal Mint. He obtained rough diamonds from India and cutters from Venice and Constantinople, as well as using cutters like de Berquen of Bruges in the Low Countries. Agnès Sorel became celebrated in her own time for her diamond jewelry.

The Three Brethren, also called the Three Brothers, is recorded in an inventory of 1419, which was probably in de Berquen's time, but it is said to date from the beginning of the century and was inherited by the last Duke of Burgundy, Charles the Bold (1433–1477) from his father. Charles the Bold had it and another jewel, the White Rose (Color Plate 11), a rose with white enameled petals with a large balas ruby as the center, with him when he lost the Battle of Granson against the Swiss in 1476. The jewels are believed to have been looted from his tent by a soldier. (This is the same story that has been wrongly attached to the Sancy Diamond).

The Three Brethren was bought by Jacob Fugger of the Augsburg merchant family from the Magistrates of Berne. His son was negotiating its sale to Henry VIII of England just before Henry died in 1547. It was still purchased, however, by Edward VI in 1551. That is one story. Another is that Edward bought it in Antwerp in that year. At any rate, it was given to his sister, Mary I, when she married Philip II of Spain, and it was later worn by Queen Elizabeth. In a new setting, it was one of the jewels, along with the Mirror of France Diamond, that was worn by the unfortunate prince who was to become Charles I on his unsuccessful visit to seek the hand of the Infanta in 1623.

Three years later, James pawned The Three Brethren in the Netherlands but redeemed it in another three years. When Henrietta Maria, wife of Charles I, did the same thing in 1642 with other items from the English Crown Jewels, it was not redeemed and was sold by the Bank of Lombardy in Rotterdam, being last seen in 1650. Although of undoubted historical interest, The Three Brethren was not a beautiful jewel despite having been altered by the addition of pearls and diamonds before it was pawned.

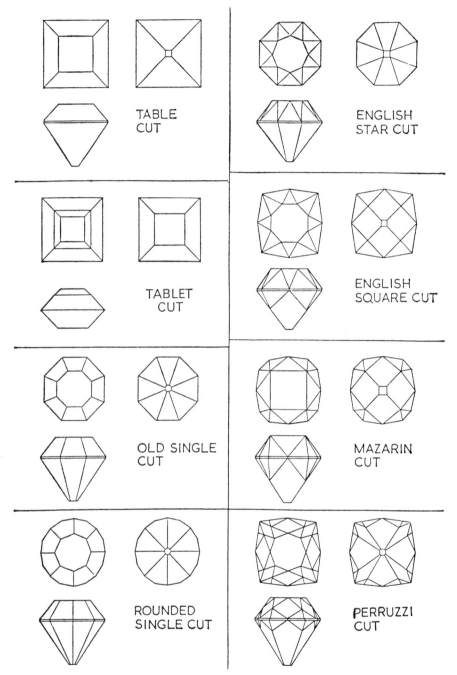

TABLE CUT

ENGLISH STAR CUT

TABLET CUT

ENGLISH SQUARE CUT

OLD SINGLE CUT

MAZARIN CUT

ROUNDED SINGLE CUT

PERRUZZI CUT

Fig. 8–1 Development of Brilliant-Cut or Full-Cut. Point-cut and table-cut diamonds, and other four-sided stones with flat tops, were popular in Tudor times. *(Courtesy of N. A. G. Press Ltd., Ipswich.)*

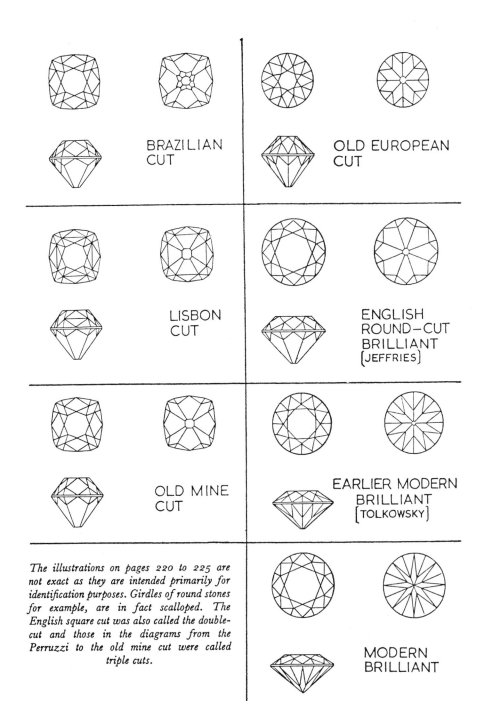

BRAZILIAN
CUT

OLD EUROPEAN
CUT

LISBON
CUT

ENGLISH
ROUND—CUT
BRILLIANT
[JEFFRIES]

OLD MINE
CUT

EARLIER MODERN
BRILLIANT
[TOLKOWSKY]

*The illustrations on pages 220 to 225 are not exact as they are intended primarily for identification purposes. Girdles of round stones for example, are in fact scalloped. The English square cut was also called the double-cut and those in the diagrams from the Perruzzi to the old mine cut were called triple cuts.*

MODERN
BRILLIANT

Fig. 8–2 Agnès Sorel. Celebrated for her diamond jewelry, she is pictured here wearing diamonds presented to her by Jacques Coeur (1395–1456), a financier and diamond merchant from Bourges. *(Courtesy of De Beers Consolidated Mines.)*

## The Colors of Ruby and Sapphire

Ruby should be of a strong red color, the finest being known as pigeon's blood red and coming from Burma. Balas rubies were generally good red spinels. They do not have the yellowish red tinge seen in rubies when viewed from certain directions, but it is not surprising that they were confused in the days before gemology and crystallography. A spinel is an oxide of aluminum and manganese that has crystallized into a single crystal, and a ruby is an oxide of aluminum, with a trace element of chromium to give it its color, that has also crystallized singly.

Confused with both in the past was the red garnet (there are green and yellow ones, too), known then when cut en cabochon (dome-shaped) as a "carbuncle." A name that appears in old inventories is "jacinth." This can mean a carbuncle or a red zircon, still another specie of gemstone.

Ruby is properly called "red corundum." Blue, yellow, pink, green, purple, violet, and colorless corundums are popularly named sapphires. In other words, ruby is red sapphire and arguments have developed as to when a pink sapphire becomes red enough to become a ruby. In trading, it may depend on whether it is being bought or sold, but the gemologist has a more scientific method.

In the old Russian Regalia, now in the Diamond Treasury in the Kremlin, was a magnificent cornflower blue sapphire cut in oval shape, $1^1/_2$ inches (3.9 centimeters) long and weighing 250 carats. There was also a "ruby" of 250 carats presented in 1777 by the King of Sweden to the Empress Catherine that was later identified as a tourmaline worth a fraction of the price.

## The Black Prince's Ruby

To the English, the most legendary balas ruby, weighing about 170 carats, is associated with the Black Prince—Edward, Prince of Wales and son of Edward III of England. It was first recorded at the coronation of William and Mary of Orange, when it was called "the King's Great Ruby." How it became associated with the Black Prince three-and-a-half centuries earlier is unknown. There was nothing like it in his will.

An inventory of the Crown Jewels made in 1858 records that it was said to have been given by Don Pedro, King of Castile, to the Black Prince, who had assisted him in the Battle of Najera, near Vittoria in Spain, in 1367. Pedro the Cruel, as he was called, is supposed to have taken it from Abu Said, King of Granada, after he was murdered. The inventory stated that the stone was pierced through "after the Eastern custom, the upper part of the piercing being filled by a small ruby," but this was done long after the Black Prince's time.

Henry V is supposed to have worn the "ruby" in the coronet of his helmet at the Battle of Agincourt against the French in 1415, as did Richard III in 1485 during the Wars of the Roses at the Battle of Bosworth Field, when he was killed by Henry Tudor, who became Henry VII. It was mounted in the crowns of the later Tudors and the first Stuarts but vanished during the Commonwealth to appear again in the crown of James II.

Lord Twining examined the history of the Black Prince's Ruby in considerable depth and came to the conclusion, unfortunately, that there is no evidence to show that the balas ruby in the Spanish crown, weighing 181 carats, was ever given by Pedro the Cruel to the Black Prince. This was the only Spanish stone it could have been. On the other hand, in the Public Record Office is a drawing (in the Plea Roll of the King's Bench at Michaelmas) made in 1553 of Edward VI's personal crown with the Black Prince's Ruby set on top but the other way up from the way it is mounted today.

This "oon grete balas" was recorded as weighing 10.1 dwt (pennyweigh) or about 157.5 carats. Adjusting the weight of the Spanish balas to the same scale would make it about 168 carats, and piercing would reduce its weight still more. So the legend is not ruled out, although Pedro the Cruel is known to have been on very bad terms with the Black Prince and was extremely hard up at the time when he is supposed to have made the gift. Perhaps it was in payment of a debt instead of being a gift.

Evidence for the generally accepted story of Henry V wearing the Black Prince's Ruby at the Battle of Agincourt is "exceedingly slender," to quote Lord Twining, and he thinks "there is no evidence at all to substantiate the claim that the stone was worn by Richard III at the Battle of Bosworth." It is sad to demolish a cherished national legend.

Another of Lord Twining's conclusions is that the stone was pierced in England for the purpose of mounting a cross perpendicularly over it. There is no reference to a hole in the stone until the inventory made under the instruction of James I. The piercing of gems was a Middle East rather than an Eastern idea and, after the fall of Constantinople in 1453, such Byzantine practices spread through Europe. The Crusaders brought back many pierced stones from the Holy Land, Constantinople, and Sicily.

This large spinel must have come from Burma or Siam (Thailand) because they were the only sources of such stones at the time (Color Plate 22). If it was ever in the possession of one of the Moguls, it would not then have been pierced. When Tavernier inspected the Mogul's gems in 1665, he saw two pierced balas rubies, one of them the Timur Ruby. They were probably not pierced in India.

There was some importance, it seems, in having a red stone in a Royal crown. That of William the Conqueror had the twelve stones described in the Old Testament of the Bible as being set in the High Priest's breastplate. The crown used at the coronation of Elizabeth I of England was also set in this way. The old Hebrew High Priest wore a bag on his breast in which were the sacred lots, the Urim and Thummim. Twelve precious stones were set in a gold breastplate mounted on the bag to represent the twelve tribes of Israel. In Exodus 28:17–20 (revised edition), the stones are listed in four rows: (1) sardius (chalcedony), topaz, and carbuncle; (2) emerald, sapphire, and diamond; (3) jacinth (red zircon or hessonite garnet), agate, and amethyst; (4) beryl, onyx and jasper.

The carbuncle—an almandine garnet or perhaps in those days, a red spinel—was placed in the most prominent position in the front of the band of a crown or on top maybe because it signified blood in its religious context. This priority can be seen also in the crowns of Austria, Bohemia, Denmark, France, Spain, and Russia.

Presumably, the Black Prince's Ruby remained among the Royal treasures after Edward VI's time, although it was not specifically mentioned. It could have been kept separately and mounted for special occasions. During the Civil War in England, the State Regalia and plate from the Jewel House at the Tower of London and St. Edward's Regalia (presumably including the Black Prince's Ruby) from Westminster Abbey were held by Parliament, which did nothing except carry out some checks until 1644. Then some plate, a font, and some gold candlesticks were pledged to the London goldsmiths for £3,000. As the money was never repaid, the articles were melted down and used for coinage.

When England became a Commonwealth, after Charles I was beheaded in 1649, all the treasures were moved to the Tower and a comprehensive inventory made of them. The Regalia was broken and defaced by order of Parliament, and the remainder preserved. The gold from the Regalia was melted down for coinage and the gemstones sold separately.

Whether the Black Prince's Ruby was sold and later recovered by the monarch or remained in the Tower is not known for certain, but there is a record of "a pierced balas ruby wrapt in paper by itself" that was valued at £4 and sold for £4 10 shillings. It seems unlikely to have been the Black Prince's Ruby, although the hole through it would have reduced its value and it was of very poor quality. It was described in the 1840s by a member of the Crown Jewelers, Rundell, Bridge and Rundell, as "a very large bad ruby balas." Its only value would have been historical, however, and that would have been very much depreciated during the Commonwealth.

Another suggestion is based on the fact that the last illustration of the "ruby" before the Puritan armies vanquished the Cavaliers was in the crown of Henrietta Maria, the French wife of Charles I, who may have taken it to sell or pawn in France, as she did the Mazarin Diamonds and the Mirror of Portugal Diamond, to help the Royalist cause. It was not listed with the others she took.

After the restoration of the monarchy, the Black Prince's Ruby was not set in the crown of Charles II, as might have been expected. But it was mounted in the State Crown of James II when it was said to be worth £10,000, apparently somewhat of an exaggeration. Because it was mounted in the front of the crown instead of on top, as with Edward VI's crown, the hole had to be hidden. This was done by setting into it an oriental ruby (i.e., a red corundum, which is a real ruby). The still uncut Black Prince's Ruby was mounted with gold foil at the back, a common practice in earlier times to improve and brighten the color of a transparent or translucent gem. In the inventory of 1858, it was estimated to weight 170 carats.

In the Royal Library at Windsor, there is a watercolor sketch made by Joseph Grisoni in 1718 showing the crown of George I with the Black Prince's Ruby in the center of the cross on the front. George IV was crowned with a new Imperial State Crown instead of St. Edward's Crown. The "ruby" was set in the front of the new crown, and the Stuart Sapphire, which had only recently been recovered, was set in the cross in front.

The old crown had what was thought to be a dome-shaped and faceted aquamarine on top before it was replaced for a time by the "ruby." In the new crown, the domed stone was replaced by a globe set all over with diamonds and surmounted by a cross. An examination in the early 19th century proved the greenish-tinted "aquamarine" to be made of glass. It was known as the Old Monde (old world, Figure 8–3) and was plated with gold and enameled over the lower facets. Part of it still exists, and it is among the Crown Jewels at the Tower of London, shown separately from St. Edward's Crown. Some say it was switched for the real aquamarine by James II when he attempted to flee.

As was the custom, many of the diamonds set in this new crown for the coronation of George IV in 1821 were hired and had to be returned to the Crown Jewelers after the ceremony. The frame of the crown is on loan to the London Museum, where it is on exhibition.

For the coronation of Queen Victoria, another new crown was de-

Fig. 8-3 Old Monde Aquamarine. George IV's crown displayed this stone, thought to be an aquamarine, surmounted by a cross and known as the Old Monde. Later, it was found to be made of glass. It is now in the Tower of London. *(Courtesy of the Twining Collection; copyright of The Worshipful Company of Goldsmiths, Goldsmith's Hall, London.*

signed, intended also to be worn as the Crown of State at the opening of Parliament on later occasions. The Black Prince's Ruby was brought to the front again and set in the cross while the Stuart sapphire was set below it in the circlet. The last change affecting the "ruby" was made after the great Cullinan Diamond was cut. The second largest stone from it, called Cullinan II or the Second Star of Africa, replaced the Stuart Sapphire in the center of the circlet, and the Stuart Sapphire was moved to the back. So the tables had been turned on the sapphire that had once relegated the Black Prince's Ruby to the back of a crown.

## St. Edward's Sapphire

The stone with the longest history among the British Crown Jewels, which contain more legendary gems than any others, is Saint Edward's Sapphire. In its original form, it was worn set in a ring by Edward the Confessor, who ruled England from the year 1042. Much of his time was devoted to religion and included the rebuilding of Westminster Abbey, which allowed his adviser, Harald, to seize the throne and crown himself on the day of Edward's funeral after his death in 1066. Harald had previously supported the candidature of William of Normandy for the English throne, and his own reign only lasted until later that year when he was killed by an arrow in the eye during William's invasion at Hastings.

Edward's body was twice removed from its resting place, and on the second translation in 1269, the Abbot of Westminster took the Saxon King's sapphire ring from his finger to preserve it as a relic in the Abbey. Soon people began to ascribe magical powers to it, including the ability to cure cramps.

What happened to it during the dissolution of the monasteries or when it was rose cut are not known. It also seems to have disappeared during the Commonwealth. It is now mounted in the center of the cross that surmounts the monde (the ball) on the top of the Imperial State Crown that was made in 1953 by Garrard, the Crown Jewelers, for the coronation of Elizabeth II. The crown follows the pattern of that made for Queen Victoria in 1838. It also carries the Second Star of Africa, the Black Prince's Ruby, the Stuart Sapphire, and Queen Elizabeth's earrings. The frame is of gold, but the setting for the stones is made of silver.

The Stuart Sapphire is another with a seemingly long history, although it is difficult to identify before the reign of Charles II. It may have been the sapphire taken by Edward IV from the miter of the Archbishop of York to set in his crown. If so, it could be the stone that Henry VIII had set in the front cross of the Imperial State Crown.

James II is believed to have taken the Stuart Sapphire with him when he fled to France and to have left it in his will to his son. It certainly came into the hands of his grandson, who was Cardinal York, who had it mounted in his miter; so it returned to its original use, but not for long, because the Cardinal sold it to a Venetian merchant. The next incident in its history is unusual. An Italian was appointed to collate the Cardinal's papers and possessions. He traced the sapphire to its owner and managed to buy it. Then he sold it to George IV for £4,000. The King gave it to Princess Charlotte, and after she died, it was added to the British Crown Jewels. The 104-carat Stuart Sapphire is now set in the back of the Imperial Crown of State.

The Crown of Charlemagne (Figure 8–4), perhaps the most famous of all crowns, first referred to in 1271, had a "very fine old ruby" weighing 206 carats fastened on top of its crimson bonnet. With or around the stone was a statement saying it had belonged to John the Good (King John II,

Fig. 8–4 The Crown of Charlemagne. Also known as the German Imperial Crown, it is perhaps the most historic still in Europe. Held together by gold pins, the crown may be taken apart and laid flat for traveling. It is in the Treasury in Vienna. *(Courtesy of the Twining Collection; copyright of the Worshipful Company of Goldsmiths, Goldsmith's Hall, London.)*

crowned in 1350). At that size, it was undoubtedly a red spinel, but in any case it was missing in 1634 when an inventory was made. Yet another large "ruby" of 200 carats was still mounted in the center of the circlet. According to an account written in 1625 (as recorded in Lord Twining's book, *A History of the Crown Jewels of Europe* [London, 1960], the crown was seized by the "Bad Leaque," which took Rhiems from the King, and *was* melted down. The gems in it were distributed to "different Persons of high standing."

## Peter the Great's Nose

Corundum—ruby and sapphire—is a dense mineral and is, therefore, smaller for its weight than, say, opal, which is much less dense. Large sapphires are much more common than large rubies. There is a giant sapphire of 548 carats known by the odd name of Peter the Great's Nose (Figure 8–5). It is, indeed, the shape of a nose. With another sapphire of pear shape,

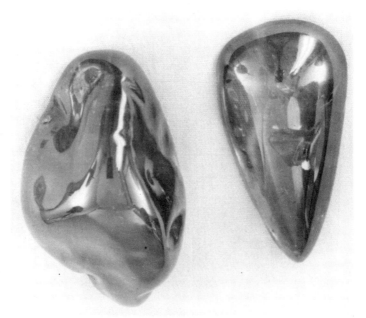

Fig. 8–5 Peter the Great's Nose. In the treasury of Saxony were two great sapphires weighing 1,884.5 and 548 carats. The largest, on the left, was traditionally known as Peter the Great's Nose. They were kept in the Green Vault at Dresden. *(Courtesy of the Twining Collection; copyright of The Worshipful Company of Goldsmiths, Goldsmith's Hall, London.)*

weighing 194.5 carats, it was one of the gems of Saxony and is now in the Green Vault in East Germany.

Peter's Nose was considerably exceeded in size by a sapphire of superb Royal blue, the finest of all sapphire colors, ranking above cornflower blue, discovered in this century. It came to light in 1929, just below the grass, when a site in the Mogok area in the Burmese jungle was being cleared by local miners (Color Plate 23). Weighing 958 carats, it was called Gem of the Jungle and was too big to be cut into a single stone because no one could have afforded it. So it was reduced to nine, the biggest two being 66.50 carats and 10.25 carats and the smallest 4.33 carats.

The Blue Mountain Sapphire, set in the front of the Crown Prince of Denmark's crown, is supposed to have been of such fine color that it shone "like a luminous mountain." It was given, when hung from a necklet, to Christian I by the Duke of Milan while the Danish King was on a pilgrimage to Rome in 1474. About a quarter of a century later, it was kept in a vault of Gottorp Castle, which could only be opened using two keys, one held by each of the joint owners of the contents, the King of Denmark and the Duke of Holstein. In 1597, the Duke presented his share in the sapphire to the King, Christian IV, but the stone was not used until 37 years later when the King's son was married and it was set in his horse's bridle over the forehead. The Siberian Amethyst, to be discussed in Chapter Nine, was apparently mounted on the harness also. The Blue Mountain was not set in a crown until 1660 when King Frederick III had to scour his treasury for suitable gems.

Balas rubies and sapphires were prominent decorations on Pope's tiaras, often mounted with emeralds, pearls, and diamonds. The tiaras vary in shape but are based on the triple crown. Some were very extravagant. Pope Paul II (1464–1471) had one on which all the space not occupied by other, larger gems was covered by pearls. Julius II (1502–1513) flaunted the riches of the Church. The traditional red stone, a 120-carat balas ruby, was mounted on the tiara (Figure 8–6) used for his coronation, but that was apparently not enough, so he engaged the famous sculptor and goldsmith from Milan, Caradosso, to make a new triple crown with an inscription set out in diamonds as well as decorations by many other stones.

This is an early but not contemporary description of it, as recorded by a writer John Talman, in Lord Twining's book:

> The wholle Crown is covered with large Pearles . . . the other three circles are likewise of beaten Gold enamelled, and sett with Jewels viz, very fine Jacinths, Balasses, and Saphirs. In the space over the lower

Fig. 8–6 The Tiara of Pope Julius II. This watercolor sketch by Bertoni shows one of Julius's many tiaras, studded with pearls, balas rubies, and sapphires with an engraved emerald on top. The original watercolor is in the British Museum. *(Courtesy of the Twining Collection; copyright of The Worshipful Company of Goldsmiths, Goldsmith's Hall, London.)*

circle (exclusive of ye small one at ye bottom) are 3 Carbuncles or Ruby-spinels of extraordinary value, and a very beautiful and large Saphir, all hanging loose; and behind on ye back part is another saphir of equal size; there are also some very large Pear-Pearls hanging loose and severall fine Diamonds; On ye top is a very beautiful and large Emeraud, placed there by Gregory ye 13th whose name is ingraved in ye fascia in ye middle of ye said stone. . .

Talman went on to explain that the jewels used in the tiara came from an unexpected find when foundations were being dug for a new Edifice of St. Peter in the Vatican. With his pickax, one of the laborers hit a stone coffin and broke it. It was found to be the resting place of the Empress, whose body was by then dust but in which lay a great quantity of her jewels.

Popes followed the examples of kings and emperors by pawning or selling their tiaras and other Vatican treasures when short of cash to finance wars or to pay debts. In 1456, Calixtus III sold all the plate and precious stones to equip a fleet to defend Christendom against Islam, in the shape of the Turks.

When, in 1804, Pope Pius VI agreed to crown Napoleon Bonaparte in Paris, he had no tiara to wear because Napoleon had taken most of the Vatican's treasures. Having gathered so many of Europe's riches into Versailles, Napoleon could afford to be generous, so he ordered a new one of traditional shape, like an elongated egg with the small end removed, which he presented to the Pope. It was set with 3,345 precious stones and 2,990 pearls.

On top of the tiara was a very large emerald, which had been one of the treasures taken by Napoleon from Rome and placed in the Museum of Natural History in Paris. The tiara still exists in the Papal Treasury, but only the emeralds and eight small rubies, now set in the stand, remain of the precious stones; the others have been replaced by simulants. Someone at the Vatican also saw fit to remove the very tactless inscriptions about Napoleon that it once bore.

Some rubies and sapphires, when cut en cabochon (dome-topped), exhibit on the dome a six-rayed star, which is especially sharp when seen under a spotlight. The rays are thin lines of light, and the star moves as the stone is moved. The effect is caused by masses of tiny needles of the mineral rutile in the stone, which lie in three directions only at 120° to each other, following the crystal structure. They reflect some of the light falling on the stones.

Star stones (Figure 8–7) were much prized in some countries in the past as well as today. One lover of them was J. Pierpont Morgan, whose col-

Fig. 8–7 The Edith Haggin de Long Star Ruby *(left)*; The Star of India Sapphire *(center)*; The Midnight Star Sapphire *(right)*. The Star Ruby from Burma weighs 100 carats and is 1¹/₂ inches long by an inch across. The two fine-star sapphires came from Ceylon: the Star of India weighs 563 carats, and the Midnight Star, which is deep purple in color, 116 carats. *(Courtesy of the Department of Library Services, The American Museum of Natural History, Neg. No. 121304; photo by Charles H. Coles.)*

lection is now in the American Museum of Natural History in New York. The Edith Haggin de Long star ruby from Burma is one of them. It weighs 100 carats and is 1¹/₂ inches long (3.8 centimeters) by an inch (2.5 centimeters) across. Two fine star sapphires came from Ceylon: the Star of India, weighing 563 carats, and the Midnight Star, which is deep purple in color and weighs 116 carats.

Sapphires and rubies are among the rarer gems used for carving because of their hardness. In fact, powdered corundum was used for carving other gems, except diamond. A celebrated early carved one was the intaglio seal of Alaric, King of the Visigoths, who died in 410 A.D. It is a bust, full face. It was in Vienna and is possibly still there. Even earlier was a head of the Roman Emperor Caracolla (188–217 A.D.), who was born in Lyons, France. A fine carving of a woman in drapery, which used the darker blue of the sapphire for the head, was in the Russian Crown Jewels but is now missing.

James and Harry Kazanjian of New York commissioned heads of American Presidents—George Washington, Thomas Jefferson, and Dwight Eisenhower—in sapphire (Figures 8–8, 8–9, 8–10). The first, Abraham Lincoln (Color Plate 13), was carved by Norman Maness from a 2,302-carat stone. The finished head is 2⁹/₁₆ inches (4 centimeters) high and weighs 1,318 carats, about 8¹/₂ ounces. The color is mainly black, but there are patches of deep blue. The carving, completed in 1951, took 1,800 hours. Heads of several other presidents have been carved subsequently.

Fig. 8–8 George Washington. Sapphire carving of Washington's head. *(Courtesy of the Smithsonian Institution, Photo No. 77-14885.)*

Fig. 8–9 Thomas Jefferson. Sapphire carving of Jefferson's head. *(Courtesy of the Smithsonian Institution, Photo No. 77-14886.)*

Fig. 8–10 Dwight David Eisenhower. Sapphire carving of Eisenhower's head. *(Courtesy of the Smithsonian Institution, Photo No.77-14888.)*

*Of all things which bounteous Earth supplies, Nothing in greeness with the Emerald vies.*
*Abbot Marbodeus (Marboeuf), 11th century.*

*Chapter Nine*

# Green Fire and Red Fire

**E**MERALDS in the ancient world came from Cleopatra's mines in upper Egypt, 15 miles north of Aswan near the Red Sea. For an unknown reason, the mines were abandoned and forgotten for so many centuries that, in the 17th century, J.-B. Tavernier thought they were a myth. Then in 1818, F. Cailliaud, a member of an expedition organized by Mehemet Ali Pasha, rediscovered them.

Cleopatra's mines were very extensive, with surface and underground workings. Cailliaud found much of the timber shoring still in good condition and estimated that as many as 400 men could have worked underground at the same time. There was evidence that provisions were brought to the mines by camel trains. Tools were found dated as early as 1650 B.C., so the mines had been worked long before the reign of Cleopatra (69–30 B.C.) and the Roman occupation. Many emeralds were taken to Rome, but the Greeks owned some before then. There are records of Greek miners being employed in Egypt in the time of Alexander the Great (356-323 B.C.). The Greek historian, Herodotus (c. 485–c. 425 B.C.), who wrote about the wars between the Greeks and Persians, referred to an emerald column in the Temple of Hercules in Tyre that emitted a fine light at night.

Two mines were worked at Jebel Sikait and Jebel Sabara, about ten miles apart in a depression in the mountains along the coast. The first was the larger, with hundreds of shafts of various depths reaching down to about 800 feet (245 meters), having been sunk in the rock. They were connected to the Red Sea by a wadi, a riverbed through which the water flow is seasonal. By the side of this, the site of a town was discovered, comprising about 500 houses, temples, and other buildings. Cailliaud reopened the mines, using Albanian miners, but closed them suddenly. It is not known why. A later expedition found baskets of ore left unemptied. Another project to rework the mines in 1899 was also abandoned.

Most of the Egyptian emeralds were of low quality, being cloudy and of light color, but deeper-colored stones must have been found there in earlier times because some were thrown up on a beach near Alexandria from sunken treasure. Mineralogical features indicated that they were from Egypt.

Although Tavernier in his *Travels in India* dismissed Egypt as a source of emeralds with these words, "As for the emerald, it is an ancient error of many people to suppose that it was originally found in the East," Pliny the Elder (23–79 A.D.) referred to the emerald mines there as did subsequent Mohammedan travelers to the region.

## South American Gems

The finest colored emeralds were, and still are, found in South America. Europeans saw them in the early 16th century when Colombian Indians offered them to Spanish conquistadores. The invaders also found them in Peru and in Mexico, although it is now known that there were no emerald mines in Mexico. It is possible that all the South American emeralds came from Colombia (Color Plate 20), although when emeralds were introduced generally to Europe at the end of the 16th century, they were called "Peruvian emeralds." Jose d'Acosta, writing of his journey from Peru to Spain in 1587, remarked on the two chests carried on board, each containing about a hundredweight (250 kilograms) of emeralds.

In the 16th century, Hernando Cortes, conqueror of Mexico, brought back to Spain five great and very fine emeralds that had been carved by the Aztecs into various shapes, including fish and flowers. An emerald bell had a fine pearl as its clapper. They were probably part of the treasure of Montezuma. Earlier in 1525, Cortes had sent to the Emperor of Spain an emerald the size of a man's palm, looted from the Halls of Justice at Tezenco, where it had been placed on the top of a human skull on a stool in front of a bejeweled ceremonial throne.

The Montezuma emeralds were the cause of the downfall of Cortes. He refused to sell them for 40,000 ducats and instead gave them to his wife on their marriage, which offended Queen Isabella, who coveted them for herself. As a result, Cortes lost favor with the King and eventually returned to Mexico. The emeralds were lost at sea in 1541 when Cortes was shipwrecked on his way to help Charles V of Germany and Spain at the siege of Algiers, stronghold of the Mediterranean pirates.

Emeralds were at first despised by the Spanish commanders in Peru. The invaders seized huge quantities of gold, which they retained, and huge numbers of emeralds, many of which were smashed by hammers. Apparently one of the Dominican missionaries with the army, Fra Reginaldo de Pedraza, declared a real emerald would withstand this test. In this cynical age, it may be thought that he was ensuring that there was no glut in the market in Spain because, when he returned, he took a large collection of emeralds with him that he sold for a fortune.

All very large emeralds are flawed in one way or another and contain tiny cavities with crystals of other minerals inside them, groups of which are called "jardin" (garden) by gemologists. Most stones with such inclusions were carved, although a few have remained uncut, such as the Devonshire Emerald (Figure 9–1), given to the Duke of Devonshire in 1831 by Dom Pedro, Emperor of Brazil, after his abdication. It came from the Muzo mine (Figure 9–2) 75 miles (120 kilometers) from Bogota in Colombia, which is still being worked but is such a dangerous place because of the Mafia-style gangs and the terrain that all but a few buyers are afraid to make the journey into the mountains even when armed.

The color of this 1,384-carat (nearly 10 ounces) emerald is rich grass

Fig. 9–1 The Devonshire Emerald. All large emeralds contain tiny cavities with crystals of other minerals inside them. Most stones with such inclusions were carved, although a few have remained uncut, such as the Devonshire. *(Courtesy of Alan Jobbins, BSc, FGA.)*

Fig. 9–2 Muzo Mine. Still worked today, the famous Muzo Mine is 75 miles from Bogota, Colombia. *(Courtesy of the Gemological Institute of America.)*

green. The emerald has been exhibited a number of times and is now in the British Museum (Natural History) in South Kensington, West London. About two inches (5 centimeters) high and the same wide, it is hexagonal in section, which is the common crystal shape of emerald. Unfortunately, nothing else is known about it.

A much bigger rough emerald is said to have been in the Viennese Treasury as it weighed 2,205 carats (about $15^1/_2$ ounces). Bigger still is the 2,650 carat (approaching 19 ounces) monster rough crystal, the Mont Vert, that belonged to an American, A. Bradley Martin, and came from the Ural Mountains in Russia. Pizarro, the ferocious conqueror of Peru, presented an emerald the size of a pigeon's egg to Pope Clement VI, which was smaller than those mentioned, but he brought back the story that the Peruvians worshiped an enormous specimen the size of an ostrich's egg.

Deposits were discovered in the Urals in 1830 after a peasant had picked up some green crystals near the root of a tree. Deposits of certain gems are not uncommonly found near tree roots because the gems were formed in pockets in the rock that have split over great periods of time and collected moisture and humus. The Russian mines produced fine but small emeralds, better than those from Egypt, and some of the smaller ones are even better than the Colombian.

Many very large crystals of poor quality have also been mined in the Urals. The Imperial Institute of Mines in St. Petersburg before the revolution had one 8 inches (20 centimeters) long by 5 inches (13 centimeters) in diameter. The largest—about 10 inches (25 centimeters) long by $4^3/_4$ inches (12 centimeters) diameter—belonged to the Czar.

Emeralds of good size that are pure are exceedingly rare and are greatly outnumbered by fine sapphires and diamonds. Consequently, they are more valuable, weight for weight, than diamonds or fine rubies. The finest, or one of the finest, emeralds from the Urals, weighing about 30 carats, belonged to the last Czar and is presumably in the Gold Treasury in Leningrad or the Diamond Treasury in Moscow.

## *The Shah's Favorites*

Shah Jahan seemed to be the Mogul who most favored emeralds because he had more emeralds than rubies set in the Peacock Throne. Tavernier reported that plenty of these were of good color, but they had many flaws. It is likely that some came from Egypt as well as South America via Europe in the first quarter of the 17th century.

The throne and quantities of gems, including emeralds, were taken by Nadir Shah to Persia, and large numbers are still among the Iranian Crown Jewels, although few are in their original form. The treasures are in the custody of the Bank Markazi (Central Bank). They were housed in the Bank Melli (National Bank) when seen by a team from the Royal Ontario Museum, which made a study of the jewels in 1966. During the last few years of the Shah's reign, until he was overthrown, they were on display in a special vault. Two entire cases were occupied by set and unset emeralds "which in number, quantity, and size, exceed any display of emeralds known elsewhere."

An English trader, Jonas Hanway, was so astonished in 1744 when he saw the harness belonging to Nadir Shah that he referred to it in a book he wrote, *An Historical Account of the British Trade Over the Caspian Sea* (London 1753):

He had four complete sets, one mounted with pearls, another with rubies, a third with emeralds, and the last with diamonds, most of which were so prodigious a size as hardly to merit belief; for many of them appeared as big as a pigeon's egg. I could not regard them but with wonder, not more for their immense value, than for the barbarous taste in which they were set; for some of them did not appear to have any art at all bestowed on them.

Hanway also revealed that Nadir Shah had informed Catherine the Great of Russia about his conquest of India and sent her a present — Hanway described it as "a specimen" — of his loot, comprising elephants, jewels, and other valuables. The elephants were presumably enameled models. These valuables are now in the Hermitage Museum in Leningrad.

Although so many are spectacular, the emeralds in Iran are too numerous to describe more than a few. Among the loose ones is an ovoid cabochon-cut bead weighing 320 carats and another of 303 carats, which is of fluted drop shape. One, of 144.44 carats, is drilled and irregular and carries an inscription. One carved hexagonal bead is blue-green and weighs 188.28 carats while another of similar color scales 184 carats with a lead plug in one end.

Many emeralds as well as balas rubies and sapphires were polished but left in irregular shape and drilled. A gold wire was passed through the hole, capped at the bottom, and twisted into a loop for hanging at the top or soldering to a gold cap with a ring. Emeralds were more frequently carved than the others because emerald is not as hard as the corundums or spinel. The Canadians suggested that the gems that have been carved — with flower, shell, melon, and other motifs — are of Indian provenance.

Two carved emeralds are the feature stones of the Crown of the Empress. Placed one above the other and surrounded by diamonds, the upper is larger and a radially fluted hexagon of 91.32 carats, and the lower a scallop fluted cabochon drop of 46.73 carats. The crown contains two other big emeralds of 66.35 carats and 63.83 carats, both in the more modern step cut.

The largest number of emeralds, three hundred of them, are contained in the Kiani Crown, the Royal crown of the Qajar dynasty that ruled Persia from 1794 to 1925. It also contains about 1,500 red stones and innumerable pearls, although most important are the many diamonds one of which is a pink and clean Golconda stone weighing about 23 carats, still in its early irregular rose cut. Several other diamonds are around 20 carats each and in the Mogul cut.

One emerald of about 100 carats, and another of about 100 carats, are set, with many other large gemstones, in the Imperial Sword (Color Plate 4). Another artifact, a majestic hemispherical bowl of gold, has a large and slightly ovoid step-cut emerald forming the center of the bottom. The inside is otherwise plain, but the outside is heavily encrusted with gems. An inscription commemorates the capture by Nasir-ud-Din Shah of the city of Herat, which precipitated a war with Great Britain. The bowl is dated 1857-1858.

Nasir-ud-Din Shah and his successors used to wear a belt of woven golden wire with a clasp in which a huge heart-shaped emerald of about 175 carats was mounted (Color Plate 19). The Mogul Jahangir was seen by an English traveler, Sir Thomas Roe, in 1616 wearing a turban with a plume and a ruby as big as a walnut on one side, a diamond of about the same size on the other, and "in the middle an emralld like a hart, much bigger." The emerald in the belt was almost certainly once this treasure of the Moguls.

Another belt buckle, probably worn by Muhammad Shah, contains an emerald of about 250 carats carved to the shape of rose petals and surrounded by large diamonds. Another of about the same weight is hexagonal in shape and has an inscription engraved on the front praising Fath Ali Shah with the date 1226 (1811–1812). It is the main pendant of a necklace.

The most spectacular item in the Iranian collection is a globe of the world about 18 inches (46 centimeters) in diameter in a stand about 43 inches (110 centimeters) high. The globe is made of 75 pounds (34 kilograms) of pure gold encrusted all over with more than 51,000 gemstones, some of extraordinary size even for this huge collection of unique and quite remarkable stones.

The oceans, seas, and large lakes are represented by emeralds and most land masses by rubies or red spinels. Iran, Britain, France, and parts of Asia are composed of diamonds, and Africa south of the Sahara and part of Egypt comprise massed sapphires. The continents are outlined in diamonds, which also indicate the equator and the ecliptic. Rubies are used for lines of latitude and longitude.

Nasir-ud-Din Shah is believed to have commissioned it to be made in 1874–1875 to ensure that some of his loose gemstones were not lost. It contains two emeralds of about 175 carats each and a number weighing about 125 carats or more each. Many real rubies weigh around 50 carats.

In the collection are two tiaras made for the Empress Farah when she was married to the late Shah in 1958. One contains the Noor-ul-Ain (Light of the Eye) pink diamond referred to in Chapter Three, and the other has five "points" each comprising a large graded cabochon emerald surrounded by round and navette (boat-shaped) diamonds. All the emeralds are described as magnificent and the biggest of them in the center, weighing about 65 carats, as superb, although another of 48 carats has the finest color. There are two irregular rows of colored diamonds of various shapes cut in a platinum frame with a lower edge of modern baguette-cut diamonds.

## The Topkapi Dagger

Moving to another country, among the golden thrones, gold and ruby bowls, and diamond crowns and tiaras that were the riches of the Ottoman Empire is a famed emerald-studded dagger. The treasures are kept in the museum and strongrooms of the Topkapi Palace in Istanbul, Turkey.

The Topkapi dagger was said to be a present from Sultan Mahmud I of Turkey to Nadir Shah of Persia, but somehow it remained in Turkey. On one side of the handle are three fine and huge emeralds, each about $1^2/_3$ inches (4 centimeters) by $1^1/_4$ inches (3 centimeters) in size. The central one is cushion-shaped, and the outer ones pear-shaped. Diamonds are set at the ends and where the emeralds meet.

In the top of the handle, a small watch signed Clarke, London, is mounted. The cover of the dial is another large emerald of octagonal cut mounted in a bezel set with diamonds. There were several watch and clockmakers named Clarke working in London in the 17th and 18th centuries. The style of the watch dial is late 17th or early 18th century, but the dagger was made in Turkey later in the 18th century. Nadir Shah ruled Persia from 1736 to 1747, so the dagger could not have been intended for him. The other side of the dagger handle is of mother-of-pearl decorated with fruit designs on enameled gold. The scabbard is of repoussé gold and large diamonds, the settings of which form a kind of filigree. The center is decorated by a panel of colored enamels showing a bowl of flowers. It is also of Turkish workmanship.

Sultan Abdul Hamid I of Turkey had a pendant in which three enormous hexagonal emeralds were set surrounded by diamonds. From the bottom was hung a tassel of small pearls, the head of which was set with diamonds. The pendant was given by the Sultan to the Prophet's Tomb in Medina. It is 17 inches (43 centimeters) long and is now in the Topkapi Museum in Istanbul.

Emeralds never played a large part in the Crown Jewels and Regalia of Europe, although it might be thought that they would be numerous in Spain after the colonization of Colombia and Peru, when Spain became one of the richest countries in the world. The reason may be that the Spanish Crown Jewels were the property of the rulers and not the state as in other European countries. As family heirlooms, they were often disposed of when their owners needed money.

The only European emerald crown is Spanish, it is true, but it was made about two centuries before the South American conquests, so the emeralds presumably came from Egypt. Called the Emerald Crown of Blanche of Anjou, it is referred to in a document dated October 23, 1313, in which James II, King of Aragon, instructs his treasurer to transfer to his daughter Isabel a number of items that belonged to Queen Blanche, who died in 1310. Anjou was a province in northwest France that earlier was attached to the English Crown. Aragon was a kingdom in the northeast of the Iberian peninsula that, when it united with Castile in 1479, led to the formation of the Spanish state.

The settlement included a number of gems and jewels along with a crown made up of sixteen pieces, the pinnacle of each being set with eight large emeralds and eight not so large. There were also sixty-four smaller emeralds and eighty-seven garnets.

A famous use of emerald, as opposed to a famous emerald, concerns the Roman Emperor Nero. It is on record that he used to peer through at gladiatorial contests. Why was not explained. The Romans polished emerald into rather flat cabochon form, which is the shape of a convex lens and would, therefore, tend to correct long sight if peered through. Alternatively, it is the shape of a convex mirror and, if more opaque, could be used in a similar manner. The color may also have offered some relief from the strong sunlight.

## Tints of Purity

Emeralds are among the gems that retain the purity of their tint in many lights, a fact noted by the Roman Pliny the Elder, who stated, "neither sunshine, shade nor artificial light" caused any change in their appearance. It is true that emerald stays the same in many versions of white light, unlike, say, the much coveted alexandrite, but colored lights will alter its tint. In fact, emeralds of good color show two colors when viewed from different directions, a characteristic of many gems. From one angle, the green is bluish and from another yellowish. The one that predominates provides the body color of the stone.

The mineral specie to which emerald belongs is beryl, a more common form of which is aquamarine. Unlike emerald, this sea green to bluish stone is often very pure, even in large sizes. The depth of tint varies from almost colorless to a fairly deep hue. There is no particular outward resemblance to emerald, but Pliny suspected it in Roman days, although the relationship was not definitely established for nearly nineteen centuries.

A large aquamarine orb representing the world on St. Edward's Crown in the British Crown Jewels, which was switched for a fake, was described in Chapter Eight. In about 1600, Leopold I of Austria bought a huge aquamarine that weighed 492 carats. The specific gravity of aquamarine is lower than that of a diamond so a stone of the same weight would be larger than the diamond. Similarly, ruby and sapphire have a lower relative density so would be smaller, although the same weight. Opal and amber are light in weight and, therefore, are particularly large for their weights.

One would expect to find some fine aquamarines in the Portuguese treasury, since they are mined in Brazil, which Portugal occupied, and a monster uncut stone of 1,650 carats is referred to in the collection of insignia of three military orders. Aquamarines were also found in Russia, and the Empress Catherine II liked them particularly because of that. In France, Napoleon Bonaparte had an aquamarine clasp to hold his coronation robe in 1804.

## Alexandrite Differs By Day and By Night

A green stone favored in Russia, especially by Catherine II, was the alexandrite, which has been described as an emerald by day and an amethyst by night. Like a good colored emerald, it shows different colors viewed from different directions — it is dichroic — but the effect is much stronger. From one direction, the color is emerald green to dark grass green; from the other, it is a columbine red with a tinge of violet. When the stone is correctly cut, it is always green in daylight but in artificial light changes to a red to violet color.

The mineral specie of the stone is chrysoberyl, and the gem was discovered by accident in one of the emerald mines in the Ural Mountains in Russia. The crystals form together into star shapes, sometimes nearly four inches (10 centimeters) across. The day when the first crystal was found happened to be the coming of age of the future Czar Alexander II, so the mineral was named after him. Another reason why it received such attention in Russia was because it embodied the military colors, green and red. In more recent times, alexandrites have been found in Ceylon. There they are grass green and change to raspberry red.

Although chrysoberyl may look like amethyst in artificial light, the two are unlikely to be confused. Amethyst is a rarer form of a very common mineral, quartz, known also as rock crystal in its colorless occurrence. The tint can range from pale, almost colorless violet, to rich, deep, and very

Fig. 9–3 The Siberian Amethyst. Weighing 1,305 carats, the Siberian stone may be the legendary Blue Mountain. Christian V of Denmark had it hanging from the canopy of his throne in the 17th century. *(Courtesy of the Twining Collection; copyright of the Worshipful Company of Goldsmiths, Goldsmith's Hall, London.*

beautiful purple. Most amethyst is cloudy, and only the clear crystals are regarded as gem material. They were prized more in the later 18th and earlier 19th centuries than they are today because they were rarer. Queen Charlotte of England had an amethyst necklace that was considered very valuable at the time but would not be remarkable now in the stock of a high class jeweler.

## The Siberian Amethyst

There is probably only one amethyst that achieved some fame, the Siberian (Figure 9–3). After the Danish monarchy became hereditary in 1660, King Frederic ordered the Keeper of the Cabinet of Curiosities to have a throne made in the style of the High Seat of a Scandinavian chief. It was made of narwhal tusks, which are a form of ivory sometimes found in jewelry. The narwhal looks like a whale about 16 feet (4.9 meters) long. It was hunted for its blubber and skin, from which the Eskimos made leather.

From the front of its head projects a single, tapered tusk up to about nine feet (2.75 meters) long. The tusk has a spiral groove and may have been the source of the legend of the unicorn, first mentioned in 400 B.C. by Ctesius.

The throne, which is still used on ceremonial occasions, has rather garish decorations. From the center of the canopy hangs the Siberian Amethyst, which has an elongated octagonal cut and is mounted in a narrow frame. The stone is now in Rosenborg Castle, Copenhagen, which has been a museum of treasures, curios, portraits, clocks, early astronomical instruments, and gemstones for more than a century.

Catherine the Great of Russia had an amethyst from the Ural Mountains described as "gleaming by night like red fire." The Vienna Treasury in Austria houses a huge, pear-shaped amethyst hung as a pendant from a mount shaped like a gold crown and set with emeralds. The Emperor Leopold received it as a gift from King Charles II of Spain (Color Plate 7). It is of 17th century provenance and is $4^2/_3$ inches (11.8 centimeters) high.

Also in Vienna is a 492-carat aquamarine and the largest precious opal known. The Hungarian Opal (Figure 9–4), as it is called, came from the mines in Cernowitz in that country, which have been worked since 1400. It is shaped as a drop and held in a frame of three clasps. The weight is 17 ounces, nearly half a kilogram.

## The Rich Opal Fields of Australia

The discovery of rich opal fields in Australia in 1877 (about the same time as the discovery of large diamond deposits in South Africa) eclipsed the Hungarian production. One of the finest Australian opals ever unearthed is smaller but breath-taking in its colorful beauty. Called the Flame Queen, it was found at Lightning Ridge in New South Wales in a shaft that some diggers had started in a desolate area and had abandoned before leaving to fight in the First World War in 1914. Some years later, two other diggers, Jack Phillips and Walter Bradley, sunk it deeper, to the opal level, but found little of value. For some reason, they continued to drive their horizontal tunnel farther than was usual, to about 35 feet (10 meters), when Bradley's pick struck a big black "nobbly." Illuminating the place by candlelight, normal practice for opal miners, he gouged it out and nipped off a small piece with steel snips. The broken part showed the exciting opal flash in the flame of the candle.

The stone was ground and polished into an oval cabochon about $2^3/_4$ inches by $2^1/_3$ inches (7 centimeters by 6 centimeters) in size and half an inch (1.3 centimeters) thick, weighing 253 carats. The Flame Queen is black opal, which shows its flashing colors—mainly bronze-red, in this case—against a black ground. Lightning Ridge is famed for its black opal. Much of the color display is lost in white opal by being absorbed into the white background.

What some connoisseurs claim to be the finest opal of all is smaller still, between 40 carats and 50 carats, and is remarkable for its strong banded colors against a black ground. It is so like the wing of a Red Admiral butterfly that it was named the Red Admiral. This, too, was found on Lightning Ridge or, to give it its original name before the diggers came, Wallangulla, in the 1920s. Four men were working the Phone Line Digging when, for no apparent reason, two of them, Canadian Bill and Jimmy Murray, moved about a quarter of a mile away. In a short time, they had dug out the Red Admiral.

Fig. 9–4 The Hungarian Opal. Said to be the largest gem opal known, it is the size of a man's fist. It was found in the ancient Cernowitz mines in Hungary, which were worked as early as 1400. *(Courtesy of the Twining Collection; copyright of the Worshipful Company of Goldsmiths, Goldsmith's Hall, London.)*

Today, almost all Australia's opal comes from Coober Pedy in South Australia. The Aborigines gave it its name, which means "man in a hole," describing the typical opal digger. The area produces white opal. In 1930, fifteen years after the first finds in Coober Pedy, a deposit that was near the surface and was easily worked, was found about 270 miles (435 kilometers) southeast at a place called Andamooka, an Aborigine name meaning "the place with no name." Some of the opal is black.

The most famous opal to come from the area is called simply the Andamooka and was found at a relatively deep level, 30 feet (9 meters). Unfortunately, it was chipped by the miner who found it and had not realized what he had come across until he had exposed more of it. The original piece of opal weighed about six ounces (170 grams) and was about 4 inches by 2 inches (10 centimeters by 5 centimeters). It was cut into a cabochon about $2^3/_4$ inches (7 centimeters) long, weighing 203 carats. It is white opal with continuous flashes of red, orange, and blue as the stone is moved, and it has no flaws or inclusions, which is exceptional for a stone of its size. In 1954, the year after its discovery, it was presented to Queen Elizabeth II set in a diamond necklace by the government of South Australia.

Opal as a material is so ordinary that few would bother to pick it up. It is a milky, blackish, grayish, bluish, or reddish glassy substance. Its beauty is not intrinsic. It comes solely from the way in which it splits up white light: in a broad sense, like a film of oil on a puddle produces rainbow colors. The electron microscope has revealed that opal comprises millions upon millions of tiny balls of silica. These diffract light so that colors of the spectrum appear at different angles. The larger balls produce most red light and the smaller ones most violet. To grasp this rainbow, men spend their lives in the desert of Coober Pedy living in underground caves to escape the intense heat of the sun while preserving what little rain that falls in corrugated drums. There, water is more precious than opal during the long periods of drought.

The most prized opal has a black ground with large moving patches of al colors of the rainbow. Next is white opal with a similar color display. Lowest in value is opal with a gray or potch (mother rock) ground. Color patches may be large (harlequin) or small (pin-point) and colors can include violet, blue, green, yellow, orange, and red, smoe opals showing only two neighboring colors. Blue is most common. An opal dealer will examine a piece cut or polished, with a light behind him and twist the stone to left and right to pick up the colors it displays. Particular colors can only be seen at certain angles.

The richest merchandise of all, and the most soveraigne commoditie throughout the whole
world, are these pearles.
*Pliny the Elder, Historia Naturalis (77 A.D.)*

---

*Chapter Ten*

# Pearls of Great Price

**P**EARLS were probably the earliest
natural objects that were prized as gems. Imagine the curiosity and surprise
of prehistoric man after cracking open an oyster for a meal to find a round,
lustrous pearl in his mouth. He would probably have been a member of a
fish-eating tribe in Ceylon or on the southernmost tip of India, or perhaps
in the Persian Gulf. Sea water pearls were first discovered in these places,
where they were venerated as talismans and symbols of wealth and importance for thousands of years.

Mother-of-pearl, the nacreous inside surface of a seawater oyster shell,
may have been used for ornamentation before the pearls themselves. Shells
have been found in Egyptian ruins of the sixth dynasty (c. 2500 B.C.) and in
the ruins of ancient Thebes, capital of the Middle Kingdom (11th and 12th
dynasties, c. 2052–c. 1786 B.C.). Graves of the 12th dynasty have yielded
necklaces of circular and oblong beads cut from pearl shells and strung on
chains with cornelian and pottery beads.

Oyster pearls are referred to in *The Shu King*, one of China's oldest
books, dated from c. 2350 to c. 625 B.C. As a tribute, Yu received pearls
from the River Hwai and strings of pearls "that were not quite round" from
the Kingdom of King Kwau. Pearls from a river are not as lustrous as those
from the sea. Called "river pearls" or "fresh water pearls" today, they come
from a large mussel (*unio margaritifera*), not from an oyster. They are
found in several parts of the world but mainly from rivers in the United
States and Europe, although pollution has taken a heavy toll of them.

Pearls from the oyster (*pinctada radiata*) are the finest and are generally known as "oriental pearls." The flesh is not very good for eating.

The most ancient pearl fisheries were those in the Gulf of Mannar, which, with Palk Strait, separates Ceylon from the southern tip of India. Although this beautiful island is usually known now as Sri Lanka, the name of Ceylon still remains in the constitution. One ancient name was Serendip, from which Horace Walpole coined the word "serendipity," — to make delightful discoveries by chance — in his book *The Three Princes of Serendip*. The fisheries are believed to have existed for about 2,500 years. There are references in the early Pali writings (Figure 10–1) of Ceylon dating back to part of that time, referring to gifts of pearls and to some being taken by an embassy to India. The waters there are only occasionally fished for pearls today.

The word "krisana" occurs several times in the Rigveda, the oldest of the Vedas, the ancient sacred texts of Hindustan, written perhaps a thousand years B.C. It is translated as "pearl." The Atharvaveda, dated about five centuries B.C. refers to an amulet of pearl shell and pearls that was employed as a talisman to bestow long life and prosperity on students of Brahma. The student would recite a prayer, of which this was one of the lines: "The shell is our universal remedy; the pearl shall protect us from straits." Another line was: "Thou art one of the golden substances, thou art born from Soma [the Moon]."

The great epics of India referred to in the Introduction, the Ramayana and the Mahabharata, use the same word, "krisana," and the former declares that a great expedition was accompanied by pearl drillers. The name may allude to the pearl's association with Krishna, the eighth incarnation

Fig. 10–1 Pali Script. The most ancient pearl fisheries were those in the Gulf of Mammar, which separates Sri Lanka from India. The fisheries are believed to have existed for about 2,500 years, based on references in early Pali writings of Ceylon.

of Vishnu, the preserver, one of the three manifestations of divine activity, the others being Brahma, the creator, and Siva, the destroyer. Krishna drew pearls from the depths of the sea to adorn his daughter, Pandaia, on her wedding day.

The fisheries of the Persian Gulf stretched from Kuwait in the north to the Trucial coast in the south and were probably exploited for pearl-bearing oysters from about 300 B.C. It was the discovery of immense oil deposits in recent times that finished the hazardous and very unhealthy diving from primitive dhows (an Arab lateen-rigged boat usually having a long overhang forward, a high poop, and a low waist) that had continued in much the same way for so long. The waters off the islands of Bahrain had been among the best for pearls. With well-paid work available in the oil fields, pearl fishing rapidly declined and was almost extinct by the Second World War.

Although no references to pearls have been identified in ancient Zoroastrian writings, there are many portraits of Persian kings and queens wearing pearls on early engraved gems and on coins. In the Persian gallery of The Louvre is a necklace of pearls and other gems that dates from at least the fourth century B.C. and is probably the earliest piece of pearl jewelry in existence. It came from the Susa or Shushan, the winter palace of the Kings of Persia, and was found in the sarcophagus of an Achmaemenid princess by J. de Morgan at about the turn of this century.

There were ancient pearl fisheries in the Red Sea, along the Arabian coast between Jedda and the Farason Islands, and also along the north African coast, near Massawa in Eritrea. They dated from about 300 B.C., and the oysters there were the small *pinctada radiata*, as in the Persian Gulf. The larger *pinctada margaritifera* also flourished there and were fished for the mother-of-pearl from their shells.

The beads cut from pearl shell suggest that the Egyptians fished for shells before seeking pearls. Their interest in pearls probably came after Egypt was occupied by the Persians in the fifth century B.C. The same Persian wars no doubt spread the love of pearls to the Greeks. Theophrastus (372–287 B.C.) wrote about their being found in a shellfish similar to the *pinna* but smaller. He declared that they were used to construct necklaces of great value.

From Greece, the desire for pearls spread to Rome, where the pearl was called *unio* because it was unique. (That, in fact, is true of every gem.) Pliny, who wrote the earliest treatise on precious stones, stated that a large perfect pearl was called *unio* and smaller, less beautiful ones were known as *margaritae*. The riches of the East, including pearls, became familiar in

Rome during the conquests of Pompey. Borne in his triumphal procession of 61 B.C. were 33 crowns of pearls, a portrait of him in pearls, a shrine dedicated to the Muses and decorated with pearls, and numerous pearl ornaments, according to Pliny.

So many treasures from Alexandria and the Orient poured into Rome that the Temple of Venus was decorated inside with pearls, and wealthy people used them lavishly on clothing. It stung Pliny into the scathing remark, "It is not sufficient for them to wear pearls, but they must trample and walk over them." There are many references to them in the decadent days of Rome. Caligula decorated his favorite horse, Icitatus, with a pearl necklace when appointing it Consul. Nero sat holding a pearl scepter on a throne decorated with pearls. He even provided masks and scepters embellished with pearls for the actors in his theater.

Pliny commented that in the first century A.D., pearls ranked first in value amongst all precious things. The Roman general Vitellus, it was reported by Suetonius, paid all the costs of a military campaign by selling one pearl from his mother's ear.

## The Making of a Pearl

How are pearls formed? The traveler Benjamin of Tudela, who visited Persia from 1160 to 1173, declared that on the twenty-fourth day of the month of Nisan, "a certain dew falleth into the waters, which being sucked in by the oysters, they immediately sink to the bottom of the sea." Then, about the middle of the month of Tisri, men descended to the bottom of the sea with the help of long cords and brought up the oysters that now contained pearls. This belief persisted for a long time. It is surprising to find that William Camden (1551–1623), the serious investigator after whom the Camden Historical Society was named, repeated the fable: " . . . the shellfish, sucking in the dew, conceive and bring forth pearls. . . . "

Another idea was that the pearl was a fossilized oyster egg. A more modern suggestion was that it was formed by the oyster around a piece of grit that had happened into the shell. The intruder is now known often to be a tiny parasite that enters the shell and causes irritation to the animal. The animal isolates it in a piece of mantle or skin and covers it with nacre in the same way as it lines the shell. Continuing the process over a number of years, it builds up a sizable pearl over the tiny dead parasite.

For a very long time, gems were credited with medical properties. Pearls were recommended particularly for the eyes and for purifying the blood. Alphonso X of Castile (1221–1282) declared in his *Lapidario* that they were a great help in palpitations of the heart and every sickness caused by melancholia (depression). "Therefore, physicians put them in their medicines and lectuaries, with which they cure these infirmities, and give them to be swallowed. They also make powders of them, which are applied to the eyes: because they clear the sight wonderfully, strengthen the nerves and dry up the moisture which enters the eyes."

Anselmus de Boot, who was physician to Emperor Rudolph II, made the even more exaggerated claim that they were "most excellent for restoring the strength and almost for resuscitating the dead." His prescription was to place the pearls in a strong vinegar, lemon juice, spirits of vitriol, or sulphur until they became liquified. "Care must be taken to cover the glass carefully, lest the essence should escape." Next, add more lemon juice, decant the milky liquid that results, and add sugar to sweeten it. Add to each four ounces of this pearl liquid an ounce of rose water, an ounce of tincture of strawberries, and two ounces of cinnamon water. From one to two-and-a-half ounces of the medicine should be taken after shaking the bottle.

Physicians gave King Charles VI of France (1368–1422) a draught of pearl powder in distilled water to cure his insanity, and Lorenzo de Medici (1448–1492), the most famous of the family that ruled Florence, was treated similarly when he was dying of fever. One of his friends asked what it tasted like, and he replied, "As pleasant as anything can be to a dying man."

## A Drink for Lovers

The most famous story about drinking pearl water centers on pride, not prescription, and was told by Pliny in his book on natural history written some 1,900 years ago. When Anthony met Cleopatra, in the words of a 1601 translator, he "strained himselfe to doe all the pleasure he possibly could, and had feasted her day by day most sumptuously and spared for no cost: in the hight of her pride and wanton braverie (as being a noble courtesan, and a queen with all) began to debase the expense and provision of Anthonie, and made no reckoning of his costly fare. . . . "

Anthony demanded how it was possible to exceed the magnificence he had provided, and Cleopatra said she would spend ten million sesterji on one supper for him. His response was to wager her that she could not. On the following day, Cleopatra provided Anthony with a supper that was "sumptuous and roiall ynough" but nothing remarkable, and he laughed her to scorn and "by way of mockerie" required to see a bill with an account of the particulars.

Cleopatra told him that what had already been served was well over the value she had declared but, because of his doubts, she herself would eat well beyond that value and her own supper would cost six million sesterji. She called for a second service, and servants set before her just one cruet of sharp vinegar.

As Pliny recounted: "Now she had on her eares hanging these two most precious pearles, the singular and only jewels of the world, and even Natures wonder. As Antonie looked wistfully upon her, shee tooke one of them from her eare, steeped it in the vinegar, and so soon as it was liquified, dranke it off." She was about to do the same with the other pearl when the judge of the wager laid hold of it and declared that Anthony had lost.

The old physicians pulverized pearl in vinegar or another liquid to make medicine. A pearl will not entirely dissolve even in boiling vinegar. So if Cleopatra did, indeed, place one of her exquisite pearl ear drops in her drink — the ransom of a kingdom in a drink to toast a lover — she must have swallowed it whole. (A cynic might say it was recoverable later. However, it did disappear.)

The remaining pearl was cut in half and made into earrings for the statue of Venus in the Temple of the Pantheon in Rome to commemorate the famous wager.

Centuries later, Shakespeare used the theme in "Hamlet:"

The King shall drink to Hamlet's better breath;
An in the cup an union shall be thrown. . .

The name "union" was often substituted for pearl in the 15th and 16th centuries. It was the river pearl, *unio margaritifera*.

J. J. Fugger, the Nuremberg banker and jeweler, made some notes in E. W. Streeter's book, *The Great Diamonds of the World*, (London, 1882) about the Three Brethren Jewel described in Chapter Eight, that once belonged to Charles the Bold, Duke of Burgundy, and was probably the most highly regarded jewel of the 15th century. As well as containing three very large balas rubies, from it hung three magnificent pear-shaped pearls, each being about half an inch (1.3 centimeters) in diameter. It passed into the hands of the Magistrates Berne after the defeat of Charles at the Battle of Granson, who sold it to Fugger with the Ducal cap, which was covered with pearls, "for no more than 47,000 florins."

## Bloody Mary and La Peregrina

The Cap was broken up, but the jewel eventually came into the hands of Bloody Mary, Queen of England from 1553 to 1558. She married Philip II of Spain, which provoked rebellion in England because of her attempt to convert the country to Catholicism. She acquired many notable gems from the Spanish Treasury. One of them was a celebrated pearl called "La Peregrina" (The Unconquerable; Figure 10–2), or the "Philip II Pearl." One story associated with it is that it was discovered by a slave pearl fisher in Panama, who was rewarded with his freedom. Other sources say it was found in the pearl fisheries of Venezuela. There are portraits in the Prado in Madrid and in Hampton Court and Winchester Cathedral in England of Mary Tudor wearing it at her wedding to Philip, so it must have been found before 1554.

Christopher Columbus was the first European to come across the pearl fisheries in the Caribbean, off Venezuela, in 1498. Columbus called the island of Cubagua "the Island of Pearls." He sent a boatload of sailors to intercept a fishing boat to discover what the local people were fishing for. One sailor had broken a dish of Malaga ware, and they traded these colored bits of pottery for strings of pearls, described as "white and large." On seeing what they had brought back, Columbus sent his sailors again with buttons, needles, scissors, and more earthenware pieces; they returned with about 18 ounces (more than half a kilogram) of pearls. This area eventually supplied the Europe of the Middle Ages with large quantities of pearls.

La Peregrina was taken originally from South America to Spain by Don Diego de Temes and presented to King Philip II. After the death of his wife, Mary Tudor, it was returned to Spain. The magnificent pearl appears in portraits by Velazquez, whose patron was Philip IV, of Isabella of Bourbon and Mariana of Austria, Philip's first and second wives. It was worn in a headdress.

There is a reference in the 1706 memoirs of Saint Simon, Grand Seignieur at the court of King Louis XIV of France, to the Queen of Spain sending a French valet with the famous pearl to her husband Philip V, who was in Versailles. Simon mentioned the pearl again in 1722, when he saw it hanging from a clasp of diamonds in a fold of the Spanish King's hat.

La Peregrina remained in Spain until 1813. Then Joseph Bonaparte took it with him to France when he abdicated. It passed to his stepniece, Hortense de Beauharnais, when she married, and then in 1837 to Prince Louis Napoleon, who got into financial difficulties and asked the Marquis of Abercorn if he could recommend an honest jeweler who might buy it, naming the price he wanted. Without a word, the Marquis examined it, opened a drawer, and wrote a check for the full amount, which he handed to the Prince.

In the afternoon of the same day, he presented the pearl to his wife. However, it became a constant source of worry to her because, having no hole drilled in it, it kept falling from its setting. At a ball in Buckingham

Fig. 10–2 Mary I of England. In this portrait by Hans Eworth, Mary I is wearing the famous La Peregrina Pearl from the Spanish Treasury. La Peregrina was sold to actress Elizabeth Taylor in 1969, for $37,000. *(Courtesy of the National Portrait Gallery, London.)*

Palace, she put her hand to her throat to discover that the pearl was missing. She was greatly distressed, wondering what on earth her husband would say. Then, while going into dinner, she saw it glistening in the folds of a velvet train to the dress of the lady in front of her.

At another event, this time at Windsor Castle, the Marquis's wife lost it and subsequently found it in the upholstery of a sofa. It vanished and reappeared on one more occasion, too, but was not drilled until it came into the possession of her son on the death of her husband. It was cleaned and polished in 1913, when its weight was recorded as 203.84 grains. It was believed to have weighed 234 grains undrilled. A pearl grain is a quarter of a carat or twentieth of a gram.

La Peregrina was worn as one earring by later Queens of Spain, the other of the set being another famous pearl of nearly equal weight known as the Charles II Pearl. It was presented to the King by Don de Alponte, Conde del Palmer, who lived in the Canary Isles. It had been discovered in 1691, nearly a century-and-a-half after La Peregrina. When a large part of the old Palace of Madrid was burned down in 1734, the Charles II Pearl was destroyed.

La Peregrina still exists. In January 1969, it was sold to actress Elizabeth Taylor. At the time of the auction, its authenticity was challenged by ex-Queen Victoria Eugenia of Spain, who claimed that a pearl in her possession weighing 223.8 grains was the real La Peregrina. Elizabeth Taylor paid $37,000 for La Peregrina, sold at Sotheby's and described as "weighing approximately 203.84 grains suspended from a foliate platinum mount set with numerous old-mine and rose diamonds."

## The Silvery Luster of La Pelegrina

Sometimes confused with La Peregrina is La Pelegrina (The Incomparable; Figure 10–3), which was also in the Spanish Crown Jewels. It was given by Philip IV to his daughter, Maria Theresa, on her marriage to Louis XIV in 1660, so it went to France. What happened to it later is not known, but it turned up unexpectedly in Russia.

For some time in its history, it is said to have been in the hands of the Zozina brothers, who were antiquarians in St. Petersburg (Leningrad), according to a little book on La Pelegrina (or Pellegrina, as it was also spelled). The booklet appeared in 1818, and the author, G. Fischer de Walkheim, claimed that the brothers bought the pearl from an English sea captain in Leghorn, who had just returned from India. But that is impossible in view of the known Spanish connection.

It weighs $111\frac{1}{2}$ grains, which is exceptionally large for a pearl of per-

Fig. 10–3 La Pelegrina Pearl. Sometimes confused with La Peregrina is La Pelegrina (The Incomparable), which was also in the Spanish Crown Jewels. It weighs 111$\frac{1}{2}$ grains, which is exceptionally large for a pearl of perfectly spherical shape and high quality. Its silvery luster was said to make it appear almost transparent, although it was not. *(Courtesy of Sotheby's.)*

fectly spherical shape and high quality. Its silvery luster was said to make it appear almost transparent, although it was not, of course. Modern references call it ovoid in shape, but according to the author of the 48-page booklet, the Zozina brothers kept it in a gold-mounted sea urchin shell with a convex lens over it as a cover. Viewed through the lens, it looked oval, but when removed and placed on a flat surface, "it rolled around like a blob of quicksilver."

There is a strange account of a wealthy Moscow merchant and a pearl in a travel book written by Johan Georg Kohl. The pearl was similar to the Pelegrina and has been associated with it, but whether or not they were the same is impossible to say.

Just before 1840, the merchant died in a convent, where it was apparently the habit of the rich to spend their last days. His wife had died so he had passed on his business to his sons. All his passions were now devoted to a large and beautiful pearl bought for him by a Persian or Arab friend. He refused all offers for it and kept it in a golden casket in the cell where he lived. He would open the casket to show it to visitors, but knowing how precious it was to him, no one ventured to touch it. When the old man died, he was clutching the pearl; it was removed from his fingers with considerable difficulty. Kohl saw this pearl in the Imperial Treasury in his travels and wrote the story later.

The real Pelegrina was sold in Moscow to Princess Youssoupoff and has been handed down in the family. It was on show in London in 1935 at an exhibition of Russian art when it was plain to see it was egg-shaped and could therefore not have been the pearl owned by the Zozina brothers.

On display with it was a black pearl of perfect drop shape named the Azra. It is hung from a necklace of the same name, comprising 110 perfectly matched pearls with a large round black one in the center. From this hangs a cross of diamonds with the Azra Pearl suspended below it.

## The Pearl of Hope

The biggest historical pearl is the Hope, which belonged to the banker, Henry Philip Hope, who also owned the Hope Diamond. It is a monster, weighing 1,800 grains or about three ounces (85 grams), and it is described as "drop-shaped baroque." This means it is not regular in form. In fact, it is reminiscent in shape of a foxglove flower about to open and is not far off the size. It is about two inches long (5 centimeters), $4^{1}/_{2}$ inches (11.5 centimeters) around its widest part and $3^{3}/_{4}$ inches (8.25 centimeters) around the narrowest. The color is pure white at the smallest end shading to greenish bronze at the large end.

It is a river pearl and when found was attached to the shell of the mollusk, which makes it, strictly speaking, a blister pearl. The part that was attached to the shell was reshaped and polished. It was mounted as a pendant being surmounted by a red enameled gold crown set with diamonds, emeralds, rubies, and sapphires. There was a bow at the top for hanging from a chain. The style of the crown is French.

The Hope Pearl was on show at the Geological Museum in South Kensington for some years with other items from the Hope collection and was sold in 1886 when the collection was put on the market. In 1908, the Crown Jewelers, Garrard and Co., were offering it at £9,000. It was privately up for sale again in 1974 for $200,000.

Hope was very fond of pearls, and there were about 148 well-shaped ones in his collection, including one of 151 grains from Polynesia, which was creamy white in color, and a bouton (of flattened round shape) weighing 124 grains that was bluish-white at the top and a dark bronze color around the body.

## A Range of Colors

Pearls can be of many colors, depending on factors that are not fully understood. Some of the colors may be influenced by the minerals in the waters where the oysters lived. Around the turn of the century, Madame Lillian Nordica was an American prima donna of the operatic world and a lover of pearls. She owned a necklace of 28 different colored pearls set in enameled gold links of floral design. Colors of the pearls ranged over white, cream, yellow, golden yellow, bronze, gunmetal, and black. The biggest, of pear shape, was a pendant of 175 grains with a greenish hue, which was said to give off red flashes when it was moved.

This particular pearl is from the abalone, which is not an oyster but comes from the sea. It belongs to the *haliotis* family of big colorful shell-fish. Their smaller brethren are found in the Channel Isles, where they are called "ear-shells." The abalone or paua, as it is called in New Zealand, is fished mainly for the colorful shell but can produce pearls of various hues, including yellows, blues, greens, and pinks. The pendant in Madame Nordica's necklace was the finest of them known.

Only oriental pearls have the irridescent nacre that is universally associated with pearls and the finest mother-of-pearl. Nacre comprises layers of tiny, platelike crystals of calcium carbonate held in place by alternate layers of an organic material with the name "conchiolin," produced by the mollusk (the oyster), that acts like cement. In an oriental pearl, all the layers are concentric like the layers in an onion. The dark brown outer coating of an oyster shell is made of conchiolin.

Gray pearls merge into the color of gunmetal, which darkens into black. One famous black pearl belonged to Count Louis Batthyani, Premier of one of Hungary's revolutionary governments. He was court-martialed and ordered before a firing squad, but before he was shot in 1849, he gave the scarf pin in which the pearl was mounted to his valet. The valet left it to his son, who pawned it.

Not having any idea of its value, the pawnbroker took the black pearl to a jeweler in Budapest, who had a suspicion that the pearl had been stolen and reported the matter to the authorities. In fact, it *had* been stolen, but not by the Count or his valet. It had been taken a century-and-a-half earlier from the English Crown Jewels. The English government redeemed it from the pawnbroker for £2,500.

## The Queen's Pearls

Queen Elizabeth I was not overfond of personal jewelry when she ascended the throne, but in later years, she developed an exaggerated love of pearls above all other gems, which led to her extravagant use of them as decorations on her dress and as jewelry. She acquired some treasures from Mary Tudor, her predecessor, and added more important pieces from the Crown Jewels of Scotland, Burgundy, Portugal, and Navarre by various means. Queen Elizabeth I also received many valuable presents and bequests of jewels.

Mary Queen of Scots's large jewel collection was sold because she left an empty treasury. Elizabeth bought some of them, including a case of pearls, for 12,000 crowns. Mary had been given the pearls by her husband, the Dauphine of France, and by his mother, Catherine de Medici, who was anxious to get back her share. The Spanish ambassador in London investigated and wrote to Catherine in 1568 to tell her she was too late: Elizabeth already had her hands on them.

They are known as the Hanoverian Pearls and are believed to be the finest in Europe, comprising six rows strung like rosary beads and, formerly, 25 loose pearls, some as big as nutmegs. They date from the 14th century, as they were given to Catherine de Medici by her uncle, Pope Clement VII, on her wedding. Other pearls added by Queen Elizabeth I of England created the exceptional collection inherited by James I, who presented them to his daughter, Elizabeth, Queen of Bohemia (Figure 10–4). Eventually, they came into the hands of the House of Hanover and the English Crown Jewels by inheritance.

Sir Thomas Gresham, the merchant and banker who originated the well-known economic law that bad money drives out good, emulated the often told tale of Cleopatra's pearl. He was said to have powdered a pearl worth £15,000 and drunk it in a glass of wine in a toast to Queen Elizabeth during a wager that he could present a more costly dinner than the Spanish ambassador. Elizabeth's portraits usually show her bedecked in pearls. Sir Horace Walpole (1717–1797), the Gothic novelist, once wrote: "A pale Roman nose, a head of hair loaded with crowns and powdered with diamonds, a vast ruff, a vaster fardingale, and a bushel of pearls, are the features by which everyone knows at once the pictures of Queen Elizabeth." Even on her deathbed, she was arrayed with pearls and other gems.

In the British Imperial State Crown are two pearls known as Queen Elizabeth's Ear-rings, a supposition that, according to Lord Twining, originated in *The Times* of January 7, 1911, when the coronation of George V was imminent. He thinks it more likely that they were two of the pearls that belonged to Elizabeth, Queen of Bohemia, just referred to. According to the report, a large quantity of articles had accumulated in the Palace by the time of Victoria's death and among them was found a packet labeled

Fig. 10–4 Elizabeth of Bohemia. In a portrait by Daniel Mytens, Elizabeth wears the great ropes of pearls reckoned to be the finest in Europe. They belonged to Mary, Queen of Scots, and were sold after her execution. They later became known as the Hanoverian Pearls. The picture is in the Royal Collection at St. James's Palace, London. *(Courtesy of the Twining collection; copyright of Her Majesty the Queen.)*

"Queen Elizabeth's Ear-rings." Edward VII ordered them to be hung in the crown. There are certainly four pearls hung from the arches of the crown.

Going back to the coronation of George IV, the Imperial State Crown was refurbished by the Crown Jewelers, who noted that the four pearls suspended from where the arches intersected were badly shaped and colored. Records at the Tower of London indicated that the pearls were of great value, having once been pawned by the Dutch government for £50,000. Nevertheless, the Crown Jewelers sold the worst one for £2 and replaced it by a better one they bought for £5. There is no record of two pearls being replaced at a later date, but that is not surprising if no money was spent on buying them.

## The Moguls: Rulers Who Loved Pearls

European monarchs were not the only rulers who loved pearls. The Moguls, although most associated with diamonds, owned many famous pearls and used them in immense numbers for decoration of clothes and furniture. They were massed in the pillars and canopy of the celebrated Peacock Throne, as well as on the umbrellas adjoining it. The finest pearl, weighing 200 grains, hung from a great balas ruby mounted in the Peacock's breast.

J.-B. Tavernier in *Travels in India* described and illustrated some of the finest pearls (Figure 10-5) he was shown when he visited the Mogul Emperors on several occasions in the 17th century. The greatest of them, according to his account, was the largest and most perfect ever discovered and without the slightest defect. It was bought in 1633 by the King of Persia, Shaista Khan, from an Arab who had received it from the fisheries at Al Katif. Tavernier illustrated it exactly like a pear with slightly concave sides but did not give the weight. His diagram, if life size, suggests it could have been as much as 500 grains.

There are five more diagrams on the same plate in his book. One shows a pear-shaped pearl with convex sides and a dimple at the bottom like the fruit. This was the pearl referred to hung on the Peacock Throne. It hung from the Peacock's neck and rested on its breast. It was the largest pearl Tavernier saw at Aurangzeb's court. The weight was not given but must have been about 200 grains.

A slimmer pearl of much the same outline but without the dimple was sold by Tavernier on his previous journey to Shaista Khan, who was an uncle of the Great Mogul and Governor of Bengal. It was the cause of a dispute Tavernier had with Shaista Khan, which cost him 100,000 rupees, to be related in Chapter Twelve. He recorded its weight as 55 carats (220 grains). It

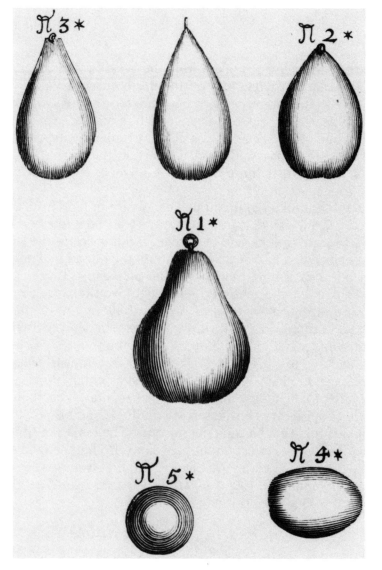

Fig. 10–5 Pearl Drawings. In *Travels in India*, J.-B. Tavernier described and illustrated some of the finest pearls of the Mogul Emperors. The greatest of them (No. 1) was the largest and most perfect ever discovered. Tavernier illustrated it exactly like a pear, with slightly concave sides. No. 2 diagram shows a pear-shaped pearl with convex sides and a dimple at the bottom like the fruit. This pearl was hung on the Peacock Throne. No. 3 is a slimmer pearl of much the same outline but without the dimple. No. 4 pearl was shaped like an olive, even to the flattened end. No. 5 illustrates a perfectly rounded pearl. The unnumbered pearl shows a pear-shaped pearl with slightly convex sides and a stalk at the top. *(Courtesy of The Oxford University Press.)*

was the largest to have been taken from the West to the East, having been found off the Island of Margarita off the north coast of Venezuela, which gave its name to the larger pearl oyster, *pinctada margaritifera.*

Another pearl illustrated was shaped like an olive, even to the flattened end, where the stalk once was. It was originally suspended from the middle of a chain of emeralds and rubies that the Mogul Emperor wore around his neck, and it hung down to his waist. It must have weighed about 125 grains.

A perfectly round pearl illustrated by Tavernier (and from the drawing estimated to have weighed about 110 grains) was, he wrote, the largest and most perfect round one he had ever seen. It belonged to the Great Mogul and, because its equal had never been found, the Mogul had never worn it, preferring to leave it unmounted with other such gems. Tavernier speculated that, if an equal had been found, the Mogul would have acquired it and made the pair into "ear pendants." A sixth drawing on his plate was unnumbered and not described. It showed a pear-shaped pearl with slightly convex sides and what looked like a stalk at the top.

Although the most prized pearls are spherical or nearly so, large pear-shaped ones seem to have been valued almost as much. Pearls occur in an immense variety of shapes, most of them irregular. The shape depends upon where the pearl was formed in the mollusk, and also on the shape of the foreign element that became the nucleus. The length of time of formation has a considerable effect on the size as well. There was an egg-shaped pearl in the French Crown Jewels, the Regent, that weighed 337 grains; another found in Panama in 1906 was 216 grains in weight. So if that seen by Tavernier was 500 grains, it outclassed the rest.

## *The Pearl of the Palatinate*

What must be the strangest of all famous pearls is the Pearl of the Palatinate (Figure 10–6), regarded as the second most valuable gem in the Wittelsbach Treasury of Bavaria. The Palatinates were two regions of Germany that comprised (from 1356) an electorate of the Holy Roman Empire. The pearl is drop-shaped, weighing about 48 grains, and the body is white but the rounded top is black with a good luster suggesting an eye. It was first noted in the Dusseldorf inventory of 1711 as part of the decoration of a box. It is now set in a cup held by three interwoven snakes in a diamond ornament. Wittelsbach has an exceptional number of fine pearls. Fresh water pearls are very occasionally seen with a dark cap.

More than one pearl can be formed in one shell and sometimes at the same time. If they are close to each other, they can join as they become big-

Fig. 10–6 The Pearl of the Palatinate. Possibly the strangest of all famous pearls, it is the second most valuable gem in the Wittelsbach Treasury of Bavaria. The pearl is drop-shaped, weighing 48 grains, and the body is white but the rounded top is black with a good luster, suggesting an eye. It is now set in a cup held by three interwoven snakes in a diamond ornament. *(Courtesy of the Residenz Museum of Munich Collection.)*

ger. One of the most extraordinary of such formations is known as the Southern Cross. It is claimed to be entirely natural, having, as it was found, seven pearls forming the shaft and one on each side, opposite each other, representing the crosspiece of a Roman cross, one pearl down from the top. The pearls are slightly flattened where they join each other and much more flattened at the "back."

The cross was whole when found, according to the boy named Clark who recovered it from an oyster in Baldwin Creek on the northern coast of Western Australia, but when he handed it over to the master pearler, James W. S. Kelly, it had become broken into three pieces. Kelly sold the three pieces for £10 to another pearler named Roy. A man by the name of Craig then bought the pieces for £40 and sold them to a syndicate. At about this time, the cross was reassembled.

It attracted much attention when exhibited at the Colonial and Indian Exhibition in 1886 and won a gold medal for the exhibitor at the Paris Exhibition of 1889. At this time, it was on offer for £10,000. One suggestion was that it should be bought for presentation to Pope Leo XIII on his jubilee in 1889.

That is the public history. According to Taunton, in his book, *Australind: Wanderings in Western Australia and the Malay East* (London 1903), it is a fake. He stated that when Kelly sold it, it was a cluster of eight pearls with only one pearl at one side. What would have been the right arm was missing. A pearl with the same luster, which was good and of suitable size and shape, was obtained at the pearling center of Cossack, which the whole fleet visited. The pearl was fastened into place by diamond cement (used by cutters to cement diamonds onto the ends of sticks when shaping them). The new pearl cost between £10 and £12.

Fine pearls of regular shape, particularly spherical or pear-shaped ones, were the most highly prized of all gems in some oriental countries in the past, particularly in Persia. Their appeal and value became outrageous in ancient Rome, and they remained very popular with Popes in Christian times, as well as with monarchs.

In the French Crown Jewels was a notable collection, much of which was sold in Napoleon Bonaparte's time. Many crowns and other regal artifacts set with hundreds of pearls are in the Treasury at the Kremlin in Moscow. Later Indian princes loved pearls too, not only to wear but to decorate their possessions. The Gaekwar of Baroda had a carpet $10^1/_2$ feet (3.20 meters) long by 6 feet (1.83 meters) wide made entirely of strings of pearls except for an 11-inch (28 centimeters) border—and that was of diamonds. It was not for walking on and was said to have been made to cover Mohammed's tomb, although this is uncertain because the carpet remained in the Gaekwar's treasury.

## Baroque Pearls

Baroque pearls occur in every shape imaginable and are not highly valued unless exceptional, like the Hope Pearl, even if they have a good luster. Jewelers like them only if they can be used to resemble something familiar in a piece of jewelry. For that reason, they became popular during the Art Nouveau period. There are some baroque pearls in jewelry in the Rothschild collection at Waddesdon Manor, Buckinghamshire, now owned by the National Trust (a highlight of this collection is a figure of Pan with a pearl in enameled gold and ivory; Figure 10–7); in Rosenborg Castle, Copenhagen; in The Louvre, Paris; in the Green Vault, Dresden; and in the Imperial Treasury, Vienna.

Baroque pearls form the main parts of jewels representing a dragon, butterfly, cockerel, horse, hippopotamus, lamb, lizard, stag, tortoise, and gondola, as well as mermaids and women's breasts. Wings of birds, bodies of fish, backs of turtles, and petals of flowers are represented mostly by fresh water baroque pearls. Baroques are often much larger than symmetrical pearls, weighing more than an ounce in some instances and in an exceptional case, as with the Hope, about three ounces.

In the Green Vault is a grotesque baroque pearl that was declared to be remarkably like Senor Pepe, the court dwarf of Charles II of Spain. Another dwarf jewel in the same collection has a baroque pearl body studded with diamonds. The dwarf's trousers, sleeves, and hat are of green and black enamel. Over his shoulder hangs a goose partly made of pearl and at his side hangs a baroque pearl in the shape of a bottle. It was made in the reign of King Augustus by the jeweler, Ferbecq. In the same collection, a drunken vintner and his dog are based on a large baroque pearl.

One of the most famous baroque pearls is the major part of the Canning Triton Jewel (Color Plate 5), usually referred to simply as the Canning Jewel, although there is a less well-known baroque pearl pendant, the Canning Siren pendant. Lord Canning was the first Viceroy of India, where he bought the jewel, which portrays a merman or triton. The torso is the pearl and the arms and face are in white enamel with gold hair and beard. The tail is enameled in bright green and set with graduated diamonds and a large carved ruby. The triton holds in his right hand a scimitar, which he flourishes over his head. In his left hand is a green and blue mask of Medusa's head with a ruby in its mouth. Baroque pearls hang from the sides and center.

This pendant is believed to have been made in southern Germany in the late 16th century and to have been a present from one of the Medici Dukes of Tuscany to one of the Mogul Emperors, who added the carved ruby and the central pendant baroque pearl with the cluster of rubies from which it hangs.

After Lord Canning's death, it passed to various relatives and was eventually sold in 1931 at Sotheby's by the Earl of Harewood. It was bought by Mrs. Edward Harkness, who presented it to the Victoria and Albert Museum in West London.

A similar history is accorded the Canning Siren Jewel, in which the

Fig. 10–7 Pan with a Pearl. This figure of Pan with a baroque pearl is set in enameled gold and ivory. It is part of the Rothschild collection now housed at Waddesdon Manor, Buckinghamshire, and owned by the National Trust.

torso of the siren is a baroque pearl with an enameled tail. She looks into a mirror (a portrait — flat — diamond) and combs her hair with a golden comb. An inscription on the back of the tail is initialed *VD*, presumably those of the maker. The piece is thought to be Italian and made about 1580. It could not have been made by the same hand as the Triton Jewel, although this was also once thought to be Italian.

The Siren was probably presented to one of the Mogul Emperors by the same Medici. After the Indian Mutiny (1857–1858), it was seized with other articles from the treasury of the King of Oudh. Lord Canning bought it from the Indian government. It was last sold at Sotheby's in London in 1970 for £40,000 to an American collector.

Much more recent, dating from the beginning of the present century, is

Fig. 10–8 Dragsted Snake Charmer Pearl. A female snake charmer nearly four inches high, based on a particularly lovely baroque pearl that forms the body from shoulders to knees. The Danish Court Jeweler, Alfred Dragsted, made it and completed the other parts of the body with gold. *(Courtesy of A. Dragsted, Royal Danish Court Jewellers, Copenhagen.)*

a female snake charmer (Figure 10–8) nearly four inches (10 centimeters high) based on a particularly long baroque pearl that forms the body from shoulders to knees. The Danish Court Jeweler, Alfred Dragsted, made it and completed the other parts of the body with gold. The snake charmer wears gem-set jewelry and charms a snake, twined around her body, with a flute.

## The Armada Pearls

Strangest of the odd-shaped pearls are four known as the O'Donnell Pearls or Armada Pearls. They are of unusual shape but regular and not baroque. Each is a small cone-shaped mother-of-pearl shell with a blister pearl inside it. The largest is about an inch (2.5 centimeters) in diameter and the smallest about three-quarters of an inch (2 centimeters). The pearls are beautifully irridescent, and the total weight is 139.93 grains.

The really curious fact about the pearls is that their formation is identical to that of a mollusk of the oyster family *Pteria phalaenocea*, which is believed to have been extinct for 35 million years. Yet the pearls are not fossilized. Some of the specialists who have examined them say they must have been from a mollusk that lived within historical times. There was a report in 1957 of a living mollusk of another specie being dredged up from about 11,000 feet (3,600 meters) under the ocean off the coast of Mexico. It was previously believed to have been extinct for 300 to 400 million years. So the pearls may have come from a mollusk that was not only living in the last few hundred years, but was in abundance because a very large number would presumably have been needed to find four matching pearls.

Hugh Roe O'Donnell was an Irishman who ruled Donegal and rebelled against Queen Elizabeth I. Captured as a boy on the Queen's orders, he was held in Dublin Castle jail, from which he escaped to raise an army that stormed castles built by the English while slaughtering everyone who could not speak Gaelic. He sought help from Philip of Spain, and when the Spanish Armada was wrecked in 1588, O'Donnell succored the survivors. The Armada Pearls were a gift of gratitude to Hugh the Red, as he was called, from the Spanish King.

When news of Hugh's aid to the Spanish came to the Queen's attention, she sent an army of 20,000 to Ireland, which routed the Irish insurgents. Hugh the Red fled to Spain in 1603, where he died. Before leaving Ireland, he handed the pearls to his heir, who lived on the lonely island of Arranmore off the northwest coast. Eventually, they came into the possession of Mary O'Donnell, who married an Englishman, Ernest Chapman, after he had rescued her from a vitriolic argument on Clapham Common about Ireland.

In 1924, Chapman took the Armada Pearls to the Empire Exhibition in Wembley to try to find out something about them. An expert there recognized that they were unique and was staggered to hear that Chapman had brought them loose in his pocket. He said they should be protected, kept in a safe place, and insured. Later, they were seen by Dr. A. Morley Davis, a paleontologist at the Imperial College of Science in London, who identified their prehistoric structure.

Ernest Chapman kept the Armada Pearls in a safe deposit and would not allow them to be shown until 1958, a few years before his death, when the Duke of Tetuan, whose family name was O'Donnell, came especially from Spain to see them at a private viewing, to which the author was also invited.

Dr. L. R. Cox, senior principal scientific officer of the Department of Geology, British Museum, took the opportunity of examining them and decided that they belonged to the *Ostrea vesiculosa* family of oysters, which was confined to the Cretaceous system. Ernest Chapman calculated that, up to this viewing, only about 100 people had seen the Armada Pearls in the previous 300 years.

## *Pearling Today*

River pearls have been mentioned several times, particularly in connection with baroque shapes. The greatest fresh water pearling area is in the Mississippi Valley in the United States, which was only fully exploited from the last decade of the 19th century. Pearls are found in large mussels in many Scottish rivers, including the Tay, Spey, Dorn, Don, Leith, South Est, Islay, Dee, Garn, and Forth. They were fished in later years by using a glass-bottomed drum to see into the water. The mussels do not attach themselves to rocks like the sea water variety but protrude a part of their bodies like a tongue to push themselves along the riverbed. There was a Scottish pearl in the Hope collection, milky-blue in color, tinged with pink, and weighing 34.75 grains.

There is only one professional Scottish pearl fisher left as of the 1980s, Bill Abernethy, although Scottish pearls were known all over Europe in the 12th century. In 1967, he found the finest large Scottish pearl in memory in a backwater of the River Tay near Stanley. It was bought by Alastair and Jimmy Cairncross, the Perth jewelers, who still sell Scottish pearls. It has a fine orient with a trace of violet in the color and is of perfect shape, weighing 44$^1/_2$ grains, so that it is about half an inch in diameter. Its true name is the Abernethy Pearl (Figure 10–9), but the press has labeled it "Wee Willie" since the Cairncross brothers while on a business trip sent a postcard to Perth to ensure that " 'Wee Willie' had had his daily bath." The pearl was wiped with a damp chamois every evening before being put in the strongroom to preserve its luster.

Wales was also a source of river pearls in earlier days, and there is one from the Conway fisheries in the British Crown Jewels. Sir Richard Wynne of Gwydir presented it to Catherine of Braganza, wife of Charles II, to whom he was chamberlain. In his work, *The Faerie Queene* (1590), Spencer wrote;

Conway, which out of his streame doth send
Plenty of pearles to deck his dames withal.

Dames still like to be bedecked with them, but now the pearls are usually cultured.

The Conway Pearl, found in the River Conway in Wales, was mounted in the Imperial State Crown but has not been identified among the pearls in the crown made in 1953 for Queen Elizabeth II.

North America has a number of sources of fresh water pearls, the most productive being in the Mississippi Valley. Pearls were recovered there by the Indians long before the Europeans even knew the continent existed to judge by the huge quantities found in burial mounds. Some were as much as three-quarters of an inch (2 centimeters) in diameter, although damaged and partly decomposed. The Mississippi now mainly provides beads of pearl shell (mother-of-pearl) for the cultured pearl industry in the East.

The biggest fresh water pearl did not come from this area, however, but from the northern part of New Jersey. A shoemaker named David Howell, who lived just outside Paterson, used to fish in North Brook for mussels

Fig. 10–9 The Abernethy Pearl. Bill Abernethy, the only professional Scottish pearl fisher, found the finest large Scottish pearl in living memory in a backwater of the River Tay near Stanley, in 1967. The Abernethy Pearl has a fine orient with a trace of violet in the color and is of perfect shape, weighs 44$^1/_2$ grains, and measures about half an inch in diameter. *(Courtesy of Cairncross Ltd., Goldsmiths, Perth, Scotland.)*

to eat. Having supper in the spring of 1857, he found on his plate amid a pile of mussels a huge pearl that turned out to weigh about 400 grains. Alas, it had been spoiled by being fried in grease. Unlike Cleopatra's, his expensive meal was involuntary.

Several of his neighbors began to fish the brook for mussels, and within a few days, a carpenter, Jacob Quakenbush, had discovered a magnificent pink pearl of excellent shape weighing 93 grains. It was bought by Charles T. Tiffany, who commented, "Here this man finds a pearl within seventeen miles of our business. What if thousands of them should be found and many, perhaps, finer than this." Tiffany's of New York could not find a buyer in the United States and passed it on to their French house. A dealer took it and sold it to the Empress Eugenie, after whom it was named the Queen Pearl.

In a few years, the small New Jersey stream had not only been depleted of pearls but of nearly all the mussels that had once lived in it.

> Let us not be too particular; it is better to have an old second-hand diamond than none at all.
>
> *Mark Twain (1835–1810)*

---

*Chapter Eleven*

# Legends in the Making

IT is extraordinary that there should be a gap of 2,111 carats between the biggest diamond crystal ever found and the next biggest. Indeed, the Cullinan was much heavier than the next *three* largest. About a century before the Cullinan was unearthed, another stone called the Braganza and weighing 1680 carats in the rough was thought to be the biggest. It was first reported by John Mawe, a London diamond cutter and dealer, in his book *Travels in Brazil* (1812).

Mawe did not see the Braganza because it had been discovered about twelve years before his visit and had passed into the private possession of the Prince Regent of Portugal. He related that three men convicted of serious crimes were banished into the interior of Brazil and forbidden to approach any civilization on pains of perpetual imprisonment. Braving cannibals and wild beasts, they determined to seek wealth in the form of gold to achieve their freedom.

While panning in a rivulet called the Abaeté, to the north of the Rio Plata, they found what they thought was a diamond weighing about an ounce. Elated by their discovery but in fear of what their reception in civilization might be (not only because of their banishment but also because of the rigorous diamond laws), they approached a clergyman for advice. He accompanied them to Villa Rica and obtained access to the governor.

Mawe wrote: "They threw themselves at his feet and delivered to him the invaluable gem on which their hopes rested, relating all the circumstances connected with it. The governor, astonished at its magnitude, could not trust the evidence of his senses, but called the officers of the establishment to decide whether it was a diamond, who set the matter beyond doubt."

The governor suspended the sentences on the men, and the stone was sent to Rio de Janeiro and thence by frigate to Lisbon. Don Juan VI, who had been appointed Regent in 1799, confirmed the pardon of the three outcasts and also "bestowed some preferment on the holy father" who had accompanied the stone. Rome Delisle made a preposterous valuation of 300 million pounds sterling for the Braganza, as it was named, and another jeweler valued it at £5,644,000.

There is one report that Don Juan VI had a hole drilled in the uncut stone and wore it suspended around his neck on special occasions and another report that Mawe really considered it to have been a "nova mina" or white topaz. It is unlikely that Mawe made such a comment, not having examined it. However, it is most likely to have been a white topaz because many are found in Brazil. Some are of truncated crystal form that could have been mistaken for octahedral diamond crystals in the days when knowledge of crystals was sparse. The Portuguese Treasury would not exhibit the Braganza, being anxious, according to some contemporary writers, that it should be regarded as a genuine diamond.

E. W. Streeter made the interesting suggestion in one edition of his book, *The Great Diamonds of the World* (London, 1882), that there was a large uncut aquamarine of 1,750 carats among the Portuguese Crown Jewels, sufficiently close to the weight of the Braganza for the two stones to be identical. The catalog stated that the stone belonged to Don Miguel.

The Braganza was without doubt the diamond that never was.

## The Deepdene Mystery

A more modern mystery concerns the Deepdene Diamond, which was on show at the Museum of the Philadelphia Academy of Sciences some years ago. Described as a 104.88-carat cushion-cut golden yellow diamond that had belonged to Cary W. Bok of the family that founded Curtis Publications, it was named after his wife's family estate. Harry Winston of New York bought it about 1954 and sold it to a London firm in 1960. It was bought by a collector in Frankfurt, West Germany.

On May 21, 1971, it was offered for sale by Christies in Geneva, where it was described as golden yellow in color, cushion cut, and weighing 104.52 carats. It was accompanied by a certificate guaranteeing its natural color and its purity as VVS1, meaning that it was almost flawless when examined by an expert using a corrected hand lens with ten times magnification. There are two tiny inclusions in it near the girdle (the edge). Its natural color was guaranteed by a German gemological institute and a department of the University of Mainz.

Before the sale, the auctioneers were warned by the distinguished gemologist, Dr. Edward Gubelin of Geneva, that the diamond had been artificially colored. He had been able to examine it at an earlier date in his own laboratory. Christies conferred with the German authorities, and the sale was allowed to go ahead with the recommendation that the stone should be examined by a fourth laboratory. It was bought by the well-known jewelers, Van Cleef and Arpels, for £190,000. They submitted it to the Gem Testing Laboratory in London, where it was examined by the director, Basil Anderson, pioneer of the modern science of gem testing.

Artificial yellow or brown is induced in a diamond by bombardment with neutrons, which turns it green, then by "soaking" or annealing at a certain temperature to achieve the final color. Anderson confirmed by spectrum analysis that the stone had been artificially colored. The buyers returned it and claimed their money back.

It is said that Harry Winston did not sell the stone as the Deepdene, but there is no doubt that it is. Originally, it was said to have an inclusion like a Maltese cross, but this is, in fact, an optical illusion, seen also in certain other stones, such as the Tiffany and the Red Cross (which is yellow, despite its name, and is a 205-carat square-cut South African stone presented in 1918 at the end of the First World War by the London Diamond Syndicate to the British Red Cross Society and the Order of St. John of Jerusalem. It was sold at auction by Christies to raise funds for the Red Cross.)

The only reason for treating such a valuable stone as the Deepdene would be to enhance its color. As previously pointed out, descriptions of colored stones are notoriously variable because people have different ideas of hues and their descriptions and there is always a temptation to glamorize the quality or color of a valuable stone, especially if it is for sale.

## The Past and the Present Intermingle

In diamonds, the ancient and the present are sometime inextricably intermingled. The Koh-i-Noor, ruined in archaeological terms by the decision to recut it, is much less interesting as a stone for this reason than the Orloff, although the Koh-i-Noor's history is more extraordinary. Recutting and artificial coloration of a diamond are irreversible. Submitting it to nuclear irradiation changes the atomic structure. When a diamond is artificially colored blue, however, the depth of color is very thin because electrons used in the process are charged and very light and cannot penetrate. Consequently, the blue "skin" can be polished off. After bombardment,

Fig. 11–1 The Briolette. This 90.38 carat diamond, shown here approximately life-size, is known as the Briolette of India. It is said to have belonged to Eleanor of Aquitaine eight centuries ago and to have formed part of a ransom for her son, Richard the Lionheart. *(Courtesy of De Beers Consolidated Mines.)*

some other gems, such as yellow sapphire, which turns to a topaz color, pink kunzite, which turns green, and pink beryl, which turns to sapphire blue (called Maxixe type), revert to their original colors in strong sunlight.

By tradition, the Koh-i-Noor is not the diamond with the oldest history. That is accorded to the Briolette of India (Figure 11–1), although there is no strong evidence to support it. A briolette is bead-shaped, although not drilled, and faceted all over. The Briolette must have been recut at some time in its history because the Indians did not originally facet stones all over. The oldest known owner of this 90.38-carat diamond was supposed to have been Eleanor of Aquitaine (c. 1122–1204), who may have obtained it on the Second Crusade (1146–1149) while in Asia Minor with her husband, Louis VII of France.

After her divorce from Louis, she married Henry II of England in 1152. According to legend, she gave the diamond to her son Richard Coeur de

Lion when he left for the Third Crusade (1190–1192), at the end of which he was imprisoned and held for ransom by the Emperor of Austria. It is surmised that the diamond bought his release.

The first authentic record of it is in the 16th century, when it was given by Henry II of France (1519–1559) to his mistress, Diane de Poitiers, because it appears in several portraits of her. Then it vanished once more, this time for four centuries, until 1950, when an Indian maharajah sold it to Harry Winston. He resold it and bought it back ten years later to sell it once more in Europe in 1971.

## Discoveries the World Over

All the long histories and most of the legends center on diamonds from India. Stories from the Brazilian mines, which supplied most of the stones from the 1730s, are relatively few. Yet many stories have come from the South African fields, which only started producing from the 1870s; perhaps because the finds were so huge by comparison that, in a few years, the volume of diamonds from them exceeded that of all diamonds found over the past three centuries. The Russian fields started producing in the 1950s and are now rivaling those in South Africa and Botswana. The biggest fields of all spread through the Congo and Angola, but they produce nearly all industrial stones.

It is odd that the Brazilian discoveries occurred by chance—because gold miners used "pretty pebbles" that turned up occasionally in their washing pans and used them for counters when playing cards—when the Indian mines were becoming exhausted. The first South African diamond digging on the banks of the Vaal River were also the result of a chance find and occurred as the Brazilian mines were becoming exhausted. The Russian fields, on the edge of the Artic Circle in Yakutia, Siberia, were, on the other hand, the result of a long and intensive search.

Diamonds were discovered in Australia in small quantities in the 1890s, but in the 1970s, vast deposits were found near Lake Argyle in the mountains at the northernmost tip of Western Australia. When the mines are in full production, the Ashton Joint Venture (the mining company) will supply about 20 million carats of lower quality gem diamonds every year. It was an extraordinary cast of fate that the area where the find was made was called Kimberley after the Secretary of State for the Colonies, whose name was also given to the greatest diamond producing area of South Africa.

The first big diamond from South Africa was seen lying on the surface and was picked up about 1868 on the northern bank of the Orange River by

Fig. 11–2 Swartboy. The first big diamond from South Africa was seen lying on the surface and was picked up about 1868 by a shepherd known as Swartboy. His find was eventually named the Star of South Africa. *(Courtesy of De Beers Consolidated Mines.)*

a shepherd boy known as Swartboy (Figure 11–2). He worked for a farmer on the southern bank and kept his find a secret because he was a subject of Captain Waterboer, ruler of West Griqualand on the northern bank, and was afraid it might be confiscated.

He did, however, tell his family, and it was decided to trust a friend, Willem Piet, to sell it to Schalk van Niekerk (Figure 11–3), part owner of another farm on the Orange River. Van Niekerk had been involved with the sale of the first authenticated diamond found in the country, the $21\frac{1}{4}$-carat Eureka, (Figure 11–4), which had been picked up as a plaything by a boy called Erasmus Jacobs (Figure 11–5), about 1867. Remembering a picture in a book of precious stones of a rough diamond, Van Niekerk thought this might be one. Although he was laughed at for this ludicrous idea, the stone was sent to Dr. Atherstone of Grahamstown, who checked its specific gravity and hardness and pronounced it truly to be a diamond.

Van Niekerk paid 500 sheep, ten head of cattle, and one horse for Swartboy's stone, eventually named the Star of South Africa (Figure 11–6). He was offered £11,000 for it by James Wykeham, a Justice of the Peace and Deputy Sheriff, but instead he sold it to two dealers, the Lilienfeld brothers, for £11,200. At this, Wykeham immediately sought and obtained an injunction to restrain the Lilienfelds from reselling it on the grounds that it had been found on Captain Waterboer's land and no authority had been given to sell it.

The Lilienfelds tried to get Swartboy to declare that it had been found

Fig. 11–3 Schalk van Niekerk *(left)* and John Robert O'Reilly. Van Niekerk, who recognized the pebble found by Swartboy as a diamond, entrusted it to O'Reilly *(right),* who had it authenticated and sold. Van Niekerk here is holding the Star of South Africa. *(Courtesy of De Beers Consolidated Mines.*

Fig. 11–4 The Eureka Diamond. Weighing 10.73 carats, it is said to be the first diamond ever discovered in South Africa. Although he was laughed at for thinking the stone might be a diamond, Schalk van Niekerk sent it to Dr. Atherstone of Grahamstown, who checked its specific gravity and hardness and pronounced it truly to be a diamond. *(Courtesy of De Beers Consolidated Mines.)*

on Van Niekerk's farm, the De Kalk, but he stuck to his first story. Swartboy was in effect kidnapped twice by the defending side to persuade him to change his story. One letter sent to the defendants suggested that they "get possession of Swartboy and bring him 'kindly' over to your side or else 'fix' a 50 lb. Wgt to his neck and drop him in a fish Pond."

When the case came before the Supreme Court in Cape Town, the ap-

Fig. 11–5 Erasmus Jacobs. At the age of 15, Jacobs found the first authenticated diamond in South Africa, probably in 1867. It became known as the Eureka. *(Courtesy of De Beers Consolidated Mines.)*

plication was refused. The Lilienfelds sold the stone to Louis Hond, an Amsterdam diamond dealer who had been advising them, and it was sent to London on MV (merchant vessel) *Celt* after being exhibited in Port Elizabeth and Cape Town. In London, after it had been cut and polished into a three-sided oval of the first water, which reduced its weight to 47.75 carats, it was sold to the Countess of Dudley for £30,000. She had it mounted in a hair ornament surrounded by 95 smaller diamonds. It was then named the Dudley Diamond but is now usually called the Star of South Africa.

In 1974, it turned up in a Christies sale in Geneva, where it was sold for 1.6 million Swiss francs, about £225,000 at the time (or about £420,000 as of 1984).

An often told story of the Star of South Africa is that it was placed on the table of Parliament in South Africa when the Colonial Secretary declared, "This diamond, gentlemen, is the rock on which the future of South Africa will be built." It is a dramatic story, but, in fact, the diamond had already been sent to London by the time Parliament was convened in 1869.

## New Surprises

Some diamonds are still being found that will be added to the history books. The latest was the Premier Rose from the mine (the Premier) that is obviously still full of surprises even after having provided the Cullinan.

Fig. 11–6 The Star of South Africa Diamond. Found by the shepherd Swartboy, this diamond earned him quite a reward. In 1974, it turned up in a Christie's sale in Geneva, where it was sold for 1.6 million Swiss francs, about £225,000 at the time (or about £420,000 as of 1984). *Courtesy of De Beers Consolidated Mines.)*

(One surprise it sprung on geologists in recent years was an unsuspected new diamond area under a gabbro sill — a large flat ledge of rock projecting into the mine.)

The Premier Rose, recovered in April 1977, weighed 353.9 carats and was of superb quality in whiteness and purity. When kimberlite rock, what miners call "blue ground," is blasted and brought to the surface, it passes through crushers to break it and release any diamonds it might contain.

There are about ten million parts of rock to one of diamond. For economic reasons, the crushers reduce the rock to a maximum size of about an inch (2.5 centimeters), so any diamonds larger than that will also be crushed. The conveyor belts are, therefore, manned by inspectors who look out for any large diamonds; an inspector can spend his working life on a belt and not find one. In this case, the diamond was picked off the belt just before it reached the jaws of the first crusher.

The stone was named after Rose Mouw, wife of the cutter and polisher who bought the stone and whose whole family, including his wife, is involved in the business. It was converted into the Big Rose of 137.02 carats, the Little Rose of 31.48 carats, and the Baby Rose of 2.11 carats.

The Mouws came originally from Antwerp, the Belgian diamond cutting center (now the biggest in the world), then went to Holland, whence they had to flee from the Nazis during the war first to France and then on to Greece and Turkey. They settled in Israel while a big cutting and polishing industry was being developed there and finally set themselves up in Johannesburg.

Even more of a surprise to the diamond trade was the appearance in March 1981 at Abu Dhabi, in the United Arab Emirates, of a pear-shaped diamond of 170.49 carats, the Star of Peace, not recorded in the standard lists. It was sold by a woman, Mrs. Salee-Amina Muhammed, on behalf of its Swiss owner, Manfredo Horowitz, for a reported $12 million. It had been found in Central Africa in 1976, when it weighed about 500 carats in the rough. It ranks as probably the nineteenth biggest rough ever found because the weight is not exactly known; it also ranks as the thirteenth biggest polished diamond. According to Mrs. Salee-Amina, it had taken three years to get it cut with perfect symmetry and clarity.

It is not often that owners of very valuable stones are named unless they are monarchs and relatively invulnerable to robbers. An exception is when a stone is bought by a diamond merchant. One such is the Idol's Eye (Figure 11–7), of which the owner was Laurence Graff of Graff Diamonds, London, until he sold it in 1982.

The Idol's Eye is of excellent purity, and its color has been described as "a dazzling light blue tint." It is roughly triangular in shape with very rounded sides, which are not regular. It weighs 70.20 carats.

Found in the diamond mines in the Golconda area of India not long after 1600, the Idol's Eye became the property of the Persian Prince Rahab. He owed money to the East India Company, who took the stone in settlement. For the next three centuries, nothing was heard of it until, in 1906, it was in the possession of Sultan Abdul Hamid II of Turkey, set as an eye in

Fig. 11–7 The Idol's Eye. A stone of excellent purity; its color has been described as "a dazzling light blue tint." It is roughly triangular in shape with very rounded but irregular sides. It weighs 70.20 carats. *(Courtesy of Graff Diamonds Ltd., London.)*

an idol in the sacred temple of Benghazi (presumably not the Benghazi in Libya).

One story now tells us that Hamid's predecessor had abducted the beautiful Princess Rasheetah from under the nose of her lover and that the diamond was the ransom paid for her return. Another story is that the Sultan feared for his throne and schemed with his minister, the Grand Azize, to smuggle certain of his gems, including the French Blue Diamond, the

Star of the East (both of which later belonged to the Hope family), and the Idol's Eye, into France. However, the Grand Azize had other ideas and planned to sell them to feather his own nest. He engaged a young Turk to take the jewels to France. But this young man was not to be trusted, either. On the train to Paris, he hid the gems and shot himself in the cheek to feign a robbery to deceive the Grand Azize. He recovered the gems later and sold them.

Whatever the truth, the Idol's Eye was later in the possession of a Spanish nobleman, who kept it for some years in a London bank. In 1947, Harry Winston bought it and sold it to Mrs. Bonfils Stanton, daughter of the *Denver Post* publisher, who had it mounted as a pendant from a diamond necklace. After her death, it went in 1962 to Harry Levinson, a Chicago jeweler, who insured it for a million dollars with Lloyds of London. In 1970, Laurence Graff bought it for his collection, but he sold it in 1982.

## Engraving Gems: A Craft of Antiquity

Another stone believed to have represented an eye is the Akbar Shah Diamond, which also has the distinction of having been engraved (Figure 11–8). Engraving and carving gems is a craft of antiquity, and the story of the historic engraved Timur Ruby has been told in Chapter Eight. Engraving a diamond is infinitely more difficult than engraving a ruby, hard as that is; yet diamond, by far the hardest substance known to man, was engraved in the early 17th century and possibly earlier.

Akbar Shah was the grandfather of Shah Jahan, who had the Peacock Throne constructed. The diamond is supposed to have been one eye of the Peacock. Shah Jahan had two inscriptions engraved on it:

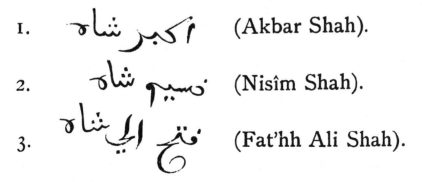

1. (Akbar Shah).

2. (Nisîm Shah).

3. (Fat'hh Ali Shah).

Fig. 11–8 Engravings on the Akbar Shah Diamond. Engraving and carving gems is a craft of antiquity. Diamond, by far the hardest substance known to man, was engraved in the early 17th century and possibly earlier.

Shah Akbar, Shah of the World 1028 A.H. (1618 A.D.)
To the Lord of Two Worlds, Shah Jahan 1039 A.H. (1629 A.D.)

Shah Jahan presumably had the diamond inscribed in 1618 because Akbar Shah died in 1605.

The diamond was carried off to Persia by Nadir Shah, and it virtually vanished until 1866, when it was recognized in Constantinople by its inscriptions — but it was then being called the Shepherd Stone. No one knows how it got to Turkey. It weighed 116 old carats and was bought by a London merchant named George Blogg.

Alas for history, Blogg was as insensitive as his name might suggest, and he had it recut to drop shape, which removed the historic inscriptions. Fortunately, a copy of the inscriptions was made. The diamond was sold by Blogg to the Gaekwar of Baroda in 1867, and its present whereabouts are unknown.

Another celebrated engraved diamond is the Jahangir (Figure 11–9),

Fig. 11–9 The Jahangir Diamond. Another celebrated engraved diamond, it still bears the inscription in Persian. The top inscription can be translated as: Jahangir 1021 (1612 A.D.). The lower inscription reads: Shah Jahan son of Jahangir Shah 1043 (1631 A.D.).

which is supposed to have hung from the beak of the Peacock in the Peacock Throne. This still bears its inscriptions in Persian, the literary language of the Mogul court. The top inscription can be translated as:

Jahangir 1021 (1612 A.D.).

It is the older and is partly obscured by a partially drilled hole, which must, therefore, have been made later. The lower inscription is:

Shah Jahan son of Jahangir Shah 1043 (1631 A.D.)

The diamond was in the possession of the Maharajahs of Burdwan for many generations until one of them, in 1954, decided to sell it. At Christies auction rooms, Stavros Niarchos, the Greek shipowner, successfully bid £13,000 for it. The Maharajah was not so fortunate. The Indian government of the time fined him the same amount as he had received for exporting it illegally.

It was sold again in 1957 by Sothebys in London to C. Patel, an Indian businessman in the Middle East, but for some reason it only fetched £14,000, although at least £20,000 had been forecast.

Still another engraved diamond, the Shah, was probably that suspended in front of the peacock, as related by J.-B. Tavernier when he was at the court of Aurangzeb. It is bar-shaped and believed to have weighed 95 carats in the rough. It was what cutters call a "lasque" and was left much the same shape when cut, with natural cleavage faces (where the stone had been split) so that the loss of weight was very small, indeed, as its present weight is 88.70 carats. It has a yellowish tint and is thought to have been found in the second half of the 16th century.

The engraving, on two cleavage faces and a curved face at the top, is most beautifully executed, the Persian script being formalized into panels. The translations are:

Bourhan Nizam Shah 1000 (1591 A.D.)
Son of Jahangir Shah — Jahan Shah 1051 (1641 A.D.)
Fat'hh Ali Shah (1842 A.D.)

The first named was the ruler of the Indian province of Achmednager, and Shah Jahan presumably obtained the stone from him in some way. The last name is that of a shah of Persia, so the stone must have been with the loot from Delhi. There is a tiny furrow cut around the stone near the top under the top inscription, which strongly suggests it took a wire with a loop for suspension from the throne.

The Shah Diamond's special claim to fame is that it averted war between Russia and Persia. Some rich territory in northern Persia was ceded to Russia under the Treaty of Turkomanchai in 1829, and, as a result, a mob stormed the Russian Embassy in Teheran, killing the young ambassador, Alexander Griboyedoff. Frightened by the thought of Russian revenge by invasion, the Persian government sent the diamond as a gift of appeasement to Czar Nicholas I, who added it to the Crown Jewels. A less romantic story is that it was presented to the Czar from the Persian Crown Jewels by Abbas Mirza when he visited St. Petersburg in 1843.

In August 1914, the Shah Diamond was sent from St. Petersburg to Moscow for safekeeping; when the strongboxes were opened in 1922 by the revolutionary government, the contents, including the Shah, were handed over to the Diamond Fund in the Kremlin, where it still remains.

These three diamonds — the Akbar Shah, the Jahangir, and the Shah — are the only three diamonds engraved by the Indians known still to exist, and one of those has been "vandalized" by the insensitive Blogg.

*I hope, Sire, that these exact and faithful accounts which I have written, since my return, from the notes which I have collected, will not be less useful to my country than the valuable articles of merchandise which I had brought back from my travels.*
*J.B. Tavernier, in the dedication to King Louis XIV in his book of 1676, Travels in India.*

---

*Chapter Twelve*

# Dealers and Collectors of Great Gems

SEVERAL names recur so many times in the history of legendary gems that they are well worth looking at in their own right. One is a thing, the Peacock Throne of the Mogul Emperors of India. Others are people, and the most outstanding of these as a contributor to our knowledge was the French jeweler and traveler, Jean-Baptiste Tavernier (Figure 12–1). No history of early Indian gems, diamonds in particular, is possible without referring to Tavernier's writings. Fortunately, he was a meticulous recorder of information about the celebrated stones he was able to see, handle, and deal in.

This remarkable man's books about his travels, the first written when he was 70 years old, showed such acuteness of observation that they give a vivid impression of 17th century life in the East as well as providing a wealth of facts. Tavernier's writing was despised by contemporary professional writers because he was literal and not literary, not conforming to the philosophical speculations that were the fashion. Voltaire was one of those who wrote disparagingly of him; but Tavernier's books were very popular in his own time, and his success as an amateur was probably the thorn in the side of the establishment.

Tavernier realized that his work was unique and ended the description of his visits to the Indian diamond mines by a comment that he had written down everything he had been able to discover with his own eyes and if anyone else had written or spoken of them before he had, the information could only have come from reports he had written before publication of his book.

Fig. 12–1 Jean-Baptiste Tavernier. Although he was not trained in the commerce of diamonds or other gems, Tavernier became a merchant by having a great interest in them and by buying and selling. *(Courtesy of The Oxford University Press.)*

Fig. 12–2 The Golconda Mine. The State of Golconda by the Kristna River was the site of the Kollur Mines in India. Tavernier's descriptions of these mines are found in his famous book *Travels in India*, which was in two volumes. *(Courtesy of the Gemological Institute of America.)*

He was obviously unaware that a man named William Methold (or Metwold), with Andreas Socery and Adolf Thomason, had visited some of the Indian mines about 1622. Methold described them as being "at the front of a great mountayne, not far from a river called Christena." His description coincides with Tavernier's of the Kollur mines in the state of Golconda (Figure 12–2) by the Kristna River. Even before then, about 1579, Caesar Fredericke had probably visited the Ramalakota mines.

Jean-Baptiste Tavernier was born in 1605 in Paris, to which city his father had fled with two brothers some thirty years earlier from Antwerp to avoid being persecuted for their Protestant beliefs. The boy became a compulsive traveler at the early age of fifteen years and by the age of twenty-two, had visited most of Europe, including France, England, Holland, Germany, Switzerland, Hungary, Italy, and, a little later, Poland, learning much of the languages as he did so. His first visit outside France was to England, when James I was on the throne, thence to Antwerp ("my father's native land") and Amsterdam, where he was able to meet many strangers who came there from all parts of the world. Perhaps those two cities gave him his first interest in the diamond trade.

Thereafter, Tavernier made long journeys to the Middle East and Far East for the rest of his life. It seems he was not trained in the commerce of diamonds or other gems but became a merchant in the usual way, still valid today, by having a great interest in them and by buying and selling. That may be another reason why his efforts at writing were denigrated by the intellectuals, who despised anything to do with trade, although their very existence in society depended upon it.

As an international merchant, Tavernier would have found it convenient to deal in portable articles of high value in order to make enough profit to pay for his travels — in modern business parlance, articles of low turnover and high margin. Nothing fitted that category better than gems.

Another interesting question is, how did he made the acquaintance of people wealthy enough to become his potential customers? That is more readily answered. One of his uncles, Melchoir Tavernier, was an engraver and printer who had become famous for his skills in France and had been appointed to work for the King. Again, Tavernier's brother, also named Melchoir, after his uncle, had followed the craft of engraving and had become a cartographer of high repute with some distinguished and wealthy clients. This concern with maps as well as the circle of learned men with whom his father apparently enjoyed discussions may also have influenced the young Jean-Baptiste.

He undertook his first journey to the East at the beginning of 1631, mainly to visit Persia via Alexandria. He bought some articles of turquoise for trading and returned to France via Aleppo, Alexandria, and Malta in 1633. For his second voyage late in 1638, Tavernier was much better equipped with the trappings of a merchant and took with him his brother, Daniel, as well as a young artist and a surgeon.

After sailing through the Mediterranean to Alexandretta, the party continued by caravan to Basra, Shiraz, and Ispahan, where they visited Shah Safavi. They seem to have remained in this area for about a year before continuing to Dacca and Agra in India during the time of Shah Jahan. Surat and Goa were the next places visited, and Tavernier set out from here to Golconda to learn about the diamond trade there and perhaps to make his first visit to the mines. He returned in 1642 or early 1643.

His third journey started at the end of 1643 on the same route with the intention of reaching Golconda again but this time to use it as a base to visit the diamond mines at Raolconda (Ramalakota, 18 miles south of Karnul) and Coulour (Kollur on the River Kristna), which was then a seven days' journey to the southeast. Tavernier may have visited other diggings. On the return journey, the ship was nearly wrecked during a storm at night when seven anchors were lost. They put into Ceylon before continuing to Batavia.

## Dealings with the Dutch

Tavernier did business with princes and also on commission for other clients, among whom were various Dutch officials. His story of one of these commissions, with an M. Constant, who had become a close friend, gives a good idea of the problems of a gem dealer of the time.

Before the English East India Company moved into Bombay, which came into the possession of the Crown as part of the dowry of the Portuguese Catherine of Braganza when she married Charles II, they controlled their offices on the Malabar coast from Surat, where they had originally established a factory in 1611 under a Captain Best. The Great Mogul (all Mogul rulers of India were called "Great") kept an officer in Surat, who was known as his Admiral. The Admiral lived in a castle, and one of his duties was to redeem the Mogul's letters of credit. Here Constant provided Tavernier with a letter of credit to be exchanged in Golconda. It was intended to provide enough cash to buy a parcel of diamond and pay Tavernier his commission.

Constant had left for Batavia by the time Tavernier returned, so the Frenchman left the parcel of stones with a friend of Constant's at the English factory then set out for Batavia himself. On arrival, he was greeted by a member of the Town Council and three other men. Several meetings followed when they disclosed to Tavernier that Constant had married the widow of the general who had been in charge. The delayed information made Tavernier suspicious, and he guessed that they were trying to find out whether or not he had the diamonds on him, so he told them the truth—that they were in Surat.

Early the next morning, he was summoned to appear before the Town Council at 11 a.m. for a hearing before the Avocat Fiscal, who alleged that Constant must have defrauded the Dutch trading company by whom he was employed, otherwise, he could not have afforded 16,000 rupees out of his salary. Tavernier could not restrain himself from laughing and pointed out that there was scarcely a servant of the company who had held M. Constant's office (a Commander), and enjoyed the opportunity of trading who had made less than 100,000 ecus (more than a quarter of a million pounds today).

In his account of the encounter, he went on to explain the many ways in which Commanders could make more than the amount mentioned in a year by trading in spices, silks, diamonds, pearls, and ambergris. For the Commanders in India, the scandal about such a deal had to be notorious before it came before the General in Batavia, and then, if the whole were confiscated, the Commanders would give a third to the Avocat to shut his mouth, a third to the hospital, and a third to the Company.

If a sailor informed a factory that a vessel was carrying private goods, more often than not, the report would not be rejected but the informer would be made very drunk while the goods were removed, and only then would the ship be "officially" inspected. The sailor or soldier would be severely punished, have his wages confiscated, and be set to work on a galley for three or four years.

Three days later, Tavernier was summoned again when demands were made for him to give details of his trading with Constant. He refused to answer this question, and the officials began to threaten him with arrest, so he gave a detailed explanation of how a Persian khan was given a very valuable present on behalf of the Dutch Company, partly subsidized by Constant, who had lost money because the golden bridle he had received in return was handed in when he got back to Batavia.

After another summons eight days later, Tavernier insisted on being addressed in French, and when the President protested that he had understood Dutch up to then, Tavernier told him that he did not understand enough Dutch to understand chicanery, adding that he was not a servant of the Company and it was not his business to observe the conduct of those who were.

The Fiscal presented the questions in French and Tavernier then stated that he needed fourteen days in which to answer. He had consulted a French lawyer, who had told him he was not obliged to reply.

By this time, he had begun to tire of the inconvenience and time wasting, despite some enjoyment of his baiting of the Council, so he called on the President in his house early one morning. The President met him while still in his night attire. Tavernier asked for the guard to be withdrawn as he wished to speak privately. He explained that Constant had given him

44,000 rupees to buy diamonds for the General himself and that the General had already bought a parcel of diamonds supplied to Constant by Tavernier as well as the two pear-shaped pearls. He added the names of other Commissioners he had bought for.

Then he asked the President if he had forgotten that when Constant had left to become Commander in Persia, the President himself had entrusted him with 31,000 rupees to invest in a parcel of diamonds. Twisting the knife, Tavernier explained that Constant had been on his way to Surat to place this money in his hands. In the event, Constant had bought the stones elsewhere and actually made a loss of 15 per cent on the transaction.

The President became very alarmed and hurried off to see the Governor-General. The next day, on his way to the Town Hall, Tavernier was encountered halfway there by the Avocat Fiscal, who asked where he was going. When told, he laughed and suggested Tavernier come to dinner with him that evening instead because he had just been presented with two cases of French and Rhine wines. That was the end of that episode, but the Dutch Company took the last trick.

On this voyage, Tavernier had bought some pay bills owing to the Dutch Company at a big discount, intending to cash them in Europe, but whether he knew it or not, this form of trading had been made illegal. He was told he had to surrender the bills, but he held out until he received a promise for them to be redeemed in Holland. This promise was never fulfilled, although his brother received part payment after a court case. After that, Tavernier had nothing good to say about the Dutch but still took advantage of local help and hospitality when it was offered.

## Off Again . . .

He returned from this voyage, as far as can be judged, in the spring of 1649 and spent two years selling the gemstones he had bought, as well as trying to recover the money owed him by the Dutch Company. He set off again in mid-1651 on his fourth journey. After reaching Persia, Tavernier landed in India on a ship belonging to the King of Golconda, again nearly being shipwrecked.

In Golconda, he had several meetings with Mir Jumla, Prime Minister and General to the King, to show him diamonds and pearls he hoped to sell to the King (Color Plate 3). He recorded his admiration of Mir Jumla as a man of great intelligence who responded to requests, gave orders, and signed dispatches with exceptional promptitude.

The sale came to nothing because Tavernier was upset by a remark by a eunuch that his prices were too high; he left at once for Surat. On arrival, he heard that the English and Dutch were at war, so he went on to Ahmadabad to show his gems to the Governor of Gujerat. Returning from Surat to Europe via Persia, he sailed in a Dutch warship that, with four others, engaged and defeated the English in a naval engagement en route.

Back home, probably in 1655, Tavernier set out once more in 1657, and this time, his ship was chased by pirates along the French coast from Marseille and had to put in at Toulon; so he returned overland to Marseille with his precious stock. Next time, he took an English ship via Italy and on to Smyrna by a Dutch one. Reaching Ispahan, he delayed his departure on hearing news of Aurangzeb seizing his father's throne in India. He wrote to Shaista Khan, who, although brother-in-law to the new-deposed Shah Jahan, backed Aurangzeb.

Tavernier had brought some curiosities from Europe for the Khan, who had a very strange family: his mother was also his sister. In exchange, Tavernier received a passport and an invitation to Jahanabad. He took the opportunity while in India to revisit the mines and returned to France in 1662.

## A Time to Marry

This time, it appears by his actions, Tavernier had decided to settle down because, at the age of 56, having amassed considerable wealth, he thought he should marry. His choice fell on Madeleine Goisse, daughter of a jeweler with whom he had done business. He had, however, to finalize some transactions in the East and planned to make a short trip, his sixth, the following year, taking with him his nephew, Maurice Tavernier. Alas for his new wife, the "short trip" lasted for five years.

In Ispahan, the King bought all his stones except the pearls and gave Tavernier the rank of Jeweler-in-Ordinary. He was presented with a robe of honor, which he is seen wearing in the engraving that appeared in the last of his books, *Recueil de plusiers Relations et Traitz singuliers ef curieux* (1679).

On arrival in Surat, he was told by the Governor that Aurangzeb was to be the first to see his stock, so Tavernier carried on to Jahanabad. After giving presents worth a huge sum of money to the Mogul Emperor and court nobles, he sold some of his most valuable stones but had a dispute over the price of a pearl, from which Aurangzeb was advised to cut 10,000 rupees. Nevertheless, Aurangzeb appeared to be pleased with his purchases because when Tavernier was ready to leave, he was pressed by the Emperor to stay for the imminent annual fête. He was promised that, if he did so, he would be shown all the jewels in the State Treasury.

This invitation was irresistible to the Frenchman and was the occasion when he handled and afterward described the Great Mogul Diamond, still the subject of much speculation and interest.

Tavernier and his companions—as well as his nephew, he had two friends with him, one an eminent French physician—eventually arrived in Dacca to give presents to Shaista Khan and his son (who alone received a watch in an enameled gold case, a pair of pistols inlaid with silver, and a telescope). He sold the Khan some stones, but when he came to present the bill of exchange he had been given, he was told by the treasurer that payment had been stopped by the Khan. The Khan insisted that 20,000 rupees be deducted from the bill. After some persuasion by Tavernier, the deducted amount was reduced to 10,000 rupees.

The blame for this contretemps had its origin, according to Tavernier, in an evil trick played on him by three rogues in the Court of the Mogul. They were two Persians, Nawab Akil Khan, who was in charge of all the precious stones, and Mirza Mu'azzam, who taxed each item, and a Banian, Nihal Chand, who checked each stone for genuineness and flaws.

Aurangzeb, who actually preferred golden rupees to gemstones, had recently instituted the law whereby all foreign merchants, when they arrived in the country, were sent by the local governor with their goods to the Emperor, either with their consent or by force. The trio had persuaded the Emperor that they should see all goods before he did and, although they had sworn to take nothing, they did not neglect to extract all they could from a merchant in order to ruin him, according to Tavernier.

Also, he added, the trio took gems to their dwellings for examination and valuation, where they wrote down the details of every piece. They circulated this list and maliciously priced items at half their true values.

The trio tried to buy Tavernier's goods to resell to the Emperor, and when this did not succeed, they wrote to Shaista Khan to state that they could have bought the goods that Tavernier sold the Emperor for 8,000 rupees to 10,000 rupees less. Shaista Khan had issued the bill of exchange to Tavernier before he received the letter.

Tavernier was so annoyed at losing the 10,000 rupees due to him that in his account of the journey, he listed the presents he was bound to give before he could do any business at all and offered advice to those wishing to do business at the courts of the Princes in Persia, India, and Turkey. They should not attempt to start anything unless they had considerable presents ready for giving and an open purse for officers of trust whose goodwill they needed.

## *Of Nobility and the Pen*

Tavernier returned home in slow stages via Agra, Surat, Ispahan, and Constantinople. It was on his return this time, at the age of 66, that he was summoned by King Louis XIV. The King raised him to the nobility and also purchased a collection of diamonds. Tavernier bought the barony of Aubonne, near Geneva, restored the castle there, and started work on his books, *Nouvelle Relation de l'interieur du Serrail du Grand Seigneur* (1675); his most important work, *Les Six Voyages de Jean-Baptiste Tavernier* (1676); and *Recueil de plusiers Relations et Traitez singuliers et curieux* (1679). All became very popular, passed through many editions, and were translated into English, German, and Italian. Two engravings of Tavernier appeared in the last book, one full length in a robe and the other as a bust.

At the age of 79, he went to Berlin, tempted by an offer from the Elector of Brandenberg, who wanted his advice on dealing with the Mogul Emperor and who had offered him the post of Ambassador in India. He returned to Switzerland and made arrangements to sell his estate and barony in Aubonne to cover the cost of fitting out an expedition. His wife conducted the transfer, and there is no hint of what she thought of the decision, but it boded ill for Tavernier. Troubles arose in France because of his Protestant religion, and it is possible that he spent some time in the Bastille.

Resolved to start trading again, he entrusted his nephew Pierre with a valuable cargo, but Pierre Tavernier defrauded his uncle and settled in Persia with the proceeds. Of Tavernier's movements at this time, very little is known except that he was in Switzerland and in Copenhagen probably in 1688.

Even of his death nothing was known until, in 1885, a correspondent of *La Bibliographie*, M. T. Tokmakof, reported having seen his grave in an old Protestant cemetery near Moscow in 1876. The name Tavernier was legible but the date of death was not. Tokmakof did discover, however, that Tavernier arrived in Russia with a Swedish passport early in 1689. So the life of this unique man — friend of the most powerful potentates of the East, gem dealer extraordinary, and popular writer — ended in total mystery and probably in penury.

King Louis XIV bought from Tavernier twenty diamonds, the most famous one being the French Blue, which became the Hope. Three others were more than 30 carats each and are known as the Tavernier A, B, and C (Figures 12–3 and 12–4). All three disappeared when the Crown Jewels of France were stolen. The Tavernier A has, however, been identified as a stone bought by Napoleon III in 1860 and presented to the Empress Eugenie. It weighs 51 carats and is of oval shape but blunt at one end. What happened to the $32^3/_8$ carat B is unknown, but C was almost certainly a stone recorded as of $31^3/_4$ carats set in the insignia of the Order of the Golden Fleece when an inventory of the French Crown Jewels was made by order of the National Assembly in 1791. In an inventory of 1810, ordered by Napoleon, it was missing.

## Describing the Peacock Throne

Tavernier was the first to describe the Peacock Throne of Shah Jahan in some detail in his *Travels in India*. Having sold gems to Aurangzeb, he was prevailed upon to stay for the fete when he went to the palace to say his farewell on November 1, 1665. Many of the gems he was allowed to inspect afterward were set in the seven magnificent thrones, the finest of which was the Peacock Throne. It had been designed by Austin de Bordeaux, who was also responsible for the Taj Mahal. Shah Jahan paid de Bordeaux 2,000 rupees a month and gave him the name "Jewel-Handed."

This principal throne was placed in the hall of the first court, and Tavernier described it as being in type and size like one of "our camp beds," about six feet long and four feet wide (1.8 meters by 1.2 meters). The four feet were massive and from 20 inches to 25 inches (50 centimeters to 62.5 centimeters.) high. Four bars attached to the top of the legs supported the base of the throne, and twelve columns on these held a canopy on three sides, one side being left open to face the court.

The feet and the bars were covered with inlaid gold set with many diamonds, rubies, and emeralds. A large balas ruby (red spinel) was set in the middle of each bar with four emeralds around it to form a cross. Similar crosses, but with four emeralds surrounding a red spinel, or vice versa, were set in the bars.

The emeralds were table cut (with flat square tops) and the spinels en cabochon (with domed tops), and although the stones did not exceed about ten carats or twelve carats each in weight, they were very "showy" stones, according to Tavernier. Some parts of the throne were set with pearls.

The throne was ascended by four steps along the long side. The Emperor sat cross-legged in the middle with a flat cushion each side of him and a large round one like a bolster behind. To each column of the throne, one of the Mogul's weapons was attached: his sword, a quiver with arrows, a mace, and a round shield. The pillows, as well as the weapons and steps, were covered with gems to match those of the throne.

Over the Emperor's seat was a canopy smothered with diamonds and pearls stitched to the underside. Above it stood the model of the Peacock

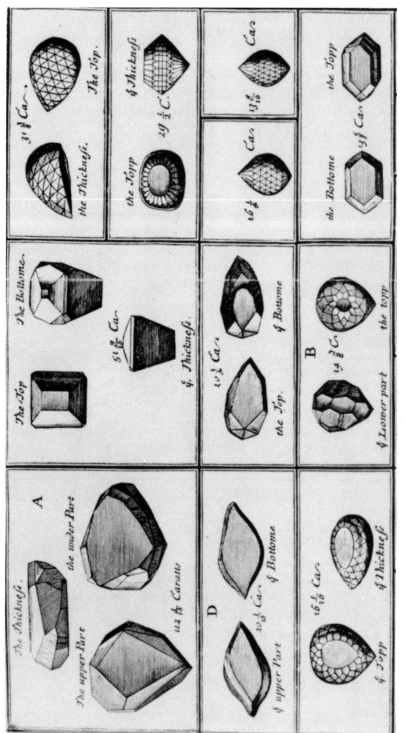

Fig. 12–3 Tavernier's A and B Drawings. King Louis XIV bought from Tavernier twenty diamonds, the most famous one being the French Blue, which became the Hope. Three others were more than 30 carats each and are known as the Tavernier A, B, and C. All three disappeared when the Crown Jewels of France were stolen. The Tavernier A has, however, been certified as a stone bought by Napoleon III in 1860 and presented to the Empress Eugenie. What happened to the Tavernier B is unknown. (Courtesy of The Oxford University Press.)

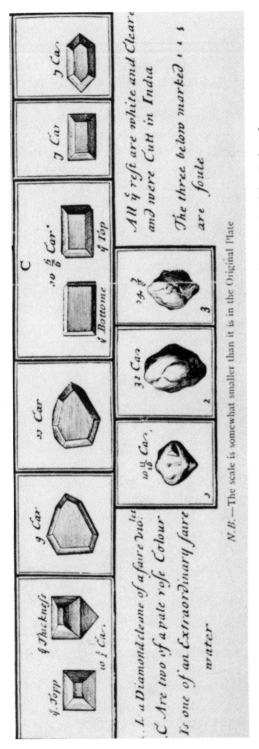

Fig. 12–4 Tavernier's C Drawing. Recorded as 31³/₄ carats, set in the insignia of the Order of the Golden Fleece, when an inventory of the French Crown Jewels was made by order of the National Assembly in 1791. In an inventory of 1810, ordered by Napoleon, it was missing. (*Courtesy of The Oxford University Press.*)

that gave the throne its name. The Peacock's gold body was set with gems, a large ruby being mounted in its breast with a pear-shaped pearl of about 50 carats hanging from it. The fanned tail was covered with stones of many colors but mainly with blue sapphires.

On each side of the Peacock was a bunch of flowers, the same height as the bird, made of gold and set with colored gems. Hanging from the throne, in a position where the Mogul could see it, was a diamond of between 80 carats and 90 carats surrounded by rubies and emeralds. There has been much speculation about this diamond, but that was all Tavernier noted. It is likely to have been the stone now called the Shah, described at the end of Chapter Eleven.

Tavernier counted about 108 balas rubies of at least 100 carats each, some weighing 200 carats or more. He could see 116 emeralds weighing from 30 carats to 60 carats, plenty of them of good color but many with many flaws, typical of emeralds. He thought the most valuable of the gems to be the beautiful rows of round pearls of between six carats and ten carats each that surrounded the twelve columns supporting the canopy.

About four feet (1.2 meters) away on each side of the throne was an umbrella made of embroidered red velvet, the stick of each being covered with diamonds, rubies, and pearls up to a height of seven feet to eight feet (2.1 meters to 2.4 meters).

Behind the Peacock Throne stood another throne, shaped like a bathtub about seven feet (2.1 meters) in length by five feet (1.5 meters) wide but without a canopy. It was covered in diamonds and pearls. Tavernier did not say what it was for.

On the right hand side of the court, a tent was erected for the principal "balandines" of the town, who were obliged to sing and dance, but Tavernier did not see them because Aurangzeb had forbidden any singing and dancing at court while he was Emperor. On the left, another tent sheltered the senior officers of the army, the guards, and the household staff.

While the Emperor was seated, fifteen horses were held by two men on one side of the throne and fifteen horses held by two men on the other. All had bridles set with diamonds, rubies, emeralds, and pearls or were mounted with small gold coins. On the head of each horse was a plume of beautiful feathers, and on the back of each was a small cushion embroidered with gold and held by a surcingle. Each horse also had suspended from its neck a diamond, ruby, or emerald.

After the first ceremonies were over, the seven bravest war elephants, covered with brocades and with gold and silver chains about their necks, were brought for inspection. Each elephant greeted the Emperor when opposite the throne by placing its trunk on the ground then raising it above its head three times, trumpeting on each occasion.

Aurangzeb was meaner than his predecessors. During this fête on the Emperor's birthday, it was customary for him to be weighed against specially minted pieces of thin silver resembling different fruits. Aurangzeb refused to have them minted, although the value even of those of Jahangir was negligible.

The throne was among the unbelievable wealth of loot taken by Nadir Shah to Persia in 1739, when he left Delhi in ruins and piled with dead. When Agha Muhammad Shah seized power in Persia by his inhuman killing of the blind Shah Rukh, he found among the Moghul treasures a replica of the throne in broken pieces. It seems that Nadir had had two replicas made, but the original and one of the replicas no longer existed. Agah Muhammad had a new throne constructed to incorporate the undamaged pieces.

Lord Curzon, British Viceroy in India from 1899 to 1905, was able to inspect what was then thought to be the Peacock Throne, which he called the "Takhi-i-Taous," in the Persian Shah's palace in Teheran. He reported that it was not of Indian construction but was made by Mohammed Husein Khan, Sadr (High Priest) of Ispahan, for Fath Ali Shah (1793–1847) when he married an Ispahani woman popularly known as "the Peacock Lady."

The Peacock Throne of Fath Ali Shah (nephew of Agha Muhammad Shah) is now in the Golestan Palace in Iran, and is clearly not one of the originals. Another throne in Iran, named the Nadir Throne (Color Plate 21), is a throne seat quite different from the Mogul thrones, although one of the original facsimiles was, indeed, known as "Nadir's Throne." There have been descriptions of several Peacock Thrones down the years, some of which were no doubt made from parts of others, but none, it seems, from the one and only true Peacock Throne, which was probably destroyed after Nadir Shah was murdered.

## Cardinal Mazarin

Another name that has persisted in the world of gems is that of Cardinal Mazarin (1602–1661). He was a remarkable statesman, who influenced the destiny of France for many years and who also assembled one of the greatest private diamond collections, which eventually became a substantial part of the French Crown Jewels.

Jules Giulio Mazarin was, in fact, an Italian by birth, who was sent as Papal Nuncio to Paris when he was 32 years old. He soon began to exert his influence through his intellect and was made a Cardinal in 1641 on the recommendation of Louis XIII and of Cardinal Richelieu, whom he succeeded as Chief Minister the following year. Cardinal Mazarin was very close to successive kings by his influence over the mother of Louis XIV, the Sun King, of whom he was godfather. Louis was four years old when his father died, and Mazarin shared the Regency with the Queen, Marie Thérèse. He arranged the marriage of Louis to the Infanta of Spain in 1660.

The Sancy and the Mirror of Portugal were the finest diamonds in Mazarin's collection, which also included personal jewels bought from Henrietta Maria, Charles I, and Queen Christina of Sweden. When Louis XIV bought the collection of diamonds from Tavernier, it is reasonably certain that Mazarin was concerned in the deal.

His name became so synonymous with diamonds that an early form of cushion cut, with 17 facets on the top and the same on the bottom, was named after him. But the so-called "Mazarin cut" was, in fact, introduced about 1620 when Mazarin was only 18 years old and certainly not collecting diamonds.

## Harry Winston

In modern times, no name has been more closely associated with famous diamonds than that of Harry Winston (1896–1978), who was the third son of a New York jeweler and who set up in business on his own at the age of 19 with a capital of $2,000.

In the Great Depression years of the 1930s, he had the courage to buy the Jonker Diamond, a superb stone weighing 726 carats in the rough named after Jacobus Jonker, on whose claim it was discovered in 1934 on the Elandsfontein farm near Pretoria. It was sold to the Diamond Corporation for £70,000. Winston eventually paid £700,000 for it, according to reports.

It was cut by Lazare Kaplan of New York into twelve perfect gems, the largest named the Jonker, weighing 142.90 carats, about which Winston commented many years later, "I priced it at one million dollars and it took me fourteen years to sell it."

In 1949, Winston bought the Hope Diamond, which he later presented to the Smithsonian Institution in Washington, D.C., for their collection. Of this notorious stone of ill fate, he said, "It is childish to suppose that gems themselves exert any influence for good or evil." The Hope's supposed evil influence did not affect Winston; he remained the diamond merchant with the biggest and most varied stock in the world and one of the trade's most colorful personalities. Although many legendary diamonds passed through his hands, dealing in them was not his main activity. Winston had cutting and polishing plants in six countries and sold small diamonds to the wholesale trade.

When Winston died at the age of 82, Harry Oppenheimer, Chairman of De Beers, said his death was "an incalculable loss to the diamond industry. His knowledge of diamonds was that of the great expert, but his quality went much further than that. He had an instinct, a feeling for great jewels which went beyond exact calculation and he had the courage to back his hunches and was very rarely wrong. He combined the qualities of an exceptional man of business with those of an artist."

Winston was of stocky build but less than five feet tall. Yet he was rarely recognized except by his business associates. A condition of his insurance policy with Lloyds of London, the largest gem policy ever issued in Lloyds's 275-year history, was that he never be photographed.

## Trying to Steal the British Crown Jewels

This book of legendary gems would not be complete without a short account of the bizarre attempt to steal the English Crown Jewels (Figures 12–5 and 12–6; Color Plates 8 and 9). If the successful robbery of the French ones was drama, the unsuccessful attempt on the English ones was farce.

It was made in 1671 by a Colonel Thomas Blood, who is supposed to have gained his rank in the Civil War fighting on the side of the Parliamentary Army. At that time, the Crown Jewels were kept in cupboards in the Jewel Tower at the Tower of London. There was no guard. The keeper, Talbot Edwards, known as "old Edwards," would let members of the public handle the jewels for a fee that went into his own pocket.

Blood dressed up as a clergyman and took a woman with him, whom he said was his wife. After several visits, the plausible and cheerful Blood became friendly with Old Edwards and his wife and was even enlisted to find a suitable husband for their daughter. Blood proposed introducing her to his "nephew," whom he said had an income of £300 a year. It was, therefore, arranged that Blood should bring the young man along to the Tower on May 9, 1671.

On the day, Blood arrived with his "nephew" and two other men. Old Edwards greeted them and said his wife and daughter were not ready, so Blood suggested they go to see the jewels. Leaving one man behind, they followed old Edwards into the jewel room, where one of them stunned him with a mallet and gagged him. Blood took the crown and hid it under his cloak; another accomplice, named Parrot, seized the orb; and the third, the scepter.

*Fig.* 12–5 The Imperial State Crown. The Black Prince's Ruby is set in the front of the crown, with the Stuart Sapphire in the cross. The globe is set all over with diamonds and surrounded by a cross. As was the custom, many of the diamonds set in this new crown for the coronation of George IV in 1821 were hired and had to be returned to the Crown Jewelers after the ceremony. The frame of the crown is on loan to the London Museum, where it is on exhibition. *(© British Crown copyright; reproduced with permission of the Controller of Her Britannic Majesty's Stationery Office.)*

Fig. 12–6 St. Edward's Crown. A large aquamarine orb representing the world was switched for a fake. An examination in the early 19th century proved the greenish-tint "aquamarine" to be made of glass. It was known as the Old Monde (old world) and was plated with gold and enameled over the lower facets. Part of it is still among the Crown Jewels at the Tower of London. *(© British Crown copyright; reproduced with permission of the Controller of Her Britannic Majesty's Stationery Office.)*

Then fate took a hand in the unexpected arrival of old Edward's son, Wythe Edwards, who, with a friend, was an army officer just home on leave from Flanders. He arrived at the Tower, saw the stranger at the door, and asked where Edwards was. Blood's accomplice told him that the man was upstairs. After that, things happened fast. The robbers were warned by the man who had let in young Edwards. They fled in such haste that the man carrying the scepter dropped it.

At this point, old Edwards, who must have been pretty tough, managed to remove his gag and began shouting, "Treason. Murder. The Crown is stolen." The daughter had by now appeared, and she, her brother, and his friend, Captain Beckman, an Ordinance officer at the Tower, took up the cry so successfully that Parrot was caught at once. Blood and a man named Tom Hunt, said to be his son-in-law, ran for St. Katherine's Gate, where they had tied their horses, but the pursuers were now within range and pistol shots were exchanged. Blood was caught on the gun wharf by the gate and Hunt outside it.

The prisoners were incarcerated in the White Tower, and it was discovered that Blood had already been in trouble in a plot to assassinate the Duke of Ormond. His pleas to have an audience with King Charles II (Figure 12–7) were naturally ignored. However, the King did at last grant him an audience with the astounding result that Blood and his accomplices were granted a free pardon and Blood was given an appointment worth £500 a year! There have been various speculations about the King's motives. One was that he was so short of money at the time that he was behind the failed attempt. Another was that Blood, who was seemingly a powerful member of the Parliamentary extremists, became an informer.

Both the son, Wythe Edwards, and Captain Beckman received rewards of £100, and old Edwards received a warrant for £200, but the authorities were so long in paying that old Edwards sold his for £100. He died three years later, probably as a result of the injury to his head.

The best part of the incident is that Miss Edwards got her man after all. She married Captain Beckman, who was of Swedish origin but had been an engineer in the English forces since 1660. Beckman later became Keeper of the Crown Jewels himself and was created Sir Martin Beckman by King James II after his coronation.

Following the Captain Blood episode, one of the Foot Guard Regiments was put on armed guard, and the scarlet tunics of the Foot Guards remain a feature of the Jewel Tower to this day.

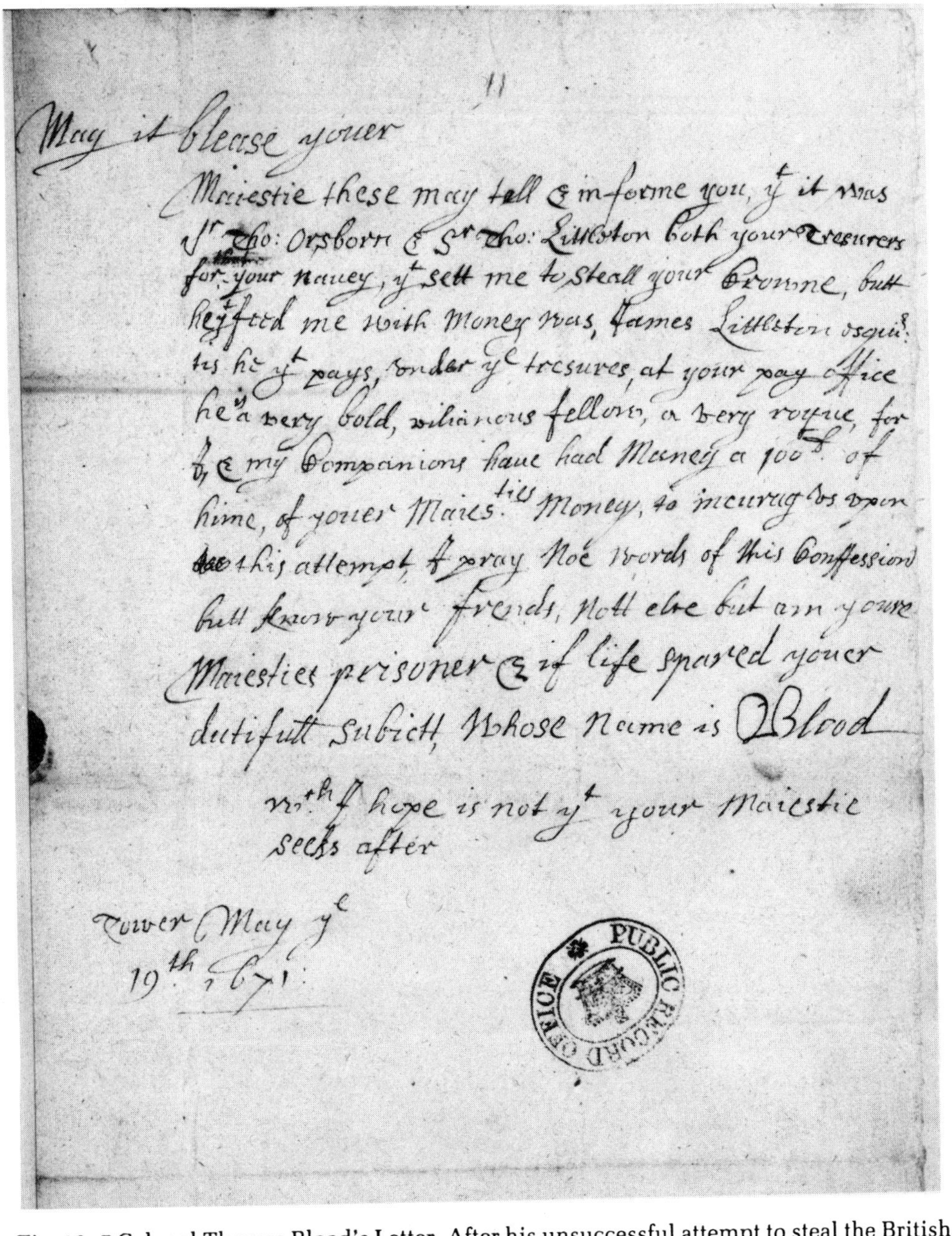

May it please your
Maiestie these may tell & informe you, y[t] it was
S[r] Tho: Orsborn & S[r] Tho: Littleton both your Treasurers
for your navey, y[t] sett me to steall your Crowne, but
hejfted me with Money was, James Littleton esq[r]
tis he y[t] pays, under y[e] tresures, at your pay office
he'a very bold, villanous fellow, a very rogue, for
y[e] & my Companions have had Money a 100[l] of
hime, of youer Mai[es].[tie] Money, to incurrag v[s] vpon
this attempt, & pray Noe words of this Confession
but know your freinds, Noll else but am youre
Maiesties prisoner & if life spared youer
dutifull Subiett, Whose Name is O Blood

w[th] f hope is not y[t] your Maiestie
seeks after

Tower (May y[e]
19th ? 671 :

Fig. 12–7 Colonel Thomas Blood's Letter. After his unsuccessful attempt to steal the British Crown Jewels in 1671, Blood appealed to King Charles II. The Colonel and his accomplices were granted a free pardon and Blood was given an appointment worth £500 a year!. *(Courtesy of the Public Record Office, London, England.)*

# Bibliography

Balfour, Iain. *Famous Diamonds* (booklet). London: De Beers Consolidated Mines.

Bapst, G. *Historie des Joyauxdels Couronne de France*. Paris: 1889.

Bruton, Eric. *Diamonds*. Radnor, PA: Chilton, 1978.

Chapman, Leo. *Diamonds in Australia*. Rushcutter Bay, Australia: Bay Book Pty. Ltd.,1980.

Dickinson, Joan Younger. *The Book of Diamonds*. New York: Crown Publishing Inc., 1965.

Dutens, L. *Des Pierres Précieuses et des Pierres Fines*. Florence: 1783.

Eyles, W. C. *The Book of Opals*. Rutland: Charles E. Tuttle Co., 1964.

Gemological Institute of America. *Diamonds, Famous, Notable and Unique*. Santa Monica, CA: Gemological Institute of America, 1966.

Hanway, Jonas. *An Historical Account of the British Trade Over the Caspian Sea*. London: 1753.

Heiniger, Ernst A., and Jean Heiniger, (eds.). *The Great Book of Jewels*. Lausanne, Switzerland: Edita S.A., 1974.

Helme, Nigel. *Thomas Major Cullinan*. Johannesburg, R.S.A.: McGraw-Hill Book Co., Pty., 1974.

Holmes, Martin and Maj. Gen. H. D. W. Sitwell (former Keeper of Jewel House). *The English Regalia*. London: Her Majesty's Stationery Office, 1972.

Howarth, Stephen. *The Koh-i-Noor Diamond*. London: Quartet Books, 1980.

Jones, Harford. *The Dynasty of the Kajars*. London: 1833.

King, C. W. *The Natural History of Gems or Decorative Stones*. London, Cambridge, 1867.

_____. *The Natural History of Precious Stones and of the Precious Metals*. London & Cambridge,1865.

Kunz, G. F. and C. H. Stevenson. *The Book of the Pearl*. New York: The Century Co., 1908.

_____. *Precious Stones and Gems*. London, 1877.

Leechman, Frank. *The Opal Book*. Sydney, Australia: Ure Smith Pty. Ltd., 1961.

Mawe, John. *Treatise on Diamond and Precious Stones*. London, 1813. Reprinted with comments. London: Industrial Diamond Information Bureau, 1950.

_____. *Travels in Brazil*. 1812.

Meen, J. B. and A. D. Tushingham. *The Crown Jewels of Iran*. Toronto: University of Toronto Press, 1968

Newman, Harold. *An Illustrated Dictionary of Jewellery*. London: Thames and Hudson, 1981.

*Notable Diamonds of the World* (booklet). New York: N. W. Ayer, 1971.

Osborne, William. *The Court and Camp of Rungeet Singh*. London: Oxford University Press, 1973.

Pallas, P. S. *Travels Through the Southern Provinces of the Russian Empire in 1793–4*. 1812.

Patch, Susanne Steinem. *Blue Mystery. The Story of The Hope Diamond*. Washington, D.C.: The Smithsonian Institution, 1976.

Roberts, Brian. *Kimberley, Turbulent City*. Cape Town, R. S. A.: David Philip Publisher, 1976.

Streeter, Edwin W. *The Great Diamonds of the World*. (2nd ed.–rare). London, 1882.

Tagore, S. M. *Mani-Mali, a Treatise on Gems*. 2 vol. Calcutta: 1879, 1881.

Taunton, *Australind; Wanderings in Western Australia and the Malay East*. London: 1903.

Tavernier, Jean-Baptiste. *Travels in India* (rare; translation of *Les Six Voyages de Jean-Baptiste Tavernier 1676*). London: Oxford University Press, 1925.

_____. *Nouvelle relation de l'interieur du Serrail du Grand Seigneur* (1675).

_____. *Recueil de plusiers Relations et Traitez singuliers et Curieux*. (1679)

Twining, Lord. *A History of the Crown Jewels of Europe*. London: B. T. Batsford, 1960.

Wilson, A. N. *Diamonds from Birth to Eternity*. Santa Monica, CA: Gemological Institute of America, 1982.

# Index

CP refers to Color Plate; page numbers in *italic* refer to illustrations.